The American History Series

Steven A. Riess
NORTHEASTERN ILLINOIS UNIVERSITY

Sport in Industrial America, 1850–1920

SECOND EDITION

WILEY-BLACKWELL

This edition first published 2013 © 2013 John Wiley & Sons, Inc.

Edition history: Harlan Davidson, Inc. (1e, 1995)
Harlan Davidson, Inc. was acquired by John Wiley & Sons in May 2012.

Wiley-Blackwell is an imprint of John Wiley & Sons, formed by the merger of Wiley's global Scientific, Technical and Medical business with Blackwell Publishing.

Registered Office
John Wiley & Sons Ltd, The Atrium, Southern Gate, Chichester, West Sussex, PO19 8SQ, UK

Editorial Offices
350 Main Street, Malden, MA 02148-5020, USA
9600 Garsington Road, Oxford, OX4 2DQ, UK
The Atrium, Southern Gate, Chichester, West Sussex, PO19 8SQ, UK
For details of our global editorial offices, for customer services, and for information about how to apply for permission to reuse the copyright material in this book please see our website at www.wiley.com/wiley-blackwell.

The right of Steven A. Riess to be identified as the author of the editorial matter in this work has been asserted in accordance with the UK Copyright, Designs and Patents Act 1988.

Library of Congress Cataloging-in-Publication Data is available for this title

Riess, Steven A.
    Sport in industrial America, 1850–1920 / Steven A. Riess, Northeastern Illinois University.
    —Second edtion.
       pages cm
    Includes bibliographical references and index.
    ISBN 978-1-118-53771-8 (pbk. : alk. paper) 1. Sports—United States—Sociological aspects.
    2. Sports—United States—History—19th century. 3. Sports—United States—History—20th century. I. Title.
    GV706.5.R54 2013
    306.4′830973—dc23   2012037671

Cover: "Coaches at Jerome Park on a Race Day," *Harper's Weekly* 30 (19 June 1886): 389. Library of Congress (LC-USZ62-10637)

Printed and bound in Malaysia by Vivar Printing Sdn Bhd

1   2013

Dedicated to the memory of my grandparents,
Alfred and Mathilde Riess and Berta and Jacob Finder.

CONTENTS

PREFACE and ACKNOWLEDGMENTS to the SECOND EDITION

I am honored to have the opportunity to write a second edition of this book. My thanks to the publisher, Andrew J. Davidson. The first edition was well received by both students and instructors for its coverage, analysis, and readability. The book was recognized as a *Choice* "Outstanding Academic Book" for 1996. I again want to thank the late Abraham S. Eisenstadt for his outstanding work as my editor on that edition. This edition has undergone some significant changes. In revision I corrected all errors I discovered, supplemented the narrative, and introduced the most current interpretations in the field. Naturally, I thoroughly revised the bibliographical essay to account for the substantial new literature in the field. The most dramatic change is the addition of an entirely new concluding chapter on the subject of American Sport in the International Arena. This topic was insufficiently recognized in the first edition, and it has been the subject of enormous scholarship since that volume was published. Permit me to single out two of the leading contributors to that subfield, Mark Dyreson and Gerald Gems, for their excellent monographs, and also for the kind assistance they gave me in creating the new chapter. I benefited from outstanding support from Andrew Davidson, who edited the manuscript, and Linda Gaio, who did a superb job hunting down photographs. As always, I am alone responsible for any errors.

Steven A. Riess
Skokie, Illinois

INTRODUCTION

Sport in modern society is one of the most popular forms of mass entertainment. People all around the world enjoy playing and watching sports. Millions attend soccer matches, horse races, and baseball games, while over a billion watch the Olympics and the World Cup on television. The United States in the late nineteenth century became one of the first countries in which sport was a widespread obsession. Great Britain was the very first, and the American fascination with sport began as a product of its colonial heritage and the nineteenth-century, trans-Atlantic, Anglo-American culture. In the mid-nineteenth century, before the United States became an industrial, urban nation, sport had not yet achieved a high level of prominence or widespread popularity. Sport appealed largely to segments of the economic and social elite and to lower-class subcultures that composed the sporting fraternity. The term *sport* had very negative connotations, defined as an object of derision, or a person with a flashy lifestyle or a mutation. As historian Elliott Gorn points out, sport intimated boisterousness, defiance of social constraint, and loutish behavior.

Historians today define sport as pastimes, primarily competitive, that require physical dexterity. These contests may be against oneself, another individual, or a rival team. The sporting games of most people around the world in the mid-nineteenth century were premodern, traditional village pastimes, such as wrestling or throwing stones, or adjuncts to religious ceremonies, such as the Native American games of lacrosse and shinny. Historians Allen Guttmann and Melvin Adelman, authors, respectively, of *From Ritual to Record: The Nature of Modern Sports* (1978) and *A Sporting Time: New York City and the Rise of Modern Athletics, 1820–70* (1986), describe premodern sports as unorganized or informally arranged athletic contests. Rules were simple, unwritten, and based on local customs and traditions, competition was local, and little role differentiation existed among participants. Reports of contests were not widely disseminated or remembered (other than by oral tradition), and no statistics or records were kept. Modern sports, on the other hand, are described as highly organized, secular activities with formal institutions at local, regional, and national levels. Rules are formal, standard, and written, and competition is theoretically open to everyone under the same conditions. Roles are highly differentiated between spectators and players, and among professionals and amateurs who specialize in particular sports and even certain positions. Finally, in modern sports, results are widely publicized and statistics and records are carefully maintained.

American sport in 1850 was only just beginning to become modernized. Furthermore, it was virtually an exclusive male preserve that defined and exemplified manly behavior as aggressive, courageous, vigorous, and unchildlike. Popular sports were primarily participatory and offered athletes an opportunity to demonstrate physical prowess, make money from prizes or bets, and fraternize with their rivals. Mass spectatorship had already become significant, particularly for elite-sponsored thoroughbred racing (although harness racing was the first modern sport organized by middle-class Americans), attended in some cases by huge audiences, and pedestrianism (long-distance running races), which matched working-class athletes. These contests provided spectators with entertainment, sociability, and gambling opportunities.

American sportsmen up to the 1850s constituted a sporting fraternity of upper- and working-class men who enjoyed traditional sporting pastimes. They composed an important segment of the male bachelor subculture that rejected middle-class Victorian morality. These men enjoyed camaraderie, sociability, and instant gratification in male-only settings in which they escaped from women, domesticity, and work. They valued such manly behavior as drinking, frequenting prostitutes, gambling, and demonstrating athletic prowess. However, sport was not yet very popular among future-oriented middle-income men, who generally frowned upon it as an immoral and socially debilitating waste of time.

The premodern, mid-nineteenth-century sporting culture was heavily influenced by the agrarian character of society. At this time 84.7 percent of Americans still lived in rural areas, and their favorite sports were contests of strength, skill, and courage that they enjoyed at taverns and in the countryside. In the early 1800s, woods and streams were readily accessible to most American sportsmen who fished, hunted, shot at targets, and rode horses. Spectators could watch horse races, combat contests like gouging (rough-and-tumble, no holds-barred frontier matches), prizefighting and wrestling, and such blood sports as animal baiting and cock fighting. Nonetheless, as early as the colonial era, cities played an important role in American sport; with their relatively concentrated populations, they provided a site for sports clubs and sports entrepreneurs. Eighteenth-century colonial cities had elite fishing, racing, and fox-hunting clubs, and by the early 1800s cities also had more democratic organizations for rowing, racquets, gymnastics, and target shooting. Colonial publicans were the first sporting entrepreneurs. They sponsored animal baiting, marksmanship contests, billiards, and bowling, all pastimes that involved wagering and attracted thirsty sporting men. Tavern promotion of animal baiting declined in the antebellum era, replaced in part by an occasional illegal prize fight. Boxing demonstrated courage and other manly traits; in 1837 the *New York Herald* argued that this sport was "far preferable to the insidious knife . . . , or the cowardly and brutal practice of biting, kicking or gouging." Spectator sports were mainly contested in cities that had sufficient gate-paying sportsmen to encourage promoters to arrange matches.

The purpose of this book is to explain how sport in the United States developed from a morally suspect, premodern entertainment in 1850 that did not attract the interest of most Americans into a respectable, modernized national obsession, culminating in the Golden Age of Sports in the 1920s. During this period the variety and number of sports rapidly increased, sporting institutions became modernized and participatory, and spectator sport became popular with men from all social classes and most demographic groups. Cities became responsible for providing public space for their residents to play, sports arenas became prominent semipublic facilities, open to anyone paying admission, and private clubs were established for the exclusive use of their memberships. In this era, star athletes like John L. Sullivan, Ty Cobb, and Christy Mathewson became national heroes. My analysis of the rise of sport and its development focuses both on the internal history of major sports (the rise of leagues, rules, records, championships, and the dissemination of information) and the influence of broader societal developments, primarily urbanization (city building) and industrialization, and, secondarily, class, race, ethnicity, and gender, upon sporting institutions. In addition, I examine the impact of sport upon the broader American culture and society.

The changes in the American sporting scene began at mid-century and then accelerated after the Civil War, primarily as a result of urbanization and industrialization. The greatest relative increase in urban population in American history occurred in the mid-nineteenth century. As a result, the proportion of the population that resided in cities tripled, from 7.2 percent in 1820 to 19.8 percent in 1860. In 1820 there were just 61 cities (population of 2,500 or more), only 11 of which had more than 10,000 residents. By 1860 there were 93 cities with over 10,000 people, including 9 with over 100,000.

American cities in this era were commercial communities, known as "walking cities" because residents usually walked wherever they had to go, seldom for more than thirty minutes. These cities were almost always located on navigable bodies of water, modest in size (the city limits extended only a couple of miles from the center of town), had small populations, and a highly mixed land use. The docks were the center of business activity. By the 1870s, the accelerated pace of urban growth led to the rise of the industrial radial city. These cities had substantial populations and were physically much larger than walking cities, their size made feasible by the emergence of extensive public transportation systems. Their economies were increasingly based on industry rather than trade. Land uses were highly specialized with distinctive commercial, residential, and industrial areas radiating out in concentric circles from the Central Business District (downtown). Organized sport emerged in the larger walking cities of the mid-nineteenth century, but the great boom in sport took place in the radial industrial cities after the Civil War. Their concentrated populations included a critical mass of potential sports participants and spectators; they provided a ready market for sports entrepreneurs who sold athletic equipment or promoted commercial sports contests.

The role of the city in the rise of modern sport was greater than simply being the site where athletes were drawn from and where sport became organized, commercialized, and professionalized. Cities were organic entities composed of physical structures, social organizations, and value systems that interacted over time to create urban change that itself helped shape the rise of sport. A city's physical structure included its spatial dimensions, demographics, neighborhoods, communication and transportation networks, and economic institutions, while its social organizations encompassed political and governmental structures, social institutions, social classes, and ethnic and racial groups. Value systems comprised individual and group attitudes, ideologies, and behavior. American sport in the industrial radial city was primarily a product of the constant blending of the elements of urbanization with each other and with sport itself.

The late-nineteenth-century sporting boom had its origins in various social forces operating in the antebellum walking city. A major factor was the emergence of a sports creed that changed middle-class attitudes toward sport from negative to positive. This transformation was produced by a broad-based reform movement that sought to ameliorate living conditions for slum dwellers as well as for sedentary white-collar workers by promoting wholesome out-of-door sports. The new sport doctrines demonstrated that athletics could be uplifting and promote public health, improve morality, and build character. It placed sport firmly within the traditional

American expectation that leisure-time activities should be useful as well as diverting.

Once sport's popularity began to grow, the rise of industrial capitalism heavily influenced its direction. The shift from an agrarian and commercial economy to an industrial economy reshaped the urban social structure, the distribution of wealth, and traditional leisure patterns. The industrial age also ushered in remarkable technological innovations. Improved communication networks made possible immediate reports of sporting events by widely read cheap daily newspapers, while the construction of railroads made sport more accessible across the country, facilitating tours by baseball teams, prize fighters, and renowned race horses. Furthermore, factories used innovative manufacturing techniques to mass-produce inexpensive sports equipment that increased opportunities for participation.

The changing spaces of towns that evolved into radial cities had a big impact on sport. Traditional playing areas were often destroyed as land use patterns shifted, such as when empty lots that formerly served as cricket pitches were used for housing or factories. Lovely boulevards and quaint rural roads used for trotting became busy city streets. Once remote streams were drained and woods were cleared, requiring sportsmen to travel further to unpolluted waterways or timberlands. Some of the problems of accessibility were alleviated by innovations such as railroads, streetcars and electric trolleys that enabled athletes and spectators who could afford the cost to get to sporting venues.

City governments responded slowly to the growing needs for outdoor space. Social reformers and boosters pressured municipalities to secure and develop public space for recreation. Cities, led by the example of New York's Central Park in 1858, established beautiful suburban public parks after the Civil War. By the early 1900s, municipalities also developed inner-city sites for small parks and playgrounds, baths, recreational piers, and schoolyards. Local governments continued to be responsible for protecting public property, maintaining order, and promoting morality. The authorities kept young ballplayers out of city streets, regulated sports crowds, issued licenses for sports promotions, fought the gambling menace, and often maintained Sunday blue laws (regulations that enforce strict moral standards, particularly on the Sabbath).

Sport in industrial America was substantially influenced by social class, which was itself heavily shaped by industrialization and urbanization. The economic changes that resulted from industrial capitalism greatly benefited the old rich and created outstanding opportunities for the new rich who made their money as industrial entrepreneurs and financiers. The upper class constituted less than 5 percent of the population, yet by 1890 owned about 30 percent of the national wealth. The elite had considerable leisure time and abundant discretionary income, which society men and women enjoyed in various ways, including participation in exclusive sports clubs and expensive sports. The rich, especially people of new wealth, organized and joined athletic, racing, and country clubs with restricted memberships. They enjoyed sports at these private organizations, and their membership certified their status and separated them from lesser sorts. Their sons proved their manliness by participating in tough sports, particularly football, and by building up an overseas American Empire, carrying the "White Man's Burden" to the third world, where they used American sports to spread their national culture.

Middle-class athletic participation grew markedly in the industrial age. Industrialization altered the antebellum middle class of independent master artisans, farmers, clerks, and shopkeepers into a largely dependent cohort of white-collar clerks, bureaucrats, and professionals who were increasingly employed by business or the growing government. Whereas the old middle class had been critical of sport and its negative social impact, the new middle class was keenly interested in sport because of the influence of the new sports creed, the emergence of upright games such as baseball (which was nonviolent and not identified with gambling, yet still manly and potentially character-building), and the positive role models of the English, Scottish, German, and Scandinavian sporting subcommunities. Besides having a newfound interest in sport, the new middle class had the time, money, and access to athletic facilities that enabled them to enjoy sport.

While urbanization and industrialization facilitated the sporting interests of the upper and middle classes, these processes hindered blue-collar participation. The industrial revolution limited workers' discretionary time and income because of onerous factory work schedules, limited leisure time, and low incomes. The shift in work-place from small craft shops to the machine-driven factory system made skills less necessary, and hence less valuable. Artisans who had considerable control over the antebellum workshop and consider-able free time lost most of their independence and control over their labor with the rise of industrialization. Like machine operators and unskilled laborers, they now worked long hours for modest wages. By 1890 the bottom 90 percent of the population owned only one-fourth of the national wealth. In addition to low incomes and limited discretionary time, lower-class sporting opportunities were hindered by the loss of traditional playing areas to urban development and the increased size of cities, which made outdoor sporting sites such as rivers, woods, parks, and baseball fields increasingly inaccessible.

Ethnicity and race were also major factors in the emerging Amer-ican sporting experience. With the exception of the Irish, who read-ily fit into the male bachelor subculture, immigrants from western Europe brought over with them a sporting heritage that provided a positive role model for middle-class Americans. Voluntary ethnic sports clubs established in urban neighborhoods or rural communi-ties helped these newcomers adjust to American life by sustaining their traditional culture. Conversely, the new immigrants from east-ern and southern Europe came to American cities without a sporting legacy, and they did not become sports-minded. Their sons, however, eager to become Americanized, became active in sports, especially those that fit in with their inner-city environment. Ironically, their athletic participation often enhanced their ethnic identity as they emulated ethnic heroes or joined ethnic sports clubs. Finally, the immigrants' athletic experience was quite different from that of African Americans, whose participation in the national sporting culture was limited and even barred because of race. Despite their skill in many sports, African Americans in the late nineteenth cen-tury were forced out of many amateur organizations as well as most professional sports.

Two of the biggest developments in sport in the industrial age were intercollegiate sport and youth sport. Intercollegiate sport, based on the so-called Oxbridge model of competition (as conducted at Oxford and Cambridge Universities in England) provided college men with a chance to demonstrate manliness, and gave both men and (briefly) women an opportunity to display their prowess, organize extracurricular activities, and promote school spirit. Intercollegiate sport emerged primarily at elite eastern institutions whose student bodies were upper or upper-middle class. By the late nineteenth century, other schools, including the more democratic state universities, copied the program. College football became the big game, and while ostensibly an amateur game, it became highly commercial, and important matches were played in major cities to draw the largest possible audiences. The commercial nature of football encouraged the rise of the professional coach, who often violated the ethics of amateurism and sportsmanship in order to win.

High-school students appropriated the collegiate paradigm, creating student-run interscholastic athletic associations that provided a focal point for the student body and the surrounding neighborhood. Sports programs were also developed by physical educators for elementary-school students, and outside of schools by boys' workers at settlement houses, YMCAs, and inner-city parks to acculturate inner-city, second-generation youth, improve their health, and train them to become productive, law-abiding citizens.

Another major theme is the boom in commercial spectator sports made possible by the great increase in the number of cities and the size thereof. By 1920, when half (51.4 percent) of the national population lived in cities, sixty-eight cities housed over 100,000 residents, led by New York with 5.6 million. Growing populations in the industrial era provided the potential audience needed to encourage a boom in sport. The three leading professional sports were prizefighting, which appealed to the sporting fraternity, horse racing, which appealed to gamblers and the elite, and baseball, which appealed to everyone. Prizefighting was almost universally banned in industrial America because of its violence, the typically low-life origins of fighters and spectators, and the gambling nexus. It was illegal everywhere until the 1890s when permitted in Louisiana, New York, and Nevada, and had a checkered history until the 1920s. Horse racing was a very popular sport in the late nineteenth century, with hundreds of tracks scattered across the country. Reformers, however, fought the sport because of the wagering, and by 1910 only a handful of tracks remained open. Baseball, on the other hand, became the national pastime, its popularity unrivaled. Professional baseball, a relatively inexpensive spectator sport, appealed to all classes, but especially catered at first to middle-class audiences. Tickets to major league games could be as cheap as 25 cents, which even the lowest classes could afford on occasion. Their attendance was hindered, however, by Sunday blue laws and work schedules. A popular baseball creed developed in the early 1900s that epitomized the finest American values, such as self-reliance, respect for authority, and teamwork. Professional teams, usually locally owned, became public symbols of their hometowns. Major League Baseball was considered a meritocracy, drawing players mainly from lower-middle-class urban backgrounds. It was, however, the first major sport to draw the color line, barring African Americans from participating after 1884.

The preeminent sports promoters were typically professional politicians or close associates whose connections provided sports entrepreneurs with protection for their investments, inside information (the best potential sites for sports facilities; plans for mass transit; and warnings about gambling raids), and preferential treatment from City Hall. The promoters built venues that were originally flimsy and dangerous edifices, but as sport became more commercialized and progressive building codes were enacted, the structures became larger, more modern, safer, and costlier. They included large, multifunctional downtown arenas and enormous outdoor facilities such as baseball parks and racetracks built on the outskirts of town or in nearby suburbs. Facilities such as New York's Madison Square Garden, Belmont Park, and the Polo Grounds were among the most prominent semipublic edifices in the industrial radial city.

A new topic examined in this second edition is the role of the United States in the globalization of sports. As mentioned, the United States was originally a recipient of sporting cultures brought over by immigrants. But in the last third of the nineteenth century, Americans began bringing *their* games overseas to prove American manliness, athletic prowess, and high level of civilization—and to make money. In addition to formal baseball tours, American educators, missionaries, and businessmen began teaching distinctly American games in the Pacific Rim and the Caribbean basin, to people who believed American sports represented democracy, meritocracy, and other important American qualities. This began as a part of the

"White Man's Burden" that Americans willingly accepted, but by the turn of the twentieth century it slowly began to become part of national foreign policy, another tool to Americanize and maintain social control over the informal U.S. empire and its new colonies.

The globalization of sport also led to higher levels of international competition, beginning in boxing when a former American slave, Bill Richmond, fought in England in the 1790s and early 1800s. The first championship contest was a boxing match between another former slave, Tom Molineaux, and titlist Tom Cribb in 1810, at Cropthorne, Sussex, attended by several thousand, in which the Englishman kept his crown. In 1811, Cribb took their rematch that reportedly drew 15,000 fans. Thereafter, Americans occasionally participated in sporting events in Great Britain, where they vied to prove their mettle against the finest athletes in the world. This culminated in American participation in the new modern Olympic Games, a quadrennial event that began in 1896. While "the Olympics" consisted of several athletic disciplines, American attention was mainly riveted at track-and-field, which U.S. teams dominated. Their success at the international level was perceived as evidence for the superior physicality of American men, but also the advanced state of U.S. civilization that had led to the production of such outstanding athletes.

By 1920, sport was one of the most prominent popular institutions in America. During the decade of the 1920s, the Golden Age of Sport, men of all social and ethnic backgrounds played and watched sport, as did many middle- and upper-class women. Attendance and rates of participation were at record highs, reflecting the decade's higher standard of living, greater discretionary income, and increased leisure time. Once-shunned gambling sports such as thoroughbred racing and boxing enjoyed great revivals. In 1927, a record 104,000 fans at Chicago's Soldier Field saw Gene Tunney earn $990,000 when he successfully defended his heavyweight title against Jack Dempsey.

Every major sport had its great heroes: Babe Ruth (baseball), Red Grange (football), Jack Dempsey (boxing), Bill Tilden (tennis), Bobby Jones (golf), and Charles Lindbergh (aviation). There were even a few heroines, most notably Gertrude Ederle (swimming) and Helen Wills (tennis). In an increasingly bureaucratic and urban society, their achievements demonstrated the continuing merit of traditional, small-town American values such as hard work and self-reliance. Team sports heroes also epitomized more modern values, such as cooperation and teamwork. Idols such as Grange and Lindbergh combined the best of both worlds, the qualities of both the pioneer and the organization man of the modern industrial society.

CHAPTER ONE

Urbanization, the Technological Revolution, and the Rise of Sport

Sport in the industrial United States was dramatically shaped by urbanization and technological innovation. It was in cities where major amateur and professional sports as well as many popular recreational sports achieved their modern form. Most top athletes were born and reared in cities and played at urban sports facilities ranging from billiard parlors and bowling alleys to arenas, racetracks, parks, and baseball fields. Yet the city was more than a place with a large population that provided a home for players and spectators, and playing sites for athletic contests. Cities performed an active role in the evolution of athletic institutions and sporting cultures that developed in interaction with the principal elements of urbanization.

The city's influence on sport dated back to the colonial era, when 5 percent of the population lived in urban sites. In towns such as New York, Philadelphia, Boston, and Charleston, the relatively concentrated populations provided tavern owners sponsoring sports events with a potential market and facilitated the formation of mid-eighteenth-century sports clubs. Residents relied on their municipal governments to regulate semipublic institutions (particularly taverns), public space (parks and streets), and Sabbath behavior to protect community norms and morality when threatened by the growing sporting interest.

Urbanization did not proceed rapidly in the early-nineteenth-century walking city, but beginning in the 1830s, the pace of urbanization accelerated greatly. During that decade the urban population increased by 63.7 percent; then 92.1 percent in the 1840s, the highest in American history, and 75.4 percent in the 1850s. Population and physical expansion increased dramatically in established cities, accompanied by the appearance of hundreds of new cities. Between 1830 and 1860, New York, the nation's largest city, grew from 202,000 to 814,000; Philadelphia from 161,000 to 566,000; and Brooklyn from 15,000 to 267,000. The town of Chicago in 1833 had merely 300 inhabitants, but it grew to 109,000 in 1860, making it the ninth largest city in the United States. By 1870, one-fourth of the national population was urban, and fifty years later, most Americans were living in cities.

The industrial radial cities of the late nineteenth century grew through annexing outlying communities, made possible by rapid mass transit systems that enabled residents to live even farther than walking distance from their jobs. The central business district (CBD) formed the nucleus of this city. Its property became extremely expensive, shaping the CBD into a highly specialized center of business, culture, and entertainment, that housed corporations, banks, and offices of professional people in newly built skyscrapers, as well as department stores, hotels, museums, theaters, and railroad stations. The high cost of land pushed heavy industry out toward cheaper peripheral areas and satellite cities and dispersed city dwellers into concentric residential zones surrounding the downtown. The first residential belt in the city was the slum, a heterogeneous, impoverished area filled with the latest arrivals to the city. It had poor-quality housing, inadequate urban services, and high mortality and crime rates. The next district was the zone of emergence, an area of upper-lower-class neighborhoods, often second-generation Irish and Germans, that was safer and healthier than the slums. Families lived in modest homes on small lots. The third residential region was known as the suburban fringe. These homogeneous, middle-class, white Anglo-Saxon Protestant (WASP) localities had large, single-family homes on substantial, grassy, tree-lined lots, employed servants, and were blessed by excellent schools and other public services, as well as low rates of crime and mortality. Middle-class husbands at first rode street cars and cable cars to their downtown jobs, but by the 1890s they were traveling by more efficient, electrically powered trolley cars. Boston and New York even had subways by 1904. Beyond the city limits were the suburbs proper, which included wealthy bedroom communities like Evanston and Lake Forest, whose residents rode trains to downtown Chicago to work, but also industrial suburbs like Gary, Indiana, and Cicero, Illinois, whose working-class residents worked close to home in local factories.

The rapid pace of urbanization influenced the rise of sport in several ways. The problems created by urbanization, such as rapid social change, growing social divisions, sedentary middle-class lifestyles, and the expansion of crowded, disease-ridden slums led Jacksonian reformers in the 1830s and 1840s to develop a positive sporting ideology that justified widespread participation in sport. The new sports creed portrayed humane, non-gambling athletic competition (or "clean sport") as socially useful recreations that would improve the health, morality, and character of alienated, poor inner-city residents and revitalize the hard-working middle class who spent little time in the fresh air engaged in exercise or physical labor. These beliefs also prompted a park movement to preserve and create public space for outdoor recreation, especially crucial for slum residents who lacked access to open space and fresh air. Empty lots, formerly used for playing areas, were lost to urban development as cities became more crowded, significantly limiting outdoor space for sport and thereby hindering participation. The push for uplifting sports and breathing spaces enabled reformers by the turn of the century to use sports to acculturate immigrant children by teaching them traditional American values.

Urbanization also had an important impact on the rise of spectator sports. The growing populations of cities created potential markets for spectator sports, although the expanding size of cities made accessibility to arenas and sports fields problematic. Along with public parks, these semipublic facilities became important city institutions that contributed to the urban booster spirit and publicized a town's progressive qualities. Star athletes became local heroes who were seen as role models, and city teams became a source of community for rootless urbanites, promoting a sense of hometown pride.

The Industrial Revolution contributed to the rise of sport in many ways, most directly through technological innovations. The four main contributions of modern technology to post-1870s sports were a) improved communications that provided fans with timely information about sporting events; b) transportation innovations that reduced the cost of travel to contests by participants and spectators; c) the mass production of inexpensive sporting equipment, which encouraged participatory sport, along with d) the invention of new types of sporting equipment.

Urban Reform and the Ideology of Sport

The emergence of a sports ideology justifying athletic participation as a positive force led to sport becoming one of the most popular American amusements. The idea that sport needed to be a beneficial and uplifting institution was rooted in Puritan values that required all pastimes to be moral, revitalizing recreations. The new positive sports creed that emerged in the Jacksonian Era was closely tied to other reform movements that promoted political democracy, social justice, and economic opportunity to address the problems created by the rapid rate of urbanization. The threat of class conflict was exacerbated by growing extremes of wealth and poverty. The urban population was becoming far more heterogeneous because of Irish and German immigration—in 1850 half of Boston's heads of households were immigrants. Traditional values and norms seemed to be breaking down, reflected by skyrocketing crime rates because of widespread poverty and transiency, especially among unsupervised young men who joined street gangs. Urban riots became commonplace due to such factors as anti-abolitionism, racism, and nativism. Disastrous public health problems characterized city life. Impoverished, overcrowded slums had inadequate sanitation and polluted water, insufficient supplies of nutritious food, and poor medical care, resulting in terrible epidemics and high mortality rates. Thus it was hardly surprising that social critics compared city life unfavorably to rural society, whose homogeneous residents presumably enjoyed closer interpersonal ties and whose lifestyle was portrayed as healthy, honest, self-reliant, hardworking, and nonmaterialistic.

Reformers sought to improve urban life for civil and religious reasons. Secular reformers were prompted by unsettling urban conditions, their social conscience, and a desire to implement republican virtues, such as self-improvement and good character. Religious reformers, inspired by the Second Great Awakening (ca. 1820s–1840s), sought to fight sin and to prepare a more perfect society for the impending Second Coming of Christ by promoting order, building character, encouraging Victorian morality, and improving public health. The reformers sought to alleviate social problems through voluntaristic societies that tried to educate the public against such vile behavior as intemperance and prostitution, and by pressuring municipalities to provide such basic services as water, sanitation, compulsory education, police and fire protection, and access to public parks.

Those reformers who identified physical fitness as a potential instrument of positive social change developed the positive sports creed that justified the uplifting value of proper physical activity. This ideology evolved slowly from: the rhetoric of eighteenth-century Enlightenment philosophers such as Dr. Benjamin Rush; the sporting traditions of ancient Greece, where fitness and education went hand-in-hand; and the ideas of early-nineteenth-century European educators such as Pestalozzi and Guts Muths, who emphasized physical activity in their new model schools. The American fitness movement began in the 1840s under the leadership of liberal clergymen such as William Ellery Channing, a Boston Unitarian; scientists such as Lemuel Shattuck, the founder of statistics, journalists such as William Cullen Bryant of the *New York Evening Post*; physicians such as Bronson Alcott; and health faddists such as Sylvester Graham, inventor of the Graham cracker.

Proponents of the sports creed described urban males as unhealthy, unproductive, and often absent from work. They were particularly critical of money-hungry, middle-class office workers who spent the entire day huddled over their desks. Fresh-air sports were recommended as a substitute for the healthier lifestyle of the yeoman farmer, serving the dual purpose of providing exercise and teaching urbanites the traditional moral values of idealized American farmers. Dr. Oliver Wendell Holmes, a Boston fitness advocate, who ran and rowed for his own health, criticized the inactive middle-class lifestyle in his column "The Autocrat of the Breakfast Table" in the inaugural volume of the prestigious *Atlantic Monthly* (1858). He pointed out that the contemporary social elite found sports and exercise socially unacceptable. The doctor disparaged "the vegetative life of the American" compared to the robust life of the English gentry. Holmes foresaw the impending rapid demise of his countrymen, certain that "such a set of black-coated, stiff-jointed, soft-muscled, paste-complexioned youth as we can boast in our Atlantic cities never before sprang from the loins of Anglo-Saxon lineage." He recommended participation in sports that sustained Victorian values such as hard work and sobriety.

Holmes' concerns were seconded by fellow Boston Brahmin Thomas Wentworth Higginson, a Unitarian minister and prominent abolitionist and feminist. In "Saints and Their Bodies," which also appeared in the initial volume of the *Atlantic Monthly*, he reproached unfit bourgeois Americans for being too concerned with making money and not enough with their mental and physical well-being. Higginson recommended enjoyable and health-enhancing outdoor activities and exercises. He wanted required exercise in schools, and he urged men to leave their office woes behind them and meet him at the local gymnasium for a good workout.

Jacksonian reformers, particularly feminist and educator Catharine Beecher, a leading advocate of domesticity and author of *Course of Calisthenics for Young Ladies* (1832), pointed out that women also needed physical fitness, perhaps even more than men. The older sister of Harriet Beecher Stowe, author of *Uncle Tom's Cabin*, Catharine encouraged women to walk, perform calisthenics, and do housework to enhance physical beauty and reproductive capacity. Reformers argued that athletic participation could prevent or cure chronic frailty and illnesses such as nervousness, indigestion, palpitations, and headaches. In 1830, for instance, the *Journal of Health* recommended horseback riding and dancing as a panacea for "women's ailments." By the 1850s, physicians and editors of popular periodicals such as *Harper's Weekly* and *Godey's Lady's Book and Magazine* were recommending gymnastics and moderate exercise to promote femininity, beauty, and grace.

Concerns over the health needs of urban residents led to the public health movement. Physicians believed that sound diets, fresh air, and moderate exercise could build up resistance to potentially fatal diseases. As urban space became more precious, reformers turned to parks for breathing space, especially for the urban poor. Shattuck proposed in 1850 that since "intellectual culture has received too much and physical training too little attention," governments should appropriate funds for "open spaces [that] would afford to the artisan [sic] and the poorer classes the advantages of fresh air and exercise, in their occasional hours of leisure."

Participation in sports would benefit society by promoting traditional American values, teaching valuable new virtues, and developing higher standards of character. By the 1850s certain social critics, frightened by the growth of urban anomie, identified sport as an institution (along with the family, police, and asylums) that would protect communities and alleviate the urban crisis. Exercise would promote manly qualities, especially courage and self-discipline. It would also help bring families closer together because fathers would make time to play and communicate with their sons.

The sports creed offered a solution for the problem of vile slum amusements. Cities were perceived as cesspools of depravity where unsupervised young farmers had gone for work and excitement. Freed from the traditional customs and social control mechanisms that regulated small-town life, they were attracted to such pleasures of the male bachelor subculture as music halls, saloons, brothels, gambling houses, and blood sports. In rat baiting, for instance, gamblers bet on the time it would take a terrier to kill all the rats confined in a pit. Perhaps the most famous locale in the Civil War era for such ignoble sports was Kit Burns' Sportsman's Hall, a popular three-story barroom with a rat pit on the first floor, frequented by New York City's best-known rogues. Burns himself was one of the last leaders of the notorious Democratic Irish Dead Rabbits Gang. He also had an arena behind the main building that held up to four hundred spectators. One of his strangest attractions was a man known as Jack the Rat, who bit off the heads of mice for ten cents, and the heads of rats for twenty-five cents.

Reformers wanted to shelter urban youth from such loathsome pleasures. They criticized such degenerative diversions for hardening men's souls toward brutality and offering instant gratification through gambling. By the 1830s, reformers concluded that wholesome sports substituted for ignoble amusements could restore participants and spectators and prepare them for more useful lives. Reformers such as Reverend Channing recognized that lower-class urbanites had a great need for leisure, and he promoted such moral entertainments as the legitimate theater, classical music, and exercise as alternatives to vile diversions.

Noted Unitarian social reformer Rev. Edward Everett Hale of Boston was the foremost advocate of rational recreation (moral entertainment that was useful in such ways as promoting good health and self-improvement). He knew that city dwellers could not readily go fishing, hunting, or enjoy other traditional, uplifting rustic pleasures, and he advocated wholesome alternatives. Hale had no confidence in commercial entertainments that catered to the lowest tastes to secure the largest possible audiences, so he sought church-state cooperation to promote wholesome recreation. He advocated muscular Christianity, recommending that clergymen promote ameliorative sports such as cricket and football to improve health, develop courage, and build character.

Muscular Christianity was a mid-nineteenth-century English philosophy that focused on harmonizing one's mental, physical, and spiritual dimensions. It advocated clean sport and exercise to develop moral, devout, and physically fit men. Muscular Christians such as Higginson repudiated the conventional wisdom that "physical vigor and spiritual sanctity are incompatible." The connection between morality and exercise was popularized by Thomas Hughes' best-seller *Tom Brown's School Days* (1857), a fictional account of Rugby, an English private school that emphasized athletics to build character.

Muscular Christianity fit in well with the Victorian disdain of libertine behavior. Its alleged benefits, which included increased potency, assuaged upper-class New Englanders' fears of depleting their sexual energies. This was particularly important in the late nineteenth century, when it seemed to old-stock Americans that their race was declining in numbers in comparison to the population of immigrant groups. Muscular Christians saw sport as a promoter of manliness, a check on effeminacy, and an alternative to sexual expenditures of energy. Moral men would earn their manhood on the playing fields, not in the bedroom. As historian Charles Rosenberg points out, "The manly Christian gentleman was the athlete of continence, not coitus, continuously testing his manliness in the fires of self-denial." Sport would enable sedentary middle-class men to maintain such "manly" physical characteristics as ruggedness, robustness, strength, and vigor rather than degenerating into foolish fops.

The muscular Christian philosophy was a cornerstone of the Young Men's Christian Association (YMCA), an evangelical organization founded in London in 1844. The YMCA was brought to the United States seven years later to help farm youth adjust to urban life in a moral milieu. By 1860, the YMCA movement supported moral athletics and gymnastics as "a safeguard against the allurement of objectionable places of resort," and soon established facilities where white-collar males could enjoy exercise with their peers in a pleasant environment. In 1869, for instance, the New York YMCA opened a gymnasium, bowling alley, and baths. The YMCA soon expanded its mission to reach more men and older boys through gymnastics and calisthenics classes.

The YMCA was the primary institutional supporter of muscular Christianity. It sought to develop Christian gentlemen through its philosophy that a strong mind and healthy body supported the spirit. The Christian gentleman was honorable, exercised self-control, avoided sentimentality or yielding to pain, abstained from sex outside of marriage, and, like Frank Merriwell, the hero of late-nineteenth-century juvenile literature, used his strength to protect others. The YMCA's work was supplemented at the end of the century by institutional churches that sought to bring the social gospel of Christ to alienated and impoverished inner-city parishioners by providing various social services, including accessible gymnasiums where they sponsored athletic programs. At a time when Protestantism was often perceived to have become overfeminized, the institutional churches used sport as a carrot to attract male parishioners.

By 1892 there were 348 YMCA gyms, 144 full-time physical education leaders, and about 250,000 members. The fitness program's emphasis shifted from gymnastics to team sports, reflecting a growing interest in athletic competition, and led to the invention of basketball in 1891 and of volleyball four years later at the International Young Men's Christian Training School (founded 1885) in Springfield, Massachusetts. Basketball was invented by thirty-year-old James Naismith as a class project to develop an indoor, nonviolent winter game. The YMCA established the Amateur League of North America in 1895, and its teams competed with colleges and athletic clubs in basketball, swimming, and track-and-field. Top players were recruited by free memberships, room and board, and travel allowances. The most outstanding YMCA team was the Buffalo German YMCA basketball team that captured the gold medal at the 1904 Olympics. By 1911, however, the YMCA deemphasized competition among top athletes to focus on serving the greatest number of participants.

The Young Women's Christian Association (YWCA), founded in London in 1855, came to the United States in 1858. The YWCA lagged behind the YMCA in sport but nonetheless was a leader in promoting women's athletics. The YWCA was founded to protect middle-class young women from the contaminating effects of city life by educating and housing them in dormitories. Historian John R. Betts found that by 1890 physical education had become a crucial part of the YWCA movement. The Boston YWCA, at the forefront of women's sports, first held athletic games in 1882. Two years later it constructed a new building that included a well-equipped gymnasium. YWCAs emphasized gymnastics and dance, along with other feminine sports such as swimming, golf, and tennis. By 1916 YWCAs enrolled over 58,000 girls in physical training programs.

Sport and Urban Space

The changing spatial patterns that accompanied urbanization had an enormous impact upon athletic participation. Overpopulation, urban development, and municipal codes that regulated streets, roads, and docks made it harder to find a place to play ball, ride horses, or swim. Furthermore, the pristine countryside became more and more distant, lessening opportunities for traditional field and stream sports. These trends first appeared in New York, and soon thereafter in other crowded cities such as Jersey City and Newark. By the mid-nineteenth century New York had already lost traditional sporting sites, where cricket had been played and trotting horses raced, to new buildings, streets, and railroad tracks. Local sportsmen moved their outdoor contests to the nearby cities of Brooklyn and Hoboken. These trends occurred later in less densely populated cities like Chicago, which in 1870 still had ample baseball fields in open prairies a mile from the town center.

One prime example of the impact of changing land use patterns on New York's sporting activities can be seen in the history of a single block at Twenty-seventh Street and Fourth Avenue in the Madison Square neighborhood. In 1842, it was a vacant lot where respectable, middle-class young men played a ball game for exercise and fun. Three years later, Alexander Cartwright, Jr., and his associates organized themselves into the Knickerbocker Base Ball Club and drew up formal rules of play for baseball. Later that year, compelled to move from their old location by the northward expansion of New York's residential and commercial properties, the Knickerbockers rented space at Hoboken's Elysian Fields, where they staged their first games.

Madison Square became the site of prestigious hotels and luxurious town houses, and the old ball field became the site of Commodore Cornelius Vanderbilt's train station, freight shed, and stable. In 1871 Vanderbilt, one of the richest men in American history (worth $100 million at his death in 1877, the equivalent today of $20.366 billion) relocated his depot to the new Grand Central Station, then leased the old site two years later to impresario P. T. Barnum. In 1874 Barnum opened the $35,000 Great Roman Hippodrome for his circus. After just one season he leased his structure to bandmaster Patrick Gilmore, lyricist of the popular Civil War song "When Johnny Comes Marching Home." Gilmore staged various events including religious revivals, the first Westminster Kennel Show in 1877, long-distance races, and boxing matches. In 1878, an executive of the dog show operated the facility, which was taken over one year later by the commodore's grandson, William K. Vanderbilt, who inherited $55 million. He took over the building and renamed it Madison Square Garden. William K. emphasized sports promotion at the arena, especially boxing. At that time the neighborhood was the center of the city's social and sporting life, with elegant theaters, shops, and restaurants.

The growth of cities also created a crying need for public play space. This became an important municipal problem, especially in rapidly growing older and densely populated northeastern cities. Even Boston Common, the finest northern public park at midcentury, rapidly became inadequate as the metropolitan area's population quadrupled between 1830 and 1870. By the 1840s a municipal park movement was underway in overcrowded New York, led by journalist William Cullen Bryant and landscape architect Andrew Jackson Downing. In the 1850s, the park movement comprised a broad-based coalition of social reformers, physicians, labor leaders, urban boosters, businessmen, and professional politicians. Advocates claimed that public parks would improve public health and cut down on sick days by increasing access to fresh air. They also hoped to alleviate class conflict and improve order by enabling social classes to mingle. The lower classes would supposedly learn proper social behavior from their social betters. In addition, proponents anticipated that public parks would encourage citizens to support their municipality on other issues in return for providing them with an important service. Park supporters further asserted that parks would aid the local economy by providing jobs, raising property values and taxes on adjacent land, and boosting New York's public image. The Tammany Hall machine, which controlled a major segment of the Democratic Party, anticipated gaining patronage jobs, which was crucial during the Depression of 1857.

The park movement scored a signal success with the construction of the 843-acre Central Park in 1857–58, then on the outskirts of New York's residential sections. The Park Board held an open competition for the park's design, which required a wooded area, a formal English garden, and a parade ground for cricket. The winning sketches were produced by Frederick L. Olmsted, a well-known journalist with political connections, and his partner, landscape architect Calvert Vaux. The inexperienced Olmsted was subsequently hired to supervise construction. Olmsted never built the cricket field because he believed the park should be reserved for receptive recreation (pleasure derived from enjoying beautiful scenery) rather than active recreation. Vigorous sports were fine, but not on Central Park's green grass. "Keep off the Grass" was Olmsted's credo. The Park Board did permit ice skating and boating, which did not mar the park's natural beauty. Central Park was considered an elite park during its first decade because of Olmsted's recreational philosophy, its remote location, and popularity with wealthy owners of horses or carriages.

The completion of Central Park demonstrated how an independent government agency could administer projects, and it encouraged municipalities to use urban planning to protect the environment. Moreover, Central Park became the model for the many large suburban parks built after the Civil War. Olmsted went on to become America's greatest landscape architect, designing parks for Boston, Brooklyn, Chicago, Philadelphia, San Francisco, and Washington, D.C.

The newly built suburban parks were mainly middle-class resorts despite the democratic ideology of park reformers and Olmsted's own expectations that they would be used by everyone as urban populations expanded toward the outskirts of town. Upper- and middle-class residents were most likely to live near these parks and, in any event, could afford the cost of travel there. Furthermore, the parks were several miles from inner-city neighborhoods, which made them inaccessible to poorer folk who could not afford the cost of riding there even after mass-transit routes were in place. Speedy electrified trolley systems developed in the late 1880s and 1890s did not help the poor access parks because the five-cent fare was too steep. An 1890s survey of Lower East Side New York youth discovered few of them had ever been to Central Park because of its inaccessibility even though their own neighborhoods had no parks. Furthermore, the enforcement of blue laws that proscribed many popular amusements on Sunday, the one day working men and women were off from work, and the presence of unfriendly police at the parks discouraged the working class from visiting city parks

If the truth be told, middle- and upper-class citizens preferred that the "riff-raff" stay out of the parks, particularly when lower-class individuals sought to use them for vigorous sports contests and rowdy parties. As upper-lower-class neighborhoods expanded in the direction of suburban parks, sections of the parks were often considered home turf by the dominant local ethnic group, typically the Irish, who would intimidate interlopers. In such cases, historian Roy Rosenzweig notes, "Parks were providing a setting for precisely the sort of behavior they were supposed to inhibit."

In the mid-1880s, pressure from middle-class park users for more active recreation led to their greater use for baseball and other sports. Baseball diamonds were constructed, soon followed by tennis courts that occupied little space and required limited maintenance. By 1885, Central Park had 30 tennis courts, and 125 of them seven years later. Chicago's South Park system had 100 courts by 1905, and more than 300 ten years later. The first public golf course, which required a lot more land and expensive upkeep, was introduced in Boston in 1898. Twenty years later there were about fifty public golf courses throughout the nation that mostly catered to the middle class.

At the same time that suburban parks were under pressure for more active use, reformers launched a complementary small park and playground movement aimed at serving inner-city residents. These small-scale facilities were located in inner-city neighborhoods where they would be readily accessible. They would provide fresh air, uplift children, and keep the poor out of middle-class parks. Park development, especially in the Northeast and Midwest, had fallen behind the growing needs of the slums, where nearly every lot was used for residential, commercial, or industrial purposes. For instance, Chicago's world-renowned suburban park system comprised 1,500 acres, second only to Philadelphia, yet the city's indigent neighborhoods were largely ignored. Three of Chicago's largest communities did not have a single park in 1900, despite a combined population of 360,000, with a high rate of disease and crime.

The use of public parks became a class issue in the 1880s, particularly since the suburban parks were largely inaccessible and inner-city boys had few places to play. Working-class residents of Boston and Worcester, Massachusetts, became increasingly resentful of limited access to their cities' beautiful middle-class parks and of restrictions placed on park use. Historians Stephen Hardy and

Roy Rosenzweig who respectively studied the small park movement in those two cities, found that both cities' working-class residents responded to the unfair situation by actively fighting for small neighborhood parks. Community organizations lobbied their ward committeemen and councilmen to seek appropriations for neighborhood parks and pass laws permitting their use as athletic fields and children's playgrounds. The local activists used their influence with Democratic Irish machine politicians to build modest neighborhood parks that fulfilled their needs for breathing space and recreation.

Despite the determination exercised by Boston's and Worcester's working class, nationally the impetus for the small-park movement in the 1880s came mostly from middle- and upper-class outsiders. In New York City, for instance, support came from reform-minded politicians such as Democratic Mayor Abram Hewitt of New York (1886–87), charity organizations such as the Children's Aid Society, social gospel ministers who wanted to bring Christ's message to the unchurched, crusading journalists, and landscape architects. The movement came to fruition around the turn of the century, led on the local level by progressive middle- and upper-class organizations such as the Outdoor Recreation League (1898), and nationally by the Playground Association of America (1906). The PAA was a coalition of progressives, particularly businessmen, settlement-house workers, and community leaders. They encountered opposition to small parks from machine bosses who preferred larger projects that involved more patronage, slum dwellers who wanted any available land reserved for cheap housing rather than baseball diamonds, and especially from proponents of cheap and limited government.

Small-park advocates believed that playgrounds should be more than merely safe places for inner-city children to play. These reformers believed that they knew what was best for inner-city youths and intended to use small parks to uplift or control second-generation kids. Slum children would be protected from their neighborhoods' deleterious influences and gain a positive alternative to the vile amusements of the streets. The Progressives were convinced by sociological evidence that adult-directed team games were more effective than independent play in teaching inner-city youth such important values as obedience, self-sacrifice, and hard work. Playing sports like baseball and basketball would improve morals, fight juvenile delinquency, and Americanize recent immigrants.

Settlement house leader Jane Addams of Chicago's Hull House successfully prodded the municipality to become the national model for small parks. The city established a special commission in 1899 that in five years opened nine small parks, each less than five acres in size. Thereafter the state legislature empowered the city's three park boards to issue bonds for recreation centers as large as sixty acres, complete with field houses, swimming pools, and athletic fields. These new facilities helped increase Chicago's park use fivefold between 1905 and 1916. President Theodore Roosevelt, honorary president of the Playground Association, described these new parks as the greatest municipal accomplishment of his day. The number of cities with supervised recreation programs rose from fewer than 10 in 1900 to 41 in 1906, and 504 by 1917. City parks became an enormously popular progressive reform that promised a relatively inexpensive way to assimilate immigrant children and promote order in the inner city.

Sport and the Promotion of Public Pride

Another function of sport was to engender pride in one's hometown (boosterism) and country (nationalism). According to conventional wisdom, people could more easily identify with their neighborhood, city, region, or nation when they cheered for athletes or teams who represented them in sporting competition. Any leading late-nineteenth-century metropolis was expected to have such cultural institutions as art museums, symphonies, and universities, as well as public parks and major league baseball teams. No large eastern or midwestern city was truly "major league" unless it had a major league franchise and a first-class baseball field. The absence of a major league team in Buffalo in the early 1900s reflected poorly on the eighth largest city in America, especially since Boston, Chicago, Philadelphia, and St. Louis had two teams each. Only New York, the nation's leading city, had three major league teams in 1903. Local boosters in smaller cities had more modest ambitions. They regarded their baseball team's minor league level and the extent of hometown support at the box office as an index of the community's progressive character. Atlanta, for instance, had a population of 89,872 in 1900, yet had a professional team in the Class B Southern League along with New Orleans, whose population was triple that of the Gate City. Atlantans demonstrated their hometown spirit with large turnouts on opening day that often surpassed that of New Orleans.

New York, befitting its status as the nation's leading metropolis, usually hosted the most important American sporting events, including amateur track-and-field championships, boxing matches, Ivy League football title games in the 1890s and, beginning in 1915, the U.S. National Tennis Championship. Other cities staged the occasional special event to bolster their status, such as the 1904 Olympics in St. Louis, or contests that became annual affairs like the Indianapolis 500, which began in 1911. On the other hand, few large cities supported disreputable sports such as prizefighting, which created a negative public image. Towns that advertised themselves through boxing were small, obscure communities, such as the Nevada towns of Carson City, which hosted the world championship heavyweight title match between Jim Corbett and Bob Fitzsimmons in 1897, Goldfield, location of the Battling Nelson–Joe Gans lightweight title bout in 1906, and Reno, site of the Jack Johnson–Jim Jeffries heavyweight bout in 1910.

In the early 1900s, cities began to build municipal stadiums to provide a facility to house important local amateur sporting events to promote tourism and bolster their civic image. The first was Buffalo's 12,000-seat Pan American Exposition Stadium, built in 1901 for the so-named world's fair. It hosted events ranging from a major eastern track meet to a day of traditional Irish Games. It was surpassed in 1915 by San Diego's 23,000-seat Balboa Stadium (1915), built for the California Panama Exposition.

In the 1920s, the construction by municipalities and other local governments of public outdoor facilities became relatively commonplace. The first important facility was the Rose Bowl in Pasadena (1922), which seated 40,000, but eventually seated more than 100,000. The Baltimore Stadium was also built in 1922, mainly for football. These two were followed the next year by the Los Angeles Coliseum, built jointly by the city and Los Angeles County in 1923 to seat 75,000 — raised to 101,000 for the 1932 Olympics — at a total cost of $1.9 million. Next came Chicago's 75,000-seat Soldier Field in 1924, expanded to seat 100,000 by 1927, at the very high cost of $8.5 million. The Philadelphia Municipal Stadium, opened in 1926, eventually seated more than 120,000.

Along with fostering local pride, sport also provided a valuable means to demonstrate national self-esteem. Nineteenth-century American sportsmen measured themselves against British standards and made a giant leap forward with America's victory in 1851 over the finest British yachts in the Royal Yacht Squadron's "One Hundred Guinea Cup" race. Nine years later, Americans took great pride when American boxing champion John C. Heenan earned a draw in his fight against English titlist Tom Sayers for the world championship.

As will be discussed later (in chapter six), in the second half of the nineteenth century and the first decades of the twentieth century, national pride in American sport and athleticism expanded well beyond old grudges with "mother England" into the wider world. International tours by professional baseball players spread American culture east and south, with the quintessentially American game of baseball soon becoming popular in Japan and enormously so in the Latin-American Caribbean basin. Finally, with the inauguration in 1896 of the modern Olympic Games, Americans were quick to take an interest. Only ten years later, a functioning United States Olympic Committee sent its first official, publicly financed, uniformed team to the unofficial intercalated (interim) games in Athens.

The Technological Revolution and the Rise of Sport

Sport and the Communications Revolution

Sports journalism played a key role in generating and sustaining popular interest in sport. In the days before radio and television, Americans depended on daily newspapers for their sporting news. In a nation of 75 million people in 1899, the average daily newspaper circulation was 15 million, led by the *New York World* at 600,000. Publishers devoted a growing amount of local news coverage to sports because it sold papers. In the 1920s, for instance, sporting news comprised 40 percent of local news in the *World*, and 60 percent in the *New York Tribune*.

American newspapers in the early republic were expensive and primarily served readers interested in business and politics. By 1831, however, penny newspapers had emerged, written for the masses, such as the *New York Sun* and the *Philadelphia Ledger*. They covered such popular topics as crime, gossip, horse races, and prizefights that reporters "accidentally" encountered. In the 1840s, James G. Bennett's *New York Herald* emphasized sport and other popular subjects to build circulation, sending up to eight reporters to cover a sporting event. The entire front page on May 5, 1845, was devoted to the Fashion-Peytona match, one of the five great North-South horse races of the antebellum era. Readers were naturally informed about the outcome of the race, but also about crowd composition, wagering, and the ambience at the Union Course. Bennett made excellent use of the latest technological innovations, such as telegraphy, which helped journalists quickly report major events at distant sites, and the speedy rotary press (1846) that printed 20,000 sheets an hour. As a result, Bennett built the *Herald* into America's most popular paper by the Civil War with a circulation of 60,000.

Subsequent inventions further speeded mass production of newspapers and cut costs. Improved presses printed on a continuous roll of cheap, pulp-based paper, cut it into sheets, and folded it, while the Mergenthaler linotype machine (1886) mechanized typesetting. Along with excellent distribution systems and the rise of yellow journalism, these inventions facilitated a boom in the penny press that resulted in huge circulations. Yellow journalism emphasized sensationalism, with large, misleading headlines, faked interviews, more than ample use of graphics, and melodramatic stories often focusing on such popular topics such as crime, sports, and sex. In the 1880s the number of New York City dailies rose from thirty-three to fifty-five, and circulation almost doubled, to nearly 1.8 million. The *New York World*, purchased in 1883 by Joseph Pulitzer, became a model for other publishers by drastically cutting production costs, using lots of illustrations, and stressing yellow journalism. Pulitzer raised the *World*'s circulation from 15,000 to 250,000 in just four years.

The *World* established the first sports department and, according to literary critic Michael Oriard, the first distinctive sports page (1896), which other papers quickly emulated. Pulitzer also pioneered sensationalist evening editions aimed at working men as well as entertainment-oriented Sunday editions with special sports coverage. He and his competitors enhanced the sports section with expensive engravings that by themselves told complete stories independent of any reporter's narrative. Halftone photographs were added in the late 1890s to further lighten up the printed page and bring readers some of the excitement of the playing field.

The baseball writer was the star of the sports page. He helped popularize the sport and linked the home team to fans who followed professional baseball in the media even if they seldom attended games. English immigrant Henry Chadwick, originally a cricket expert, was the first baseball journalist and the inventor of the all-important statistic, the batting average. Chadwick started covering baseball for the *Herald* in 1862, and also wrote for other newspapers and sports weeklies, especially *The Sporting News*, which began in 1886. He edited the first baseball guide, the *Beadle Base-Ball Player* (1860–81), and then the *Spalding Official Baseball Guide* until his death in 1908. He was a staunch proponent of sportsmanship and rule reforms. As a member of the rules committee of the amateur National Association of Base Ball Players, founded in 1857, Chadwick led the effort to make baseball manlier by advocating the fly-out rule, adopted in 1864, which required a fielder to catch a batted ball without a bounce to record an out. He established a widely emulated, straightforward manner of reporting a game's major events, but in the late 1880s a more entertaining and creative style was developed in the competitive Chicago newspaper market. Leonard Washburn began the trend in 1886 by spicing up his stories with an appealing, light-and-breezy tone soon adopted by Finley Peter Dunne (though he was best known for the character he created, "Mr. Dooley," a South Side Irish saloon keeper who pontificated in dialect on various political and social issues). Another member of the so-called "Chicago School of Sports Writing" was Charles Seymour, who employed slang, metaphors, and similes instead of dry and formal reporting.

The first major sports weeklies were John Stuart Skinner's rurally oriented *American Turf Register and Sporting Magazine* (1829), which emphasized horse racing, and William T. Porter's more urbane *Spirit of the Times* (1831), which promoted angling and horse racing, but also covered cricket, rowing, and yachting. Porter aimed his weekly, which cost $10 for a one-year subscription, at gentlemen of property and standing. By the mid-1850s the *Spirit* had a weekly circulation of 40,000 copies. Other urban periodicals included George Wilkes' sensationalist *National Police Gazette* (1845) which began as an anti-crime tabloid, and Frank Queen's *New York Clipper* (1853), a popular advocate of baseball and a leading defender of prizefighting. In 1856, Wilkes sold the plebeian *Police Gazette* and bought the *Spirit*, which in a slightly altered form remained in business through 1902. The *Spirit* covered track-and-field better than any other magazine and was the preeminent horse-racing weekly of its day. The *Police Gazette* fell on hard times until Irish immigrant Richard Kyle Fox took it over in 1877. Fox emphasized crime, sex, and working-class sports, primarily boxing. He made the *Police Gazette* the bible of boxing and promoted several major matches. Fox donated jeweled belts to honor champions in different weight classes, as well as medals and trophies for other sports, such as pedestrianism and weight lifting, both of which were popular with the male bachelor subculture.

The *Gazette* was printed on garish, red-tinted paper and amply illustrated with sketches of athletes and scantily clad women. Its average weekly circulation stood at 150,000, one of the highest of any American weekly, topped by a 400,000–copy print run following the Paddy Ryan–Joe Goss boxing championship in 1880. By comparison, the circulation of *Harper's Weekly*, a prestigious middle-class opinion maker, was only 85,000. The *Police Gazette* was extremely influential among working-class sports fans, whose interests it irreverently and constantly defended. The magazine was ubiquitous in saloons, barbershops, hotels, and other centers of the male bachelor subculture, where each edition passed through dozens of hands.

Popular general-interest periodicals provided considerable sports coverage as well, especially baseball. In addition, by the 1890s, these magazines were second to the daily press in the coverage of football, but still mainly emphasized baseball. The more high-brow weeklies and monthlies like *The Independent* were much more critical of sports than the hugely successful middle-brow magazines such as *Colliers* or the *Saturday Evening Post*. In the early 1900s, middle class periodicals enjoyed a remarkable surge in readership. For instance, the *Saturday Evening Post* had 1 million subscribers by 1913.

Communication innovations not only enhanced and made sports reportage more accessible, but they also had a big impact on illegal gambling. In the late nineteenth century, Western Union, which controlled the nation's telegraph lines, sold information on sporting events not only to newspapers, but also to poolrooms (illegal off-track betting parlors), billiard halls, and saloons where a lot of betting on sports occurred. The bet takers needed instant reports about baseball games, boxing matches, and especially horse races to prevent cheating by their clients. By 1891, Western Union's racing department was its most profitable, earning $18,000 a week just from New York City poolrooms. In the early 1890s New York tracks temporarily barred Western Union because they were losing too much of the betting business to off-track sites. Wire-service employees responded by initiating several imaginative schemes to secure racing results, including sending in female agents with carrier pigeons hidden under their dresses to forward the outcomes. In 1904, the racing bureau was bringing in $5 million a year, but one year later the moral opposition of Helen Gould, daughter of robber baron Jay Gould (who had at one time a controlling interest in Western Union), and other major stockholders forced the telegraph company out of the racing business. A new racing wire was established that ended up six years later in the hands of Chicago bookmaker Mont Tennes, who thereafter monopolized racing news for sixteen years. Along with the telegraph, another communication innovation that had a great influence on illegal gambling was Alexander Graham Bell's telephone, invented in 1876. Gambling syndicates at first used the telephone to warn poolrooms about impending raids, and later to distribute race results from a central office to neighborhood bookmakers. It was not until the 1920s, however, that bookmakers used the telephone to take bets directly from their clients.

Sport and the Transportation Revolution

Transportation innovations, especially the railroad and the trolley car, were crucial in facilitating the rise of sport. The railroad substantially shortened long-distance travel, making it easier for top athletes to compete in distant cities, outdoorsmen to reach far-away hunting and fishing sites, and the rich to get to their remote exclusive resorts. The development of mass transit within cities also had a huge impact, by greatly increasing access to sporting facilities, particularly for spectatorial events.

As early as the 1840s, New York horse-racing fans used railroads to reach distant racecourses at the outskirts of town like the Union Course in Queens County. The railroad's potential to stimulate long-distance trips for sport was initially demonstrated in 1852, when the Boston, Concord, and Montreal Railroad sponsored the first American intercollegiate athletic contest, a Harvard-Yale crew race at Lake Winnipesaukee, New Hampshire, where the railroad hoped to promote tourism. The competitors were given a free vacation for their efforts.

Shortly after the Civil War, trains played an important role in the growth of baseball. The 1869 national tour by the undefeated Cincinnati Reds, the first all-salaried team, was made feasible by railroads, and one year later, Harvard's nine toured by rail as far west as Milwaukee. The first professional teams in the National Association of Professional Baseball Players in 1871, as well as its successor leagues, depended on trains to complete long-distance trips that might start in Boston and end in St. Louis. Rail lines competed for the baseball trade by offering teams special rates and proudly advertising their patronage. Local rail lines solicited business by selling reduced-rate tickets to fans or by running special trains to the ballparks.

Railroads contributed significantly to the survival of prizefighting, universally banned until the 1890s. Even major bouts, including heavyweight champion John L. Sullivan's title defense against Jake Kilrain in 1889 for a record $20,000 purse, had to be clandestinely staged. The sporting fraternity gathered for the bout in New Orleans, and on July 7, 2,000 boxing fans who had paid $10 to $15 for excursion tickets were whisked out of town on three trains on an unannounced route. The trains stopped after crossing the state line into Richburg, Mississippi, where a ring was laid out the next morning. This was the last heavyweight championship fought under the London Prize Ring rules of 1838. Pugilists brawled bare-knuckled and were permitted to tackle their opponents, but were forbidden from hair-pulling or head-butting. Rounds were unlimited and lasted until one fighter was downed. He then had thirty seconds to come to the middle of the ring and resume fighting. The Sullivan-Kilrain bout lasted for about two hours, until the challenger failed to appear for the seventy-sixth round.

Railroads had a major impact on horse racing by transporting trotters and thoroughbreds across the country to compete at various racecourses. This made feasible the creation of harness racing's Grand Circuit, a regular schedule of racing dates at major eastern and midwestern tracks. Trains also brought spectators to suburban racetracks as well as to more distant, out-of-town tracks. In 1870, for instance, the Harlem, Rensselaer and Saratoga Railroad shipped thoroughbreds from New York City to Saratoga Springs at cost in an effort to promote the resort and thereby increase future ridership.

The railroads recognized that racing was good for business, and they employed their political influence on behalf of the turf. The Pennsylvania Railroad, for example, did considerable business in the late nineteenth century carrying New York and Philadelphia bettors to neighboring New Jersey tracks. The Penn's lobbyists in Trenton were among the strongest supporters of racing from the mid-1880s until the state banned horse-race gambling in 1894.

Railroads also catered to cyclists, anglers, hunters, and other sportsmen by offering special rates or free baggage. Touring cyclists going to rustic destinations could bring their bicycles on board without any charge, while the Chesapeake and Ohio Railroad, known as "the Route of the Sportsman and Angler to the Best Hunting and Fishing Grounds of Virginia" and West Virginia, proclaimed, "Guns, fishing tackle, and one dog for each sportsman carried free."

The emergence of mass transit in antebellum New York and Philadelphia, the nation's most populated cities, was tied to the physical growth of the walking city. The horse-drawn carriage (omnibus) and the horse-drawn streetcar that rode over rails were mainly used between 1850 and 1880 for going to work, shopping, or recreation. New Yorkers, for instance, rode streetcars to reach Central Park, located several miles north of the principal residential areas. They also commuted by ferry to popular Brooklyn and Hoboken athletic fields.

As walking cities grew into radial cities, urbanites increasingly had to travel farther than they could comfortably walk. Big innovations after the Civil War greatly enhanced the speed and comfort of mass transit, primarily by supplanting horse power with mechanical power. The first big advance was the cleaner and faster cable car, introduced in 1873 in San Francisco to replace horses that struggled to climb the city's steep hills. However, they were expensive to set up, requiring the digging up of streets and the laying of lengthy cables that connected each vehicle to its steam-driven power source. Furthermore, the system was unreliable, and when a cable broke, it put all of the cars on that route out of commission. In other cities, the cable car was quickly surpassed by the electrified streetcar, first employed in South Bend, Indiana, in 1882, although the standard system was not implemented until 1888 by Frank Sprague in Richmond, Virginia. Sprague's big innovation was the use of an electric pole ("troller") to connect the vehicle to an overhead DC electric source. Within a few years it virtually eliminated all competition, although in Boston the subway was introduced in 1897, followed by one in New York seven years later. This circumvented the dilemma of trying to move large trolleys on overcrowded downtown streets. The principal transit routes extended outward from the central business district toward middle-class residential neighborhoods and anticipated sites of development at the urban periphery. Lines often terminated at a distant suburban park, and sometimes at ballparks. Trolleys made sports facilities and municipal parks very accessible to middle- and upper-lower-class urbanites.

Mass-transit traction companies frequently encouraged traffic by developing recreational sites near their terminals. Over one hundred lines sponsored amusement parks that included roller-skating rinks, shooting galleries, and arenas for bicycle, dog, and foot racing. Their success encouraged traction interests to support professional baseball. Streetcar companies subsidized club-owned teams and built ballparks at the ends of their routes. Historian Ted Vincent found that in the late nineteenth century, transit firms in seventy-eight cities were financially involved in professional baseball. Streetcar interests even owned or sponsored major-league teams. Cleveland fans in the late 1890s could buy a round-trip ticket and admission to the ballpark right on the trolley, both of which were owned by the Robison family. The close ties between rapid transit and baseball provided a nickname for Brooklyn's team in the 1890s when they played in Brownsville at Eastern Park. The club became known as the "Trolley Dodgers," or Dodgers for short, because fans walking to the field had to be careful to avoid getting struck by passing trolley cars.

Lights, Camera, Action

Certain technological innovations contributed to sports development by recording outstanding achievements and preserving great athletic moments. The measurement and evaluation of athletic feats was greatly enhanced by the stopwatch, which originally recorded times in fifths of seconds, and the camera, which helped determine winners of close horse races. Motion pictures provided a means to keep a permanent visual record of a sporting event in action. In 1889 Thomas A. Edison invented the kinetoscope, the first practical motion-picture camera. In 1894, one of his first subjects was boxing matches, because he felt there was a market for fight films. Three years later the James Corbett–Bob Fitzsimmons heavyweight championship fight was filmed, grossing $75,000.

The introduction of electric lighting had an important impact on the viewing of indoor sports. Indoor arenas were originally poorly lit by dull, flickering, and dangerous gas lamps. Edison's incandescent light bulb, invented in 1879, was a superior alternative, emitting an adjustable and consistent illumination that used independently operated outlets. In 1880 William K. Vanderbilt's Madison Square Garden became one of the first semipublic buildings to use electric lighting. Vanderbilt admired the quality of incandescent lighting, and he also wanted to advertise Edison's Electric Light Company, which his family helped to finance. Athletes complained, however, that the lights were too bright, and the Garden returned to gas until 1885. Nevertheless, electric lighting was clearly superior to other forms of illumination, and by 1890 its use became commonplace at leading indoor sports facilities. Historian John R. Betts believed that the improved lighting systems helped draw athletes and spectators to athletic clubs, armories, and sports arenas.

Artificial lighting was seldom used out-of-doors, although the first night baseball game was played in Fort Wayne, Indiana, in 1883. The quality of the illumination was originally inadequate for baseball, but the technological problems had apparently been resolved by 1909, when an amateur game was played under artificial lighting at Cincinnati's Palace of the Fans. One year later a semipro night game at Chicago's Comiskey Park drew 20,000 spectators. Still, conservative baseball-team owners did not implement night baseball until the Depression.

Technological Innovations and Sports Equipment

One of industrialization's principal influences on sport was the fabrication of cheap sporting goods and the invention of new and superior equipment. Factories utilized the American system of manufacturing, which involved strict division of labor and standardization of parts to mass produce sporting goods and sharply lower consumers' costs. A top-of-the-line major league baseball manufactured by Spalding cost $1.25 in 1892, but customers could buy a lesser Spalding baseball for as little as five cents. Consumers in the late nineteenth century had several options when it came to buying the equipment they needed, ranging from specialized sporting goods stores to mail-order catalogues like those of Sears, Roebuck and Montgomery Ward. A shop-at-home buyer perusing his Sears, Roebuck catalogue in 1895 had more than sixty pages of sporting goods to choose from. A new option emerged in the early 1900s when Macy's established the first sporting-goods section in a department store.

Albert G. Spalding was the preeminent manufacturer of sporting goods. Originally an outstanding pitcher for the Boston Red Stockings of the National Association from 1871 to 1875, Spalding compiled a record of 204–53, over fifty more victories than anyone else. In 1876 he became player-manager of the Chicago White Stockings of the new National League, where he went 47–12, and led the NL in wins. When Spalding came to Chicago he opened a sporting-goods store and a publishing company that printed a full line of sports guidebooks. These books instructed readers how to play a particular sport, provided them with information about its rules, history, and records, and advertised Spalding's products. Spalding expanded his firm into a well-integrated and efficient sporting-goods company that manufactured athletic equipment. By the 1890s he nearly monopolized all aspects of the sporting-goods industry. He increased market share by advertising heavily in sporting magazines and sponsoring tournaments to promote his merchandise. A. G. Spalding and Brothers became closely identified with the governing agencies of various sports by publishing their guidebooks and rules, and by becoming their official supplier of equipment, a status that seemingly certified their products' quality. Spalding employed the same business methods as other captains of industry who restructured their businesses to control the supply of raw materials and the distribution of finished goods. For instance, Spalding bought his own lumber mills to guarantee a steady supply of wood for manufacturing baseball bats.

Entrepreneurs developed new products that improved the performance of sandlot players as well as elite athletes. For example, the speed of racing crews was enhanced in 1870 by the introduction of sliding seats, and subsequent innovations such as swivel oarlocks, and smooth, lacquered, lightweight racing shells. Harness racing was dramatically enhanced by streamlined sulkies with pneumatic tires (1888) that cut the mile record by about five seconds. Baseball was improved by the introduction of the catcher's mask and chest protector, enabling the receiver to move closer to the batter. Ball games were ameliorated by the use of vulcanized rubber that produced more elastic and resilient balls. A particular improvement came in golf, the new rubber-cored golf balls of the early 1900s enabling players to hit up to seventy-five yards farther than with the old gutta-percha ball, a development that required architects to design larger golf courses.

The bicycle was one of the most important of the new sporting goods, providing urbanites with personal transportation to go wherever and whenever they wanted. A "machine in the garden," the bicycle enabled millions of middle-class men and women (who could afford its high cost) to escape modernity and the crowded industrial city for pastoral landscapes and a slower pace of life on a vehicle that was itself a testament to modern technology. The first bicycle was Pierre Lallement's velocipede, invented in France in 1865. He brought the "boneshaker" (nicknamed for the quality of its ride) to America one year later. A riding fad began in 1868 in eastern cities that caused many municipalities to pass regulations curtailing cyclists who interfered with horseback riders and pedestrians.

The velocipede was superseded by the English ordinary, an odd-looking vehicle first exhibited in 1876 at Philadelphia's Centennial Exposition. It had a large front wheel, sixty inches in diameter, and a tiny rear wheel that lightened the machine's weight. The ordinary had some distinct disadvantages. A new bicycle cost a steep $100, was hard to master, uncomfortable to ride, and dangerous to maneuver. Most riders were middle-class daredevils who had conquered the difficult techniques of mounting, riding, and braking, and traveled at high speeds. Manufacturer Albert A. Pope championed the ordinary by promoting cycling magazines and cycling organizations. In 1878 he established a cycling club in Boston, the first in the United States, and also helped organize the League of American Wheelmen. The LAW was a national pressure group with the goal to galvanize riders into a voting bloc to rapidly secure access to city streets and parkways. The league also provided other services such as publishing road maps and evaluating routes to make cycling more enjoyable.

The invention of the English safety bicycle in the late 1880s created a secure, comfortable, easy-to-ride, lightweight vehicle with equal-sized pneumatic tires and efficient coaster brakes. Although the newer bicycles were still not cheap—a medium-quality vehicle cost $100—cycling rapidly became enormously popular. The new vehicle led to a new bicycle fad in the mid-1890s enjoyed by some 4 million cyclists. By 1896, 1.2 million bicycles were produced annually, and at the turn-of-the-century Americans owned 10 million bicycles. Riders often joined cycling clubs that provided them an instant community of people who shared the same passion. There were over 500 cycling clubs by 1895. One of their duties was to sponsor races for their members, including 100-mile events (known as a "century"). Just completing the course was victory enough for most riders. There were other local amateur events, such as the annual fifteen-mile Chicago-to-Pullman Race that attracted up to 400 participants.

Manufacturers promoted the safety bicycle by subsidizing professional riders whose victories ostensibly confirmed their machine's high quality. Six-day indoor bicycle races dated back to 1879, and ten years later, the first professional women's six-day event was staged at New York's Madison Square Garden. Major races at the Garden in the 1890s drew up to 10,000 spectators. In addition to the long-distance events, professional sprint racing was also very popular. The sprints were dominated by African American Marshall "Major" Taylor, world champion in 1899 and American champion in 1898 and 1900.

Cycling was the most popular physical activity among middle-class women. Most health professionals and other advocates applauded cycling for women because it provided exercise, an affordable and independent mode of transportation, and an escape to the countryside. Cycling necessitated the wearing of less-restrictive sports clothes that signified women's growing liberation from Victorian patterns of dependence and subservience. Riders discarded corsets and floor-length dresses for slightly scandalous bloomers and split skirts. Conservative critics found the sport stressful and feared it might encourage housewives to shun domestic chores. Detractors also pointed out that cycling threatened Victorian respectability by fostering coed activities and making women too independent and visible. No woman challenged prevailing criticisms about cycling more than Annie "Londonderry" Cohen Kopchovsky, a first-generation American, and a married woman with three children, who bicycled around the world in 1894–95!

Historian Richard Harmond has pointed out that safety bicycles epitomized progress, symbolized the victory of technology over environment, and provided a means to escape the negative features of urban industrialization. The bicycle was a machine, yet it freed people, albeit temporarily, "from the disruptions and stresses of a machine-based society." Nature became more accessible for riders who exercised while enjoying visions of beauty and peace of mind.

These could be brief jaunts or more substantial tours on well-organized routes, along which riders could stay at LAW-approved inns.

By the turn of the century, well-to-do men seeking a more exciting and prestigious experience turned to the more complex, speedier, and expensive automobile, which originally cost several thousand dollars. The car's early history recapitulated that of the bicycle, which it displaced as the primary mode of individual transportation. By World War I the bicycle was mainly a toy for children. The automobile and the internal combustion engine were invented in Germany in the late 1880s, and their cars set the early standard. Several of the first American automobile manufacturers, including Henry Ford, came from the cycling business, and they applied their experience to car production. They tested their vehicles and advertised their quality by participating in car races, starting in 1895 with a fifty-three-mile round-trip contest from the South Side of Chicago to Evanston. Six cars started the race, which was won by automobile manufacturer Charles Duryea. Only one other car finished. Henry Ford got into the racing business seven years later. He originally drove his own cars before turning them over to professionals such as Barney Oldfield. Races in enclosed ovals were sponsored by local boosters in Atlanta, Daytona Beach, and Indianapolis to promote tourism and draw attention to their cities. The first Indianapolis 500 in 1911 drew 80,000 spectators. There were also road races that tested endurance and publicized the need for good highways, such as the long-distance Glidden Tours inaugurated in 1904.

The first race across the United States was in 1905 from New York to Portland, Oregon, by two old runabouts, later described as "motorized buckboards," which the winner completed in forty-four days. Just three years later, six cars set out west from New York to cross the continent and then the world, ending in Paris, 22,000 miles away. (They ferried across the Pacific.) The race was won by American George Schuster in a Thomas Flyer. The following year, Alice Huyler Ramsey, at the age of twenty-two, became the first woman to drive across the United States in her Maxwell DA, doing so in fifty-nine days.

By the 1920s, cars were readily available mainly because of Henry Ford's innovative production and marketing of the Model T, which brought the cost down to $290, as well as an improved standard of living, installment buying, and the emergence of a secondhand market. Car racing remained a significant sport in the 1920s, but the automobile's primary role in sport was mainly transporting fans to ball games and golfers to the links.

Conclusion

The unparalleled rate of urbanization and industrialization in the nineteenth century and the emergence of a positive new sports creed in response to the problems created by rapid urban growth shaped the emergence of American sport in the period between 1850 and 1920. Justification for widespread sporting interest came from the new creed that encouraged physical fitness and athletic competition in nongambling, humane sports as a substitute for traditional vile amusements and the lost pastoral life. Sports were seen as a partial antidote to such urban problems as the antisocial behavior of the male bachelor subculture, unacculturated immigrants, high rates of disease, and the fear of declining vitality and manliness among middle-class urbanites. Yet as cities grew, access to healthful outdoor playing space became more difficult because of competing needs for ever-more-valuable space. Urbanites in the industrial city relied heavily on public parks near their homes for sporting opportunities.

Cities provided an ample market in a physically concentrated area to encourage industrialists to manufacture sporting equipment; and sufficient numbers of potential ticket buyers stimulated entrepreneurs to promote commercial spectator contests. It was in the cities where major technological breakthroughs were employed to facilitate the growing interest in sport, ranging from communication and transportation innovations to mass production of sporting equipment. Once a sound base was established for the rise of a modern sporting culture, people from different social classes and ethnic groups operating within the constraints of the industrial radial city shaped the emergence of sport as a popular mass institution.

The Yacht *America* Winning the International Race, 1851. Commodore John Cox Stevens of the NYYC and five others formed a syndicate and hired George Steers to design a 101-foot yacht to race in England. America won the race around the Isle of Wight against fifteen British rivals in a huge upset, demonstrating the prowess of American seafarers and naval architects. This was the first major victory of American sportsmen over Great Britain. Painting by American Fitz Henry Lane. *Courtesy, The Athenaeum.*

William Walker Martin (1860–1942) on an ordinary bicycle with its large front wheel and small rear wheel. Martin was an outstanding professional rider who, in 1891, won a six-day professional race at Madison Square Garden, New York, covering 14,66 miles, for which he earned $2,000. Considered the long-distance champion of the world, in 1894 he won the 10-mile and 20-mile world championships. *Library of Congress, (LC-USZ62-105442)*

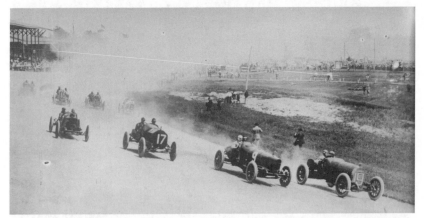

Indianapolis 500 in 1913. Ten of 27 cars starting the third Indy 500 race finished the entire distance. The race was won by Jules Goux of France, driving a Peugeot in 6 hours: 35 minutes and leading for 138 laps. He earned $21,165—more than double the second place finisher. *Library of Congress, (LC-DIG-ggbain-13113)*

Central Park, Winter. The Skating Pond. Currier & Ives lithograph, 1862. Co-ed ice skating became a popular fad in the early 1860s following the construction of New York's Central Park. It was one of the few active pleasures that men and women could enjoy together. *Library of Congress, (LC-DIG-pga-00646)*

In 1886, elite racing fans rode their luxurious carriages to Jerome Park in New York, dressed in their finest attire. They had the option of watching from the infield or the lavish clubhouse. Drawn from photographs by Bidwell. *"Coaches at Jerome Park on a Race Day."* Harper's Weekly *30 (19 June 1886): 389. Library of Congress, (LC-USZ62-10637)*

The Morris Park Racetrack's $240,000 clubhouse opened in 1891 in what is today part of the borough of the Bronx, New York. The six-story building, open year-round, had sixty-rooms, including forty-two bedrooms. It combined the finest features of the country club and the downtown city club including a huge ballroom. The piazza overlooking the race course seated 1,000 people. *"The Club-House of the New York Jockey Club,"* Harper's Weekly *335 (29 June 1891): 465.*

The Horse in Motion. "Sallie Gardner," owned by Leland Stanford, running at a 1:40 gait over the Palo Alto track, 19th June 1878. These photographs were taken by Eadweard Muybridge (1840–1904), a noted British photographer who pioneered the study of animal and human locomotion in the late 1870s, employing multiple cameras to capture motion in stop-action photographs. His work demonstrated that running horses actually have all four feet off the ground at one moment. *Library of Congress, (LC-DIG-ppmsca-06607)*

Upper-class racing fans enjoyed a gracious ambience at the Saratoga Racetrack on 5 August 1905. The day's highlight was the Saratoga Special for two-year-olds, won by Mohawk II, owned by state racing commissioner John Sanford. *"The Racing Season at Saratoga: The Running of the 'Saratoga Special,'"* Harper's Weekly *49 (19 August 1905): 1191.*

Isaac Murphy, America's Leading Jockey of the Nineteenth Century.
Murphy (1861–1897) won three Kentucky Derbies (1884, 1890, 1891),
and four of the first five American Derbies (1884–1888) in Chicago.
The most respected and admired African American athlete of his era, he
reportedly won a remarkable one-third of his races, with earnings that
ranged up to $20,000, excluding bonuses. Murphy holds records that
remain unbeaten to this day. *Library of Congress, (LC-USZ62-50261)*

One of the earliest photographs of women playing golf, at the Jackson Sanatorium in Dansville, New York, 1890. Established in 1854, Jackson was renowned for its health-inducing waters. The women wore long dresses and shirtwaists which was the accepted costume for female golfers. *Library of Congress, (LC-USZ62-63587)*

Twenty-year-old Francis Ouimet, a local boy, at Brookline Country Club at the 1913 U.S. Open. He was the first American amateur to win the event, defeating renowned British professionals. Ouimet's success helped to bring the sport into the mainstream. *Library of Congress, (LC-DIG-ggbain14173)*

Men and women playing and watching tennis on public courts at New York City's Central Park in the early 1900s. The middle-class had been playing the game on public sites for around two decades. *Library of Congress, Detroit Publishing Company Collection, (LC-D401-17424)*

Boys Playing Ball in a Boston Alley. Space in inner-city neighborhoods was at a premium. Youths playing baseball had to be creative in inventing their own ground rules to adapt the game to the available spaces, such as the narrow alley in this Lewis Hine photograph. *Kheel Center for Labor-Management Documentation and Archives, Cornell University Library (5780PB32F25B)*

The "Manly Art of Self-defense" Newsboys' Protective Association, Cincinnati, Ohio, 1908. Lewis Hine was an investigative photographer for the National Child Labor Committee, and documented working and living conditions of American children in the early 1900s. Newspaper boys sold papers on city streets at the turn of the century, earning about thirty cents a day. They were often living on their own, and needed to defend themselves against bigger boys who would steal their papers. *Library of Congress, (LC-DIG-nclc-03176)*

The *National Police Gazette* Appeals to the Male Bachelor Subculture. Publisher Richard K. Fox overtly sold sports, violence, and sensuality to his working-class readers. It was renowned for its engravings and photographs of scantily clad women, notably strippers, burlesque dancers, and prostitutes. His covers seemed to just avoid violating the Comstock Law of 1873 that banned the distribution of salacious publications through the mail. *Courtesy of National Police Gazette Enterprises, LLC. Used by permission.*

Gymnastics room at Turner Hall, Milwaukee, Wisconsin ca. 1900. George Brosius (second from left, in suit) was Turner Hall's first salaried gymnastic instructor in the mid-1800s. Brosius promoted physical education in Milwaukee's public schools. A Brosius student would later introduce his training methods to West Point Military Academy. *From: George Brosius,* Fifty Years Devoted to the Cause of Physical Culture, 1864–1914 *(Milwaukee: Germania Publishing, 1914), p. 69. File:Milwaukee Bundesturnhalle.jpg*

CHAPTER TWO

Sport and Class

Americans like to believe that sport has always been a democratic institution that crossed class, racial, and ethnic boundaries. Today, everyone has access to parks, and most people can afford to play games like tennis and golf that once were considered elite sports. Furthermore, sport is meritocratic, and any athlete with the necessary skills and coaching has the opportunity to become a star in his/her chosen sport. However, the sporting experience of Americans between 1850 and 1920 was anything but democratic, and was largely a product of social class. An individual's social class was determined primarily by his or her occupation and income, along with such social variables as education, religion, race, ethnicity, and residency. The American social structure in this era was strongly influenced by the rise of industrial capitalism. At the apex was a tiny upper class of white, native-born Americans. The urban middle class, also predominantly white and native born, comprised 30 to 40 percent of a city's population, depending on the extent of local industrialization. The majority of urban residents were lower-class, blue-collar workers, mainly immigrants and their children. Members of these three major social classes had dissimilar lifestyles, a result of differing amounts of discretionary income and leisure time, as well as distinctive social values, attitudes, and behavior.

The upper class was the richest 5 percent of the population, and at the apex of the upper class stood the elite. The social elite comprised about 1 to 3 percent of Americans and were drawn from the most socially distinguished families. Their status depended on how their affluence was achieved, their access to power, and individual social characteristics. The antebellum elite of leading merchants and great planters had the wealth, time, and self-confidence to indulge themselves as they pleased, and they emulated the English gentry, their role models in leisure activities. In the post–Civil War period, sport was particularly important to the new rich, people who made their fortunes from commerce and industry, as a way to gain recognition and social status.

On the other hand, antebellum northern, middle-class citizens largely frowned upon such sports as horse racing, boxing, cock fighting, and animal baiting as immoral and wasteful. Evangelical Protestants were the leading critics of early American sport, and even in the late nineteenth century they remained opposed on moral grounds to gambling and blood sports. The middle class' abhorrence of sport changed over time as antebellum reformers created the positive sports creed, which portrayed so-called clean sports as health-promoting and character-building activities. Middle-class men began to become active sportsmen, participating in ball games and other forms of exercise. The growing bourgeois interest in fitness increased toward the end of the nineteenth century as a new professional and bureaucratic middle class evolved for whom sport had important social and cultural functions.

Manual workers, especially artisans, were often very active members of the antebellum sporting culture, but the rise of industrial capitalism and urbanization curtailed their athletic opportunities. As historians Benjamin G. Rader and Elliott Gorn point out, working-class options were particularly hindered by the decline of small artisan workshops in certain industries, including textiles and shoemaking, in which employees originally had considerable control over the pace of work and substantial free time. Such a working environment was supplanted by an increasingly proletarianized, modern capitalist production system characterized by time and work discipline and weakened ties between workers and management. The rise of the factory system eliminated or devalued the skills of many artisans. By the late nineteenth century, 85 percent of industrial workers were semiskilled or unskilled employees working in increasingly larger factories. For example, in 1919 Chicago, more than 70 percent of manufacturing wage workers labored for companies with at least a hundred employees, and nearly one-third of them worked in firms with over a thousand workers. They had modest incomes, back-breaking jobs, and limited discretionary time (although free time was often involuntarily increased because of underemployment and unemployment) all of which hindered their recreational choices.

Sport and the American Elite

The American elite were prominent sportsmen ever since the colonial era, when they raised fighting birds, raced horses, and hunted foxes. The first voluntary associations established to encourage sports were upper-class organizations, including Philadelphia's Schuylkill Fishing Club (1732) and the Charles Town Jockey Club (1735). In the antebellum era, the elite sustained their historic interest in expensive sports such as horse racing, while certain rakish sons slummed among the demimonde, becoming members of the male bachelor subculture. For those "swells with money to burn," debaucheries like spending a night at a fashionable brothel or a cockfight provided a rite of passage into manhood.

The leading antebellum sportsman was John Cox Stevens, son of John Stevens, a rich Hoboken, New Jersey, inventor and engineer. The younger Stevens made his fortune in promoting the development of steam-powered boats. Stevens' first major sporting achievement was the revitalization of thoroughbred racing to New York in 1823 when he orchestrated the Eclipse–Sir Henry race, the first great competition between northern and southern horses. Twelve years later, Stevens promoted the first major pedestrian race after he wagered that a person could run ten miles in under an hour. Previously, in 1831 he had established the Elysian Fields in a corner of the family estate in Hoboken. The Elysian Fields became a popular site among the metropolitan elite in which to picnic and play sports, and in 1845, it became the first major site of antebellum ball sports.

Despite these important accomplishments, Stevens was best known in his time as a yachtsman. In 1844 he organized the New York Yacht Club (NYYC) among elite Knickerbockers to promote pleasure, sociability, good health, and American naval architecture. In 1851, Stevens' yacht *America* won the Royal Yacht Squadron Regatta held in conjunction with London's Crystal Palace Fair. This remarkable victory over eighteen squads representing the masters of the seas was a source of great national pride, and it symbolized the coming of age of American seamanship. The winning trophy became known as the America's Cup. The NYYC became one of New York City's leading men's clubs, and the nation's preeminent athletic organization. Membership tripled, and the makeup of members shifted away from the old elite to such *nouveau riche* (new rich) as John J. Astor and Cornelius Vanderbilt, who believed that membership in such an elite club, would certify their social status.

Stevens died in 1857 and was soon replaced as the leading elite American sportsman by James G. Bennett, Jr., son of a Scottish immigrant who had made a fortune publishing the plebeian *New York Herald*. Bennett used his inherited wealth and athletic proficiency to achieve recognition and social cachet. In 1857, at the age of sixteen, he joined the New York Yacht Club, and nine years later he won the first trans-Atlantic yacht race. Bennett was also active in track-and-field, promoting the first intercollegiate track meet at Lake Saratoga in 1871 and financing professional pedestrians like Daniel O'Leary. Bennett was an avid horseman who belonged to the American Jockey Club (AJC), rejuvenated fox hunting in Virginia, and, in 1876, organized the first polo club in the United States, the Westchester Polo Club in New York. Bennett also built the Newport Casino Club in Rhode Island, site of the first thirty-four U.S. men's tennis championships between 1881 and 1914.

The upper-class fascination with sport remained strong throughout the century. Social critic Thorstein Veblen argued that late-nineteenth-century elites enjoyed sport because it was fun, provided opportunities to be trendsetters or conspicuous consumers, and promised prestige based on prowess and the exclusivity of their games. Sport provided a means to separate themselves from lesser folk. Men of new wealth tried to gain acceptance from the established elite by marrying into old aristocratic families and emulating their lifestyles. They built costly mansions and estates, staged extravagant balls, financed cultural institutions, secured membership in high-status men's clubs, and participated in fashionable sports.

Upper-class young men looked to sport as a means to prove their manliness. Social commentators, as well as the elite young men themselves, felt that upper-class men had lost power and influence. There was a lot of questioning about their courage and manliness in a society whose culture seemed to have become increasingly feminized and excessively refined. These men did not seem to stack up well compared to their fathers and uncles who had demonstrated their bravery during the Civil War. The elite eastern establishment worried that the Anglo-Saxon male had become effete and was losing his sexual potency. There was a lot of fear about declining family size, although that had less to do with virility than with planned parenting. For example, Congregationalist minister Josiah Strong in *Our Country: Its Possible Future and Present Crisis* (1885), argued than native-born white Americans and their small families would soon be overtaken by hordes of fertile new immigrants from eastern and southern Europe. The future of the Anglo-Saxon race and its control of the United States seemed threatened by the failure of the sons of leading families to measure up. Historian George Fredrickson argues that by the 1890s, one answer was participation in tough sports, especially football, considered a moral equivalent of war, and even boxing, which enjoyed a brief fad in the 1890s.

Theodore Roosevelt, who promoted the concept of the strenuous life, exemplified the elite manly spirit. He had been a sickly child, but he had built himself up through physical activity. Young Teddy boxed, rowed, and wrestled on intramural teams at Harvard. He also enjoyed swimming, mountain climbing, and big-game hunting. Roosevelt was typical of elite Americans concerned about the future of their country and their class, who viewed sport as a means to facilitate social, sexual, and cultural regeneration. In 1898 Roosevelt organized the Rough Riders, a volunteer company to fight in the Spanish-American War, which he composed of former cowboys and college football players from elite eastern institutions.

A strenuous lifestyle was instilled at elite prep schools. Sociologist Christopher Armstrong credits Groton's headmaster, Endicott Peabody, with making athletics compulsory in emulation of English public schools and elite eastern colleges. Peabody's goal was to build his students up physically, morally, and spiritually. They would learn to play by rules, control their aggression, work as a disciplined unit, and do their best. Once-pampered boys would be ready for New Haven, Cambridge, and Princeton playing fiends or the battlements of San Juan Hill. They would also be prepared for the next test of manliness, the building of an overseas American empire.

The Elite Sports Club

Sports clubs were voluntary associations organized to facilitate athletic competition among people of similar backgrounds. Clubs obtained the necessary playing space, built facilities, purchased equipment, and arranged contests. Elite clubs provided a socially segregated, nonthreatening environment that fostered camaraderie. They guaranteed the integrity of competitors by establishing eligibility requirements, and they formulated playing rules in cooperation with local, regional, or national associations.

Elite athletic organizations had secondary functions that often became more important than their primary purposes. Membership was restricted by high initiation fees and annual dues and by requiring the unanimous approval of applicants by members. The sports club became a comfortable community of like-minded people who shared the same social origins, beliefs, values, customs, and lifestyles. It offered a safe haven from the problems of the industrial city. Members could close ranks against social inferiors and integrate their families into an elite subculture. The club also provided a place to strengthen bonds between the well-born and the new rich. By the late nineteenth century it was no longer possible to personally know everyone that counted, but members knew that fellow club members were the proper people with whom to socialize and do business. Membership also provided a stepping stone to higher status nonathletic men's clubs. The sports club was an integral part of the elite social world that encompassed patterns of speech and fashion, prep schools, Ivy League colleges, and Episcopalian parishes.

Late-nineteenth-century sports clubs catered to a wide range of interests. A small segment of the elite enjoyed field sports, particularly big-game hunting. The one-hundred-man Boone and Crockett Club, which included Theodore Roosevelt among its members, arranged expensive wilderness trips led by professional guides. Cricket became an exclusive upper-class sport in metropolitan Philadelphia although it had nearly disappeared elsewhere in the United States. The city's five major cricket clubs had up to thirteen hundred members whose elaborate clubhouses and pitches were located in the most prestigious neighborhoods. The new sport of polo acquired enormous status, which reflected the skills needed to ride well but especially the high cost of maintaining a string of polo ponies. Polo soon joined yachting at the apex of sports clubs, even if yachting had much more public exposure whenever the NYYC defended the America's Cup against foreign competition. Most elite sportsmen had to satisfy themselves with membership in the still rarified air of jockey clubs, athletic clubs, and country clubs.

Thoroughbred Racing and the Jockey Clubs

Thoroughbred racing was sponsored by rich men who craved public attention and social acceptance. The sport of kings was the leading elite colonial sport, but its gambling and aristocratic British connotations made racing inappropriate during the Revolution, when it was widely prohibited. This ban continued in northern states for three decades because of religious objections and the perceived need for citizens of a Republic to be especially virtuous. Northern racing was revived by the Eclipse–Sir Henry race and four subsequent intersectional contests, culminating in the Fashion-Peytona match in 1845, which drew crowds estimated at well over 50,000. Victory went to the first horse to win two four-mile heats. These races symbolized to fans the relative progressive state of culture and economic development, not to mention the breeding of thoroughbreds, in the free, relatively urban North and the rural, slaveholding South. Northern racing largely died out following the 1845 match as a result of track mismanagement, rising costs of operating stock farms, the expense of attending races, competition from harness racing, the lingering impact of the Depression of 1837, and widespread opposition to

gambling by evangelical reformers. Racing remained popular in the antebellum South, centered in wide-open New Orleans, with its staunch male bachelor subculture abetted by great planters and wealthy merchants. However, the coming of the Civil War all but killed the sport in the South.

Northern thoroughbred racing made a comeback in 1863 when professional gambler and ex-heavyweight boxing champion John Morrissey, together with upper-class New York City sportsmen, organized a four-day meet at the elite Saratoga Springs resort to promote gambling at his casino. The event was a success and racing became a fixture at Saratoga. The results encouraged capitalist Leonard Jerome, financier August Belmont, the long-time chairman of the national Democratic Party, and their friends, to restore racing to New York City. They organized the American Jockey Club (AJC) in 1865 to make thoroughbred racing fashionable again, improve the breed, and promote social intercourse. The American Jockey Club established Jerome Park Race Track one year later. It attracted the carriage trade by building a luxurious clubhouse, banning liquor sales, facilitating gambling, and offering large purses to attract the finest thoroughbreds in North America.

Membership in the AJC or comparable jockey clubs was less prestigious than belonging to the New York Yacht Club or the leading metropolitan men's clubs, yet it offered horsemen public recognition and status. Historian Melvin Adelman found that the American Jockey Club's original 862 members were mainly New Yorkers of new wealth in finance or commerce who lived in the best parts of town, especially along fashionable Fifth Avenue. Among them, one small group, the 50 life members of the Board of Governors who actually ran the AJC, were more than twice as rich, and of significantly higher social status, than the other members. There were a number of prestigious jockey clubs in operation over the next several decades, running such new elite racetracks as Pimlico (1870) in Baltimore, Churchill Downs (1875) in Louisville, Sheepshead Bay (1880) in Brooklyn, Washington Park (1884) in Chicago, and Belmont Park (1905) in Long Island. Opening day at these courses marked the start of the social season, and elite families turned out in droves, riding to the race track in luxurious carriages and dressed in the lat-

est fashions. By the turn of the century, major races at these tracks regularly drew over 30,000 spectators. Some of the thoroughbreds racing there cost as much as $40,000 and competed for stakes that might exceed $50,000.

The elite operated the most prestigious tracks, owned the most valuable horses, and governed the sport. In 1891 major track owners in New York established the Board of Control to regulate racing, primarily because of problems such as the fixing of bets and abuse of animals at the more plebeian, profit-oriented proprietary tracks. Widespread dissatisfaction with the board's performance, and fears that the New York State legislature would ban horse racing, compelled leading turf men to create The Jockey Club (TJC) in 1894 to establish national standards of conduct and behavior. The Jockey Club licensed racetrack workers, divided up racing dates among the tracks in the state, investigated dubious races, boycotted substandard tracks, and banned horsemen who raced at outlawed facilities. TJC received quasi-governmental status one year later when the state legislature established a racing commission to supervise the sport in New York in conjunction with TJC. The State Racing Commission was the first state organization created to oversee sports in the United States.

The Athletic Club

Right after the Civil War, well-to-do sportsmen organized athletic clubs that emphasized track-and-field. The sport was previously dominated by professional pedestrians and Scottish Caledonian clubs that sponsored traditional Highland games. In 1868 three upper-middle-class New Yorkers established the first athletic club, the New York Athletic Club (modeled after the London Athletic Club) to arrange competition among men of similar backgrounds. By the mid-1880s nearly every major city had an athletic club.

The New York Athletic Club (NYAC) played major roles in track-and-field as an innovator in the sport—in 1876, it built the first cinder track and sponsored the first national track-and-field championships; it was an archetype for other athletic clubs and the major proponent of strict rules of amateurism. Amateurs were considered athletes who participated purely for the sake of competition.

They were sportsmen who never competed for money, never vied with professionals for a prize, or taught athletics to earn a living. This differed from the antebellum era, when amateur cricket players regularly played with one teammate (usually the bowler) who was paid to play. The new and stringent regulations largely copied those in Great Britain, where strict constructionists barred professionals, people who devoted themselves to sport as a full-time job and therefore had an unfair advantage; they worked at play, training more diligently and practicing against other full-time athletes. Historian Benjamin Rader further argues that athletic clubs supported strict amateur rules out of fear that social inferiors would take over their games and their status in their communities.

Benjamin Rader, in his *American Sports: From the Age of Folk Games to the Age of Televised Sports* (2008), argues that in 1882 the NYAC's focus shifted from athletic competition to social rivalry. Status depended less on championships than the social backgrounds of members. The club altered recruitment policies to seek members from among "the most prominent and successful men" without regard to athletic prowess. Membership shifted from young athletes to older, more socially oriented men in the Social Register. By 1885, the New York Athletic Club reached its limit of 1,500 members despite raising initiation fees to $100 and annual dues to $50.

The social emphasis displeased many original members, who resigned in the mid-1880s, but demands for victories did not slacken. The athletic clubs began heavily recruiting outstanding white (primarily Protestant) athletes, regardless of social background, to assure victories and enhance the club's prestige. Inducements included free initiation, room and board, cash, and even jobs, a clear breach of the amateur spirit. In 1884, the prestigious Manhattan Athletic Club recruited the great Jewish athlete Lon Myers, a bookkeeper by profession, by hiring him as club secretary. Myers was invincible at races from 300 to 1,000 yards, and at different times held American records from 50 yards to the mile. He took advantage of his opportunities to compete to win medals, silverware, gold watches, and other prizes, which he could turn into cash.

In 1879 the National Association of Amateur Athletes of America (N4A) was established by the most elite athletic clubs to oversee

the strict enforcement of amateur rules. Myers was a prime target of the N4A since his actions seemed to violate the association's ban on professional athletes, but a hearing in 1884 sustained his amateur standing. The NYAC was so dissatisfied with the association's position on the amateur question and jealous of the Manhattan Athletic Club's success that it dropped out of the N4A in 1886. The NYAC continued its fight against professionalism by helping establish the Amateur Athletic Union (AAU) in 1888 to organize competition and better monitor amateurism standards. The AAU banned from its meets athletes who participated in N4A competitions and ended up destroying its rival after one year.

Athletic organizations were on the lower rung of metropolitan men's clubs, although membership in one could serve as a stepping stone into a more prestigious sports club or male association that emphasized wealth, ancestry, culture, or politics. Hierarchies existed among particular sports (yacht clubs were still more prestigious than athletic clubs) and between individual sports clubs. For example, the New York Athletic Club was less prestigious than the Manhattan Athletic Club or the University Athletic Club (which required a college degree), but had far more status than many other athletic clubs in New York. In addition, because the NYAC was in New York, it was far more prestigious than the top athletic clubs in lesser cities such as Rochester or Buffalo.

Upper-class athletic clubs flourished in the 1880s, constructing superb facilities. The New York Athletic Club's $150,000 five-story downtown clubhouse built in 1885 included a gymnasium, swimming pool, bowling alley, billiard tables, dining rooms, a wine cellar, and sleeping quarters. Within three years, the club secured a country site where a clubhouse, tennis courts, running track, and boathouse were built, and in 1892 a lavish new clubhouse was constructed. Yet as wonderful as the NYAC's facilities were, certain New York clubs and a few out-of-town clubs such as the Boston Athletic Association, with its $300,000 clubhouse, were more sumptuous. Unfortunately, the over-building of expensive facilities and the Depression of 1893 killed many prominent associations despite the AAU's efforts to help athletic clubs survive as status communities.

Women and the Elite Sports Clubs

Upper-class women constituted a leisure class whose ostentatious lifestyle reflected their fathers' or husbands' economic success. Contemporaries saw them as heavily dependent upon men for sustenance and physically debilitated "by modes of dress and enforced idleness." Yet elite young women were among the first sportswomen. Their social prestige protected them from ridicule or a challenge to their femininity, which made it easier for them to break social conventions. Lower-status women, on the other hand, could not participate in a traditionally male sphere such as sports without having their femininity and place in society seriously questioned. Elite daughters may have been unwelcome at the workplace or the voting booth, but fathers and male friends supported their presence at country clubs and tennis courts. As historian Cindy Himes points out, the elite women "used sport to establish more casual and friendly relations between the sexes, to discredit myths about feminine weakness, to adopt more practical forms of dress and to reject physical idleness and disability as a lifestyle."

Women were admitted to male athletic clubs as spectators, social guests, and competitors. The Brooklyn Athletic Club, for instance, opened its billiard and bowling facilities to women on Mondays and Fridays, and they hired a female fencing instructor. In 1889 New York's Berkeley Athletic Club constructed a $200,000 midtown clubhouse (library, gymnasium, pool, and dressing rooms) for women members, set aside tennis courts and a running track at the Berkeley Oval in the Bronx for them, and allotted time for female scullers at its boathouse. These sporting clubs also provided extensive social calendars with various activities for members and their wives.

Upper-class women also organized their own athletic clubs and in 1901 established the Federation of Women's Athletic Clubs. The Women's Athletic Club of Chicago (1898) was the first and most outstanding private athletic club opened for women. Its goals were to provide them with the same chances for exercise, relaxation and sociability men had in their athletic clubs. The building opened in 1903 at a cost of $100,000 donated by the city's leading women, including club president Mrs. Philip Armour. Its 275 members paid $100 for initiation and $40 for annual dues. The club had a billiard room, bowling alley, gymnasium (for fencing, basketball, and gymnastics), and marble pool (for swimming, diving, and water polo). It also offered dance lessons and lectures on topics like nutrition, literature, and current affairs.

The Country Club

The country club, modeled on the lifestyle of English country gentry, was a particular focal point for elite sportsmen and sportswomen. Country clubs were large suburban resorts used for a wide range of activities. Himes maintains that because women had more leisure time than men, they spent as much or more time at country clubs than did men. The first, simply called the Country Club, was established in Brookline, Massachusetts, in 1882 and became a model for subsequent facilities. Members were drawn from families of the highest rank, with names like Cabot, Forbes, and Lowell—a genuine *Who's Who* of Boston Brahmins. As historian Stephen Hardy has pointed out, half of the founders were Harvard men; 30.5 percent of them belonged to the Union and 69.7 percent of them to the Somerset, Boston's most prestigious men's clubs. Hardy described the club as "part of an interlocking constellation of financial, cultural, medical and industrial institutions."

The suburban country club provided an asylum or escape from the anxieties of work and the problems of urban life. As journalist Caspar Whitney observed, it was a serene rustic oasis that encouraged a sense of identity, community, and stability. The club was a resort that preserved traditional values and insulated, protected, and taught upper-class youth essential social skills. Elite sons and daughters socialized with their peers at club dances and parties, sometimes finding romance and future spouses.

Tuxedo Park, built by tobacco magnate Pierre Lorillard in 1885 in the fashionable New York suburb of the same name, was America's most stylish country club. Members living in nearby mansions enjoyed the huge clubhouse's glass-enclosed verandas, ballroom, theater, and billiard room. Outdoor sports included fishing, hunting, pigeon shooting, golf, steeplechasing, ice skating, ice boating, sleigh riding, and tobogganing on a mile-long electrically lighted slide.

The country club set dominated the new sports of golf and tennis. Golf was an expensive sport enjoyed by the English elite, who served as role models for rich Americans. The first American course was St. Andrews, originally a nine-hole facility constructed by Scotsman John Reid in Yonkers in 1887. Most courses, however, were modeled after the professionally designed Shinnecock Hills Golf Club, built in 1891 for William K. Vanderbilt and his friends in swank Southampton, Long Island. Golf required eye-hand coordination, timing, and concentration, but the sport was not physically taxing, which appealed to rich older men. It quickly became the principal country-club game, in part because foursomes offered a comfortable grouping in which men could socialize and consummate business deals. The sport spread rapidly, and there were about one thousand golf clubs by the turn of the century, mainly on the outskirts of cities.

Golf was considered an appropriate sport for well-to-do women because it did not require much physical exertion. Women were rarely barred from men's courses, although they were usually restricted to certain off-peak hours. In the 1890s women not only established their own golf organizations but even their own golf course, New Jersey's Morris Country Club. The women's national championship began in 1895, just one year after the men's, both under the U.S. Golf Association. Five years later golfer Margaret Abbott became the first American woman to win an Olympic championship.

Lawn tennis was an English game developed in 1873 by Major John Wingfield. One year later Mary Outerbridge brought lawn tennis to the United States from Bermuda. Her brother laid out a court with an hourglass shape at the Staten Island Cricket Club, which he managed. A ladies club was organized and given exclusive use of the courts on weekday mornings. The game quickly became popular at Philadelphia cricket clubs and fashionable summer resorts such as Newport, Rhode Island. In 1881 the United States National Lawn Tennis Association was established in New York City to supervise the new game and hold its first men's championships. Tennis was not considered a virile sport, and many courts were specifically built for country club wives and daughters who enjoyed doubles matches that did not require strength or vigorous exertion. "The game is well enough for a lazy or *weak* man," noted the Harvard *Crimson* in 1878, "but men who have rowed or taken part in a nobler sport should blush to be seen playing Lawn Tennis." Male interest emerged mainly after the turn of the century because of international competitions such as the Davis Cup (1900).

Women preferred a sedate baseline game, positioning themselves as far from the net as possible, because they played in full-length skirts; running around was considered unladylike. May Sutton, America's first Wimbledon champion (1905), pioneered by playing more vigorously and shedding her high collar and long sleeves for more comfortable clothes. The women's national championship began in 1887, and it was an important venue for America's first outstanding sportswoman, Bostonian Eleanor Sears, four-times doubles champion. She was also the first national squash champion, a sport that was even more elite than tennis. Renowned for her fashion and her romances, Sears wore men's trousers, rode horses astride instead of sidesaddle, raced cars and airplanes, and challenged men in sports contests.

The elite sportswoman provided a model for the athletic Gibson girl of the 1890s who participated in coed cycling, golf, tennis, and horseback riding. She abandoned the corset in favor of a shirtwaist and long skirt that provided greater freedom than most contemporary apparel. This ideal American woman was attractive, tall and slim, physically fit, "aglow with the ruddy color of physical health and energy." She was well-to-do and independent, sexy yet innocent. Elliott Gorn, author of *The Manly Art: Bare Knuckles Prize Fighting in America* (1986), argues that the athleticism of the "new woman" symbolized the more active role that upper-class and upper-middle-class women were taking in American life.

Sport and the Middle Class

The middle class in 1850 comprised professionals, shopkeepers, clerks, prosperous farm owners, and future-oriented labor aristocrats, who were well-paid craftsmen. Middle-class skilled workers were "loyalist" artisans who worked in small shops. They supported capitalism, lived by Victorian norms, and had considerable control over the pace of work. Middle-class workers at midcentury were usually their own bosses, except for ambitious young clerks who were learning a business and had realistic expectations of advancement. These men believed in hard work, had little discretionary time, and found many contemporary sports to be time wasting, immoral, and debilitating, if not illegal. They did not seek to demonstrate manly traits through the vile pleasures of the sporting fraternity, but through hard work, providing for their families, and making the home the center of their lives.

The antebellum middle class abhorred the sporting fraternity with its culture and social ethic that emphasized immediate gratification and whose favorite sports, such as baiting contests, cock fighting, and boxing, attacked the moral fiber of society. As Gorn points out, boxing inverted the Victorian value system and posed a dangerous threat to capitalist values such as hard work and deferred contentment. Clergymen, journalists, physicians, and other social reformers ardently criticized such immoral and time-wasting pastimes that undermined self-control, promoted disorder, and often defiled the Sabbath. Such games stimulated gambling, debased humanity, and encouraged the assembling of potentially dangerous crowds. Hence middle-class reformers sought to civilize and restrict the male bachelor subculture. Henry Bergh's American Society for the Prevention of Cruelty to Animals (1866) opposed blood sports that harmed animals, while Anthony Comstock's Society for the Suppression of Vice (1874) sought the elimination of gambling sports.

Ironically, given their opposition to gambling, the antebellum sport first identified with the middling sorts was harness racing. Historian Melvin L. Adelman argues that harness racing was the first modern American sport. It gained popularity in the 1820s because standard bred horses were relatively cheap, cost little to maintain, and were useful for transporting people or freight, unlike thoroughbreds whose only function was to race. About seventy harness tracks existed in the 1850s, when it had become the most popular spectator sport. The trotter was seen as a democratic "American" horse in comparison to the aristocratic and foreign thoroughbred. Trotting was an urban sport, centered in New York City—where contests were originally staged on city roads—the locus of the breeding and training industry. Trotting provided an exciting diversion that enabled owners to display their property, demonstrate their prowess, and make wagers. The sport first became organized in 1825 when the New York Trotting Association (NYTA) was formed by middle- and upper-middle-class horsemen. The association arranged semiannual meets instead of the customary spontaneous races, known as brushes.

Trotting's middle-class nature was reflected by the sport's modest origins and by the low cost of many top horses. For example, the great Lady Suffolk, winner of over $35,000 in purses, was discovered pulling a butcher's cart during her racing career. By the 1850s, however, the sport began to attract the interest of the nouveau riche, such as Cornelius Vanderbilt of the New York Central Railroad and *New York Ledger* publisher Robert Bonner, both self-made men who used the sport to gain publicity and promote their status (although Bonner never raced his horses in public because he abhorred gambling). These rich owners bought up the best trotters (Bonner paid $40,000 in 1884 for Maud S., the mile record holder), began to scientifically manage the breeding industry, and made it hard for less affluent horsemen to compete.

Negative middle-class attitudes toward sport that prevailed among the middle class of the early nineteenth century dramatically changed with the development of a positive sports creed prior to the Civil War. The new ideology asserted that clean sport would be a positive, uplifting social force to promote Victorian manliness. The new sport creed claimed that physical exercise and participation in new moral sports would provide sedentary men with a substitute for the lost rustic world of vigorous agricultural work and fresh air. The middle class became convinced of the salutary power of sport to remake the character and personality of Americans, enhance public health, and promote order in the cities. A modern middle-class leisure ethic arose that encouraged men to stop working themselves to death and to take time off for exercise and other recreational activities. Now the middle class became fascinated with sport. Team games furnished fun, camaraderie, excitement, and healthy outdoor competition. By the 1870s and 1880s, nonmanual workers were employed about eight hours a day with a half-holiday on Saturday that left considerable discretionary time for sports or other uplifting recreations.

The advocacy of participation in a strenuous lifestyle was an important response to changing middle-class conceptions of manly behavior. Like their upper-class counterparts, middle-class young men in the last third of the nineteenth century exhibited considerable uncertainty about their manliness. Football historian Michael Oriard points out they faced conflicting calls for pugnacity and constraint. Social critics feared that these men were becoming "over civilized" and losing their sexual identity through the feminization of culture at home, church, and school. New terms such as *sissy, stuffed shirt*, and *mollycoddle* emerged. Manliness used to be perceived as the opposite of childishness, but now had become the antithesis of femininity. Middle-class men had previously relied upon their work as a means of demonstrating manliness. In the post–Civil War era, however, white-collar workers were less likely than in the past to be independent workers or entrepreneurs and more likely to be bureaucrats in the growing corporate world or the expanding government. Consequently they often lacked the sense of self-worth, creativity, and accomplishment that their predecessors enjoyed. Instead of getting satisfaction from their job, they turned to their leisure to gain a feeling of self-esteem. Sport became a means for middle-class men to demonstrate physical prowess, strength, and other manly characteristics and to gain the kind of recognition that work had previously supplied. Vigorous physical activity became a solution to the loss or imagined loss of masculinity. The strenuous life of hunting or competitive sports would prove one's manliness as warfare or feeding the family had done in the past. The emerging cult of manliness was a popular middle-class response to feared inadequacies, and fit in with the jingoistic spirit of the 1890s.

Clerks particularly saw in sport a means to demonstrate their manliness. They were typically younger men whose occupation in the late nineteenth century was becoming increasingly feminized (becoming pink collar jobs), as women were hired as sales clerks and office workers, especially the new occupation of typists. Furthermore, the job of junior clerk, if measured by level of income and lessened opportunities for advancement, was becoming a working class occupation where employees had little input into working conditions.

Middle-Class Sports Clubs

The emergence and popularization of uplifting athletic contests, particularly team sports that provided camaraderie, excitement, tests of physical skill, and healthful open-air competition, was a major boost to middle-class sport. Team sports prior to the 1840s were mainly for children and students playing various versions of football, cricket, and baseball. Thereafter they became a welcome source of recreation for young, middle-class men. Voluntary associations were established among people with similar backgrounds to socialize, arrange contests, and compete. These clubs provided the means to gain a sense of self-esteem and identity.

The first organized team sports played by adults in North America were Native American contests, such as lacrosse. Euro-Americans did not, however, respect the culture and institutions of the First Americans, and so did not copy their sporting pastimes, which was different in Canada, where lacrosse became one of the nation's most popular sports in nineteenth century. The first organized team sport in the original thirteen colonies was the English game of cricket, which colonials played on an informal basis. Englishmen regarded cricket as a manly (batters defending wickets might be hit by bowlers throwing an extremely hard ball), complex, competitive sport that required considerable skill and mental exertion. One of the men most responsible for promoting cricket in the United States was the English émigré, sportswriter Henry Chadwick, who asserted that cricket taught its American players such virtues as sobriety, self-denial, fortitude, discipline, fair play, and obedience. Organized cricket in the United States began in the 1830s among English textile-mill workers in Philadelphia, but formal matches were rare until the 1840s. Thereafter, cricket enjoyed nearly two decades of widespread popularity, and English merchants and workingmen organized teams throughout the Northeast.

At midcentury, cricket was the preeminent American ball game, with competition highlighted by intercity and even international matches. Games were played on Saturday afternoons, betting was commonplace, and some teams featured professional bowlers. The first international test match took place in 1840 between a team from Toronto and another from New York City. Such contests lasted two innings during which all eleven players would bat and have to be put out. These matches could take as long as two or three days to play out, although teams playing less consequential games might agree to a score or time limit. By 1860, about 400 clubs operated with 10,000 players. Cricket would not, however, sustain its popularity with middle-class Americans, for whom time was money. They preferred the simpler, more dramatic, fast-paced game of baseball.

Baseball evolved in the early nineteenth century from the English game of rounders, a ball game played on a square field with stones or posts at the corners, twelve to twenty yards apart. The batter hit the ball, and then ran clockwise around the stones. A number of American versions developed, most notably the Philadelphia game of town ball, first played regularly in 1831. The Massachusetts game, popular in the late 1850s, was played on a square field with bases or tall stakes at the corners. The batter was stationed halfway between first and home. An inning lasted until an out was made, and the game continued until one side scored one hundred runs. One popular way to put a batter or base runner out was to hit him with the baseball ("soaking"). The New York version, known as baseball, was played as early as 1842 by a group of respectable and prosperous upper-middle-class young men, who three years later became known as the Knickerbockers. Historian Melvin L. Adelman has described this team as the "first important and long-term club," which played a three-inning intra-club game on October 6, 1845. The first known interclub game was played on October 22, 1845, between the New York Base Ball Club, already at least two years old, and the Brooklyn Base Ball Club, with the former winning 24–4. One year later the New York Club defeated the Knickerbockers 23–1 at the Elysian Fields in Hoboken, in what had long been considered the first game of baseball.

Historians have long debunked the myth that Abner Doubleday, best known as the second-in-command of Ft. Sumter, South Carolina, where the Civil War began. A baseball commission in 1907, financed by Albert Spalding, asserted that Doubleday had invented baseball in 1839 in his hometown of Cooperstown, New York, on the basis of no creditable evidence at a time when Doubleday was actually a cadet at the United States Military Academy in West Point, New

York. Thereafter historians mainly pointed to Alexander Cartwright, a member of the Knickerbockers, as the person most responsible for creating baseball, unaware that some of the evidence later discovered was misrepresented by family members. Scholars now believe that credit should be shared with fellow club members Daniel Lucius "Doc" Adams, William Rufus Wheaton, and Louis Fenn Wadsworth. The Knickerbockers as a group formalized the basic patterns and rules of baseball in writing and provided an organizational model for future teams. The club played on a diamond-shaped field, with the batter stationed at home plate, one of four equal distant bases (the ninety-foot distance was not established until 1857), with space outside the baselines designated as foul territory. The offensive team had three outs per inning, which could be made by striking out the batter, catching the batted ball on a bounce (which made the game easier to play for boys as well as "less manly" than cricket) or on the fly, forcing runners out, or tagging them when off base. "Soaking" (also known as "plugging") was abolished. The first team to score twenty-one runs, called aces, won.

Baseball, like cricket, fit in well with the new sports creed, promoting good health by providing exercise in the fresh air, and encouraging cooperation through teamwork and morality by adherence to the rules. Yet baseball had several important advantages over cricket, the former became the most popular team sport in the 1850s. Baseball was based on widely enjoyed childhood games, considered a sport of "American" origins, and did not demand as high a level of skill, important for a newly popularized sport. The new game was more exciting, with rapid changes from offense to defense, and took less time to play (in 1857 games were limited to nine innings and usually lasted less than two hours), an important quality in a time-conscious society. In addition, baseball did not require as large and level a plot of ground as did high-level cricket contests, something that by midcentury was becoming hard to find. In short, urban expansion made such parcels of land too valuable for sporting purposes.

The research of Melvin Adelman on New York sports has taught us a lot about the first baseball teams, which were mainly voluntary associations of middle- and upper-middle-class men in metropolitan

New York, although the game spread quickly along the Atlantic seaboard to Philadelphia, Baltimore, and other cities. In the early 1850s, three-fourths of the leading Brooklyn and New York players were white-collar workers, and as late as 1870, about 70 percent of all ballplayers were still nonmanual workers.

Amateur baseball clubs in the 1850s had a constitution, by-laws, elected officers, and charged dues. They secured the necessary playing field, organized practices, and arranged contests. Teams gave themselves patriotic names or referred to themselves by the occupation, neighborhood, or political affiliation of their members. They wore uniforms — like volunteer firemen, an important segment of the male bachelor subculture — that set them apart as a community of respectable athletes, who contemporaries identified as "the baseball players' fraternity." The ballplayers largely stressed the serious nature of play and practiced on a regular basis. However, they also emphasized sociability, inviting girlfriends and wives to watch games. Competition ranged from friendly intrasquad games to earnest matches against other clubs, highly ritualized proceedings that often included public advertising, the presentation of the game ball to the winning captain, and a dinner hosted by the home team.

In 1858 the top metropolitan New York teams organized the National Association of Base Ball Players (NABBP), defined the rules of play (adopting the Knickerbockers' rules), resolved disputes, and controlled the sport's future. The game became increasingly democratized, and by the late 1850s three-fourths of the ballplayers were low-level white-collar workers or artisans. The lowest classes were largely unrepresented, even though one-third of New York's labor force was unskilled. These men lacked the time, money, and access to playing fields, as well as the status necessary to gain acceptance into the early ball clubs.

At first, pre–Civil War employers criticized playing ball as a waste of time that led workers to neglect their duties. The new sport ideology, however, convinced bosses that baseball would make their employees healthier and more productive by teaching values congruent with the needs of the white-collar workplace. Chicago entrepreneurs John M. Farwell and Marshall Field were among the first businessmen to sponsor white-collar company teams. They believed baseball was a rational recreation that would keep young men away from saloons, gamblers, and loose women and teach such values as thrift, sobriety, virtue, and hard work, which in turn would produce reliable, cooperative, and self-sacrificing employees. Furthermore, sponsoring baseball would promote employee loyalty, advertise the company's name, publicize a positive image of the city, and help maintain social stability at a time of incredibly rapid change. By 1870, Chicago companies supported over fifty baseball teams.

In addition to team sports, the middle class organized athletic (track-and-field), cycling, target shooting, and other sports clubs to hold competitions, and, in emulation of the elite, promote sociability and gain social status. Target-shooting companies, the largest sports organizations in New York after the Civil War, were a substitute for traditional field sports that were becoming too expensive. Upper-middle-class athletes joined clubs such as the Boston Athletic Association, with its expensive costs ($40 initiation fee; $30 annual dues) as a stepping stone to a more prestigious club. These sportsmen also enjoyed less competitive and more social sports such as croquet, a popular coed fad in the 1860s. Tennis became popular with the middle class once public courts were constructed in municipal parks in the 1880s. Golf was considerably less accessible because of its high costs. In 1895 the first municipal golf course (nine holes) was opened at New York's Van Cortlandt Park, and was mainly used by middle-class duffers. Shortly thereafter, Boston opened a public course at Franklin Park, and Chicago at Jackson Park. By 1914 there were at least sixty-three municipal courses, most of which belonged to the newly formed Association of Public Golf Courses.

Middle-Class Women

Victorian women were held up on a pedestal for their piety, morality, and self-sacrifice. These attitudes, known as the cult of domesticity, meant that wives occupied a separate sphere from men, with a focus on raising children and creating an upright and godly domicile. Men, on the other hand, lived a more public life outside the home, which included earning a living. Urban women were typically pale, physically unfit, and often ill. As we have noted, reformers during the 1830s and 1840s had asserted that physical fitness was important for women to alleviate Victorian frailty. Renowned feminist Catharine Beecher championed such activities as walking, swimming, horseback riding, and exercise to prevent common female maladies.

Physicians in the post–Civil War era, concerned about women's physical, emotional, moral, and mental afflictions (abetted by ill-fitting clothing, inactivity, and diet), continued recommending moderate exercise as a preventative and partial antidote. By the 1880s, general-interest magazines gave serious attention to women's health and exercise. Women educators advocated physical training to prove that mental strain did not cause reproductive and nervous disorders and to improve their students' health, attractiveness, and strength—all good preparation for motherhood. Anne O'Hagen's "The Athletic Girl," which appeared in 1901 in the popular *Munsey's* magazine, argued that sport would improve women's morality (an antidote to narcissism) and provide freedom, fun, vigor, and health. Journalist Christine Herreck asserted in *Outing* in 1902 that women athletes learned logic, patience, and discipline in place of selfishness, snobbery, and over-emotionalism. Athletics did not make women unfeminine, but graceful and efficient, superior companions to men. Health crusader Bernarr McFadden, whose motto was "Health is Beauty, Ugliness a Sin," was among the most-noted advocates of women's fitness in the early 1900s. McFadden argued in books such as *Power and Beauty of Superb Womanhood* (1901) and in his *Journal of Women's Physical Development* that better nutrition and exercise would make healthier, more beautiful women.

Many prominent critics of women's physical culture, among them the Englishwoman Dr. Arabella Kenealy, felt that women had no place in sport. Kenealy claimed in *Nineteenth Century* magazine that women could not be both athletic and feminine since their bodies had limited constitutional capital that physical activity would squander. James Cardinal Gibbons of Baltimore feared "the restless women" who moved into traditionally male spheres, such as business, politics, and sports, and gave inadequate attention to women's traditional domestic role. Opponents of women athletes also asserted that sport taught qualities appropriate for business, not the home, citing as evidence that athletes tended to be single and, if married, had fewer children than the norm.

Early proponents of female fitness emphasized gymnastics systems ranging from calisthenics and precision drills, known as Swedish gymnastics, to Dr. Dio Lewis' system of light gymnastics that relied heavily on apparatus. Lewis became prominent in the late 1860s for a program that emphasized rhythmic exercises with rings, wands, and wooden dumbbells to promote flexibility, agility, and grace. Lewis' regimen was supplanted in the 1880s by Dr. Dudley Sargent's "corrective gymnastics" program, which stressed programs tailored to ameliorate the individual student's weaknesses. Sargent taught at Harvard University for forty years and directed its new Hemenway Gymnasium. His Sargent School of Physical Education became the preeminent institution for the training of women physical educators. Sargent claimed that women's preference for passive entertainment and sports such as bowling, tennis, and swimming was evolutionary because their narrow waists, wide hips, and sloping shoulders made them genetically less capable of vigorous physical activity

Even women's fitness advocates stressed moderation in sport because they were concerned that too much activity might induce women to become overly boisterous, competitive, sexual, and exhibitionist. In addition, physicians feared that highly competitive sport could seriously damage reproductive organs. Doctors and educators believed that women's psyches were highly vulnerable and prone to stress and nervous illnesses, making them less competitive than men. Over aggressiveness would badly damage women by allowing sexual passions to get out of control. Sport was perceived as situated at the border of civilized behavior and primitive aggression, so too much competition might erode women's self-control. Hence, where women were concerned, moderation in sport was necessary to protect modesty and prevent immorality.

The few fashionable middle-class women's sports at midcentury included horseback riding, sledding, ice skating, and croquet, often enjoyed in company with men. Evening skating in the park under gas-lit lamps was an extremely popular social sport. A skating fad emerged in the winter of 1858–59 after a frozen pond was opened in New York's Central Park. In the late 1860s the park reportedly averaged 20,000 skaters a day (100,000 for Christmas, 1860), including 2,000 women. Good skates cost from $13 to $30, but skates could be rented for a dime, plus a $1 deposit. Along with horseback riding, skating was about the only exertive sport appropriate for Victorian ladies in the Civil War era, and it gave middle-class women an opportunity to exhibit skill, exercise vigorously, and socialize with men. By the 1890s, acceptable coed sports included cycling, tennis, and golf.

Women's participation in sports identified as physically demanding did not readily gain social acceptance. When college girls participated in team sports such as basketball, baseball, and crew, it was only suitable if the sport was adapted for women's physical capabilities, did not stress competitiveness, and limited spectators to other women. One of the rare middle-class women who dared participate in a male sport with men was Alta Weiss, of Ragersville, Ohio, daughter of the town physician. In 1907, when just seventeen, she pitched for a semipro men's team, the Vermillion Independents, wearing a gym suit with a long skirt (shedding the skirt the following year). Her first season was highlighted by a victory against one of Cleveland's top semipro teams at League Park, home of the American League's Naps (known since 1915 as the Indians). Alta subsequently starred with the semipro Weiss All Stars of Cleveland, which helped pay her way through college and medical school.

Working-Class Sport

As Adelman has pointed out in *A Sporting Time: New York City and the Rise of Modern Athletics, 1820–70* (1986), skilled, well-paid antebellum workers, including printers, construction workers, and food tradesman, were prominent sportsmen. These "labor aristocrats" had considerable control over the pace of work and their free time. However, many craftsmen began to be displaced by labor-saving machinery, particularly shoemakers.

Labor aristocrats could be categorized by their value systems: loyalist, radical, or traditionalist. Loyalists and radicals shared the same Victorian work and leisure ethic embraced by white-collar workers, although the former two had greater esteem for physical prowess and strength. In the first half of the nineteenth century, loyalists were part of the middle class that identified with capitalism. They believed that Victorian virtues and self-discipline would result in personal advancement. In the second half of the nineteenth century, however, their incomes did not keep pace with most nonmanual workers, and their lifestyles grew closer to those of all other blue-collar workers. Labor radicals also championed self-restraint and Victorianism to prepare themselves to fight capitalism through unions and cooperation. They wanted to preserve their traditional control of the workplace against mechanization, the factory system, and the growing power of capitalists. Labor radicals believed that libertine values that rejected hard work, piety, sobriety, and sexual continence were destructive to the labor movement.

Traditionalist artisans wanted to maintain customary values, which included respect for physicality, honor, and toughness. These blue-collar sportsmen drank on the job, occasionally took off extra days from work to extend their weekend, and earned sufficient discretionary income to enjoy themselves as they chose. They enjoyed illegal blood and gambling sports, as well as the more respectable sport of baseball. Adelman argues that baseball enabled them to demonstrate they were not simply rowdy carousers, but respectable men. The traditionalists included shoemakers, handloom weavers, and food tradesmen, especially butchers who were renowned for their strength.

Traditional artisans were an important segment of the male bachelor subculture that included semiskilled and unskilled workers—and before the Civil War a smattering of slumming wealthy young men. Members of this community did not believe in work before pleasure, deferred gratification, humanitarianism, self-control, accumulation of property, or devotion to domesticity. They preferred the company of other young men and encouraged such manly values as courage, honor, prowess, strength, virility, and violence. Most members of this subculture had little control over their work; instead they turned to their leisure for fulfillment, identity, a sense of manliness, and satisfaction. They enjoyed such vile pleasures as drinking, frequenting prostitutes, gambling, and watching such bloody sports as boxing and cock fighting. Adelman argues that, for them, participation in sport reflected a veneration of physical prowess and an effort to preserve traditional values.

Members of urban street gangs and volunteer fire companies were particularly prominent members of the antebellum sporting fraternity. Their overlapping memberships were composed of journeymen, apprentices, and casual laborers. They were very involved in municipal politics and in sustaining the male bachelor subculture's traditional way of life in opposition to the core middle-class value system. Boxers often headed the gangs, appropriate enough, because one of their major activities was fighting with rival gangs. The sporting fraternity supported a preindustrial sporting world that centered around plebeian billiard halls, firehouses, gambling halls, and especially taverns.

Working-class volunteer firemen typically had boring jobs, yet at the firehouse they could drink and play cards with their buddies and look forward to the excitement of the fire alarm ringing, when they would rush breathlessly to the scene of a fire. One historian described fire companies as "frat club-cum-athletic teams," renowned for their fights with rival companies from different neighborhoods or ethnic groups at the scene of blazes. As Gorn points out, they recruited boxers such as Yankee Sullivan, the American champion (1849–53), and street toughs such as Butcher Bill Poole, a nativist politician and gang leader (and the model for Bill "The Butcher" Cutting, the villain in the film *Gangs of New York*, 2002), to bolster their fighting crews. Antebellum fire companies also organized sports competitions that encompassed various athletic contests related to fighting fires, such as hook-and-ladder races. These matches were attended by as many as 2,500 spectators. One scholar has described these contests as an early equivalent of modern spectator sports, wherein firemen gained respect and pride by displaying their physical prowess.

After the Civil War, the male working-class sporting tradition was hindered by urbanization, immigration (most new immigrants from eastern and southern Europe had no sporting heritage), and the effects of the industrial revolution. The growth of cities and the loss of traditional playing sites limited blue-collar sports. In post–Civil War Pittsburgh, for instance, workers originally had easy access to sites for baseball, aquatics, and hunting, but increasing demands on open spaces for residential or industrial purposes in the 1880s and

1890s curtailed traditional sport. In addition, the large new suburban parks were largely inaccessible to inner-city youth. Consequently slum children were forced to compete with pedestrians and trucks to play in crowded streets where they ran the risk of getting run over.

Industrialization in the last third of the nineteenth century, beginning with its transformation of the workplace, had a very negative impact on working-class recreation. The rise of the modern factory system weakened the relationship between master craftsmen and journeymen, reducing their personal relationships to conflicts over wages, hours of work, control of the shop floor, and productivity. Factory workers were given little latitude and were closely supervised. Workmen who came in late, took off an extra day, or drank on the job would be severely disciplined or fired. The change from the small antebellum artisan shops to the factory system created a low-skilled, low-wage proletariat labor force that worked long hours and had few holidays. Native-born white Americans and the old immigrants from western Europe shunned the least desirable, lowest paying, and most dangerous factory jobs that were largely held by hard-working eastern and southern Europeans who had no alternatives. At the turn of the century, unionized skilled employees worked about fifty-four hours a week, with only Sunday off, while nonunion semiskilled and unskilled workers averaged sixty hours a week. The worst case was steelworkers, who worked twelve-hour days, with only every other Sunday off. In general, the men engaged in physically exhausting work were often too tired for any after-hours activity more exerting than raising a beer mug to their mouths.

This is not to say that industrial workers labored all the time. They often had unwanted free time when underemployed, laid off because of seasonal unemployment, or unemployed for long periods during recessions and depressions. During these periods of unplanned leisure, older employees could not afford to buy tickets to sporting events because of familial responsibilities. In 1910 about 40 percent of the workforce fell below the $500-a-year poverty line, and entire families had to work just to survive. A visit to the neighborhood saloon for a nickel beer or a small bet with the local bookie was about all the recreation low-income married men could afford, even in flush times.

Blue-collar sporting options were further curtailed by Sunday blue laws. An American Sabbath of restricted Sunday activities was especially commonplace in the pietistic South, where it was maintained by custom and social pressure. The only exceptions were the cosmopolitan and relatively heavily Catholic port cities of New Orleans, Mobile, and Memphis, as well as Texas cities with large Mexican and German populations. Sabbatarianism was weakest in the West and Midwest, where Sunday baseball was widely played in the late nineteenth century. Influential Midwestern German and Irish communities used their clout to prevent enforcement of the blue laws, and both regions had a strong tradition of social democracy that discouraged any one group exercising social control over another.

In the Northeast, small-town WASPs who controlled state legislatures used their power to impose restrictive blue laws to regulate Sunday behavior in cities dominated by immigrants and their children. Local machine politicians who sympathized with their constituents' desire for Sunday recreation sought lax enforcement of Sabbatarian laws, pointing out that the rich could go golfing, but city boys were hassled for playing ball in the streets. Amateur or semiprofessional ballplayers were often allowed to circumvent the blue laws by selling programs rather than admission tickets. Such was not the case, however, for professional games. Major-league Sunday baseball was banned in New York City until 1919, when the legislature liberalized the state's Sabbath laws. The first Sunday games held there drew about 35,000 fans, which reflected the size of the pent-up interest among the working class for good, clean fun on Sundays. Blue laws prevented Sunday ball in Boston until 1929, and in Philadelphia and Pittsburgh until 1934.

As a result of these circumstances, the typical working-class sports fans in the late nineteenth and early twentieth centuries were mainly native-born Americans, German artisans, and Irish municipal workers. These men had grown up familiar with sports and had a sufficiently high standard of living to enjoy athletic entertainments. Artisans earned about twice as much as laborers (skilled workers' wages rose by 74 percent between 1890 and 1914 as compared to 31 percent for unskilled workers), toiled shorter hours than most blue-collar workers, and lived in neighborhoods where public parks and commercial sporting facilities were relatively accessible. Many, such as bakers or policemen, worked evening shifts so they could go to afternoon sporting events without skipping work.

The Working-Class Saloon

The local tavern, situated on nearly every corner in urban blue-collar neighborhoods or across the street from most factories, was the most accessible working-class sporting site. The "poor man's club" was the most important semipublic institution in working-class neighborhoods and the center of the male bachelor subculture. Historian Perry Duis, author of *The Saloon: Public Drinking in Chicago and Boston, 1880–1920* (1983), describes Chicago's saloons as quasi-gymnasiums. The largest among them had full-sized handball courts in the back room, while smaller rooms might hold billiard tables, bowling alleys, and dart boards. By 1909 half of the city's 7,600 saloons had a billiard table, which, according to Duis, was "almost as much a necessity as the bar itself." Taverns had been important sites for sports since the colonial era, when they provided facilities for table sports, animal baiting and gambling, and rooms for clubs to meet. In the mid-nineteenth century, less respectable taverns were still the primary site for blood sports. The most famous animal-baiting arena was Kit Burns' Sportsman's Hall in New York, a barroom hangout for some of the city's roughest and toughest criminals. Despite the American Society for the Prevention of Cruelty to Animals' opposition to animal baiting in the late 1860s, cock fighting remained a popular sport, especially in southern backwater areas and bachelor communities such as mining camps, where it reportedly detracted from efforts to organize labor unions.

Taverns served as a major center for the boxing crowd, or "the fancy" as fans were known in the mid-nineteenth century. There sportsmen could pick up a copy of the *Police Gazette* and admire pictures of champions on the walls, especially the ubiquitous John L. Sullivan, heavyweight champion of the world. Pugilists, who were virtually all products of poverty and the mean streets of urban slums, were among the leading working-class heroes. Early bouts were usually arranged at taverns, with the saloonkeeper acting as promoter and stakeholder. In the 1870s, when Harry Hill's Dance

Hall in New York was the sporting fraternity's leading hangout, Hill helped many prominent boxers get their start. In the late nineteenth century, when prizefighting was illegal virtually everywhere, many minor matches were secretly held in saloon darkrooms for twenty-five cents a ticket. Gorn points out that combat sports epitomized a lower-class style of raucous play that affirmed lower-working-class values such as prowess, bravery, honor, and valor. Well-trained boxers were admired for their well-proportioned bodies and craftsmanship, exhibiting expertise at a moment when workingmen's skills were threatened.

The saloon was a popular site for sports gambling with bookmakers, who also worked barbershops and other bastions of maleness. Off-track bookmakers were accessible, paid track odds on any horse in a race, accepted bets as small as twenty-five cents, and extended credit. The largest cities, primarily New York and Chicago, also had poolrooms, located mainly in midtown or the local vice district, where clerks were reportedly their principal clients. In the late nineteenth century, workingmen avoided elite race tracks that had high entrance fees, were located an expensive ride away at the outskirts of town, and were inhospitable to the small bettor. They preferred business-minded proprietary tracks that catered to mass audiences, such as Brooklyn's Brighton Beach, or "outlaw" tracks such as New Jersey's Guttenberg, owned by bookmakers and machine politicians. Outlaw tracks were unsupervised by any racing regulatory agency, and they were frequently guilty of abusing horses, holding meets year-round, and fixing races.

If the saloon was the most accessible site of working-class sport, pool halls were a close second. In 1900, some 30,000 businesses had pool tables, which included saloons and stand-alone pool halls. New York City alone had 300 poolrooms in 1900 and more than 4,000 by the 1920s. Billiard table games were not inherently evil. Wealthy people often had their own tables in a room set aside for the sport, and Judge Ben Lindsey, the renowned Denver juvenile court judge, recommended that middle-class fathers buy tables for family entertainment. Pool halls in the inner city, however, had a well-earned terrible image as public menaces. They were considered hangouts for inner-city ne'er-do-wells who gambled, drank, and plotted crimes.

Track-and-Field

Young blue-collar athletes competed successfully in those sports most appropriate to their socio-economic situation and their overcrowded neighborhoods, particularly sports that did not require expensive equipment and could provide an avenue for social mobility. Youth who grew up in working-class zones of emergence played baseball, inner-city lads boxed and played basketball, and all of them participated in track-and-field.

The top amateurs in track-and-field in the last decades of the nineteenth century were rarely blue-collar workers, hardly surprising considering their lack of regularly scheduled free time, long working hours, and low wages. Furthermore, they lacked suitable equipment, sound coaching, and sponsorship. Most amateur champions in the 1880s were either students or clerks, some of whom were subsidized by prestigious athletic clubs. Blue-collar athletes who participated on a high level were mainly labor aristocrats such as printers, who were well paid and worked relatively short hours, or municipal workers such as policemen who had job security, decent wages, and worked flexible hours so that they could train—inherently vital for a job that depended upon physical fitness and strength. In fact, several New York policemen starred in the early Olympics in field events (see chapter 6).

There were just a handful of working-class track-and-field clubs in the late nineteenth century, so most blue-collar track-and-field athletes mainly competed at annual picnics sponsored by their employer, union, benevolent society, ethnic organization, or political party. A number of ethnic-based track clubs did spring up at the turn of the century, most notably New York's Irish-American Athletic Association (1898), which sponsored several world-class track and field stars. Picnic games dated back to the mid-nineteenth century, organized as fund-raisers for middle-class charities. Companies in the 1880s began sponsoring picnics to curry favor with their employees, primarily the office staff, and to gain publicity. Sporting events included bowling, marksmanship, and track-and-field contests, some of which were exclusively for employees and others open to all competitors. In addition, there would often be a couple of events for professionals to compete for cash purses. The outings typically ended with a dinner dance.

Union picnic games in the late nineteenth century were staged by local chapters of the Knights of Labor, as well as unions of artisans such as typographers, plumbers, stonecutters, and bricklayers. They were typically held on Decoration Day, Independence Day, or Labor Day, in conjunction with marches and other demonstrations. Some of these meets in the 1880s were significant enough to be covered by the middle-class *Spirit of the Times*, but usually with a condescending tone. William Curtis, the *Spirit*'s editor, was a founder of the New York Athletic Club and regularly criticized the annual games of the Printers' Benevolent Association of New York for sloppy preparation and bad judging. By the early 1890s, however, both the *New York Times* and the *Clipper* were impressed by the quality of the "type stickers'" athletic picnics.

The purpose of the union-sponsored picnics, historian John Cumbler reminds us, was to promote the recreational life of their members and keep alive a sense of community, class consciousness, and interdependence. Unions encouraged sociability and camaraderie at their halls, where they sometimes set aside a room for pool. Union leaders were in a constant struggle with management for the loyalty of the workforce (see below, *Industrial Sport*) and sought to demonstrate their concern about their members' quality of life, which transcended such workplace goals as the eight-hour day, higher wages, and safer working conditions.

Neighborhood political organizations sponsored picnics to improve relations with constituents. Machine politicians were leaders of the sporting fraternity and played a prominent role in promoting participatory sports as well as commercialized spectator sports. The most famous affair was New York City's East Side ward boss Tim Sullivan's annual outing, paid for by local businessmen to curry favor with the machine. The event drew up to 6,000 participants, mainly Irish-American, who would enjoy the sports, a parade, and a political rally.

The working class dominated professional track-and-field sports, which originated with pedestrianism in the 1830s and the Scottish Caledonian Games of the 1850s. Professional long-distance runners in the late nineteenth century were mainly clerks and blue-collar workers who competed in highly organized events, most notably six-day-long marathons. The most prestigious was the 1878–79 International Astley Belt races for purses of up to $20,000 at arenas such as Madison Square Garden. The event was sponsored by Sir John Dugdale Astley, a British member of parliament, to determine the "long distance champion of the world." The winners routinely exceeded five hundred miles. Marathon events remained popular throughout the 1880s. Other professional athletic contests — including sprints which became popular in the 1870s — were staged at Caledonian Games, working-class picnics, and amusement parks. The runners were often sponsored by saloonkeepers or local politicians who bet on the matches and shared their winnings with the athletes. By the 1880s, amusement park races were staged at resorts in Coney Island, New York, Hoboken, Newark, and Paterson, New Jersey, and Philadelphia for purses of $100 to $300. They drew up to 2,500 spectators at twenty-five cents a ticket.

Blue-Collar Baseball

The first blue-collar ballplayers were artisans, primarily loyalists who supported capitalism, rather than traditionalists, who wanted to maintain the old male bachelor subculture. Their teams were regimented and serious and gave players a chance to temporarily escape their problems, demonstrate prowess, make friends, gain a sense of belonging, and enjoy themselves without the boss looking over their shoulder. There is little evidence, however, contrary to the views of Marxist historian Bryan Palmer, that baseball established a collectivist subculture antagonistic to core American values.

The first artisan baseball players were from metropolitan New York. Historian Melvin Adelman found that nearly one-fourth (23.4 percent) of players active in Brooklyn or New York clubs in the first half of the 1850s were artisans, and virtually none were unskilled laborers. By the late 1850s, almost half (48.2 percent) of the most active players were skilled craftsmen. Furthermore, workers also played a prominent role in the sport's leadership. Roughly one-third of Brooklyn club officials were blue-collar workers, and one-fifth of Brooklyn and New York delegates to the NABBP were artisans. The Brooklyn Eckfords, founded in 1855, was the first blue-collar club, comprised mainly of prosperous shipwrights and mechanics (77.8

percent), economically middle class with bourgeois, modern values. Well-to-do dock builder–president Frank Pidgeon believed in "business first, pleasure afterwards." He advocated amateurism because he wanted to give all teams a fair chance. Pidgeon feared that with professionalization, the wealthier clubs would hire the best players and ballplayers would lose their independence, a common concern among midcentury artisans. However, sporting journals such as the *Clipper* and Porter's *Spirit of the Times* supported professionalism as a means to democratize baseball by making it easier for gifted working-class athletes to participate.

The best blue-collar team was the Brooklyn Atlantics, mainly composed of Irish Catholic food-industry employees with strong ties to the Democratic Party. In 1860 they played a series with the middle-class white Anglo Saxon Protestant Brooklyn Excelsiors that drew enormous interest because the teams represented opposing ethnic, political, and class groups. The first two games were split, but the third and decisive game, attended by more than 15,000, was halted after the fifth inning with the Excelsiors up 8-6, due to rioting Atlantic fans, and declared a draw.

Early working-class teams were organized along occupational lines, neighborhoods, and political divisions. They mainly played other workers because higher-status groups did not want to play beneath their station. These clubs had a strong fraternal and social aspect, and games were usually followed by a dinner; nonetheless, they played to win. Club officials expected players to be disciplined, trained, and well-drilled. A generation later, in the 1880s, blue-collar teams were sponsored by ethnic groups, unions, benevolent societies, political parties, and factories. Union teams publicized the labor movement, drew crowds to rallies and demonstrations, raised money to aid striking comrades, and promoted issues such as the eight-hour workday. Employers who had once feared that baseball disrupted work habits now appreciated the sport: disciplined, moral, and healthy young men made good workers; the games provided clean fun for other employees who attended them; and facilitating sports for workers might lessen their support of labor unions.

Manual workers were well represented on early professional baseball teams. The *New York Times* in 1869 claimed that the first professionals were mainly young mechanics. That opinion has recently been corroborated by Adelman, who found that three-fifths (61.8 percent) of New Yorkers in the National Association of Professional Base Ball Players (NA), which lasted from 1871 to 1875, were blue-collar workers. Adelman argues that young artisans tried professional baseball more readily than older white-collar workers who had better job alternatives and less time for arrested adolescent behavior. Furthermore, white-collar ballplayers were put off by the low status of the new occupation, and they were less eager to leave home for a new and untried enterprise, especially if they had a family.

Industrial Sport

When the Industrial Revolution emerged in antebellum America, capitalists justified low wages, long working hours, and constant supervision as essential to keep workers in line and prevent dissipation from vile amusements. In the late nineteenth century, however, they learned from British capitalists the benefits of industrial relations in producing a happy, contented, loyal workforce that would be punctual, efficient, hardworking, and non-union. American industrialists used sport as well as other features of welfare capitalism, such as bonuses and healthcare programs, to improve relations with their employees and kill unions by demonstrating to workers how much their company cared about their needs.

As early as 1872 railroad moguls relied on the YMCA to provide programs for their workers, and they greatly increased their support of the Y movement following the nationwide rail strikes of 1877. The company-sponsored YMCAs provided food and shelter, baths, libraries, work-related classes, religious instruction, and athletic facilities to discourage future labor disputes. During the 1880s, the YMCA reached out to such alienated workmen as Pennsylvania miners and Wisconsin lumbermen, although it remained a predominantly middle-class evangelical association. Workingmen found the YMCA too expensive, too Protestant, and too moralistic, and they largely resented having a middle-class value system imposed on them. In 1902 the YMCA tried to improve its working-class appeal by organizing an industrial department. Many memberships were paid by employers trying to ingratiate themselves with their workers. By 1903, 98,000 industrial workers belonged to the YMCA, but they made up just 20 percent of its membership.

In the 1880s, companies began sponsoring their own athletic programs, and within twenty years these programs became an integral element of welfare capitalism. Industrialists supported athletic programs for several reasons. They wanted to promote morale and bolster their firm's public image. Management believed sports programs would attract new workers, maintain control over the workplace, forestall the rise and growth of unions, and encourage company loyalty. Sports would help instill workers with proper behavior and values such as punctuality, while helping the firm oversee some of their discretionary time. Finally, management believed welfare capitalism would keep taxes down by averting any need for the construction of municipal recreational facilities.

Bosses felt that welfare capitalism allowed them to make a positive contribution to their workers' lives while simultaneously increasing profits and fighting unions. Welfare capitalists felt responsible for helping workers adjust to the dislocations caused by the Industrial Revolution on and off the job. Among native-born white Americans, these problems were particularly acute in southern textile-mill towns, where workers had been torn away from their traditional, independent, rural lifestyle.

The first outstanding industrial sports program was sponsored by industrialist George Pullman, builder of the world-renowned Pullman sleeping cars at his newly built company town of Pullman, Illinois. The town, established in 1881 (and annexed by Chicago in 1889), was a model community for blue-collar employees located on the outskirts of Chicago. Pullman wanted to skirt Chicago's political corruption, unionization, and demon rum. He attracted a highly skilled workforce by providing them with competitive wages, quality housing, good schools, and clean streets. There he tightly exercised social control over his employees, banning saloons and unions, even spying on them. The town offered such amenities as Sunday concerts, a public library, and sports programs. The Pullman Athletic Association (PAA) was organized in 1882 and was open to all employees. It helped attract workers, provided a moral alternative to vile amusements, and gained the company considerable positive recognition. The PAA stressed highly competitive sports, especially cricket and crew. The oarsmen, among the finest in the United States, were experienced athletes, many of whom had been recruited from Great Britain by a job offer. In 1883 the town hosted the national crew championships, attended by 15,000 spectators. Track contests were also very popular, so much so that they were not even disrupted by the famous Pullman strike of 1894.

Industrial sports programs were adopted in the early 1900s by huge companies such as the Pennsylvania Railroad, National Cash Register, and U.S. Steel. The latter's president, Andrew Carnegie, was a leading proponent of welfare capitalism who believed that leisure-time activities influenced his workers' mental, physical, and moral development. Industrial sports programs proliferated among major firms, and by 1918, 152 of the 400 largest manufacturers provided indoor recreational facilities and about half of them sponsored outdoor recreation or annual picnics. By 1920 Ford Motor Company workers in Dearborn, Michigan, enjoyed a twenty-acre athletic park with facilities for football, baseball, and tennis, while in Pittsburgh, the Pennsylvania Railroad had thirty-two baseball fields, thirty-three tennis courts, seven athletic fields, and even a golf course. Certain firms even sponsored semiprofessional and professional sports teams to improve labor relations, exercise social control over the workers, and make a profit. In 1897 when a miners' strike hit eastern Pennsylvania, one prominent mine owner responded by organizing and funding an entire minor league. In Paterson, New Jersey, the local Atlantic League team was owned by Garret Hobart, soon to become William McKinley's vice president. His club was expected to deflect public interest from labor issues at a time when the local silk mills and locomotive works were on strike.

The first professional football teams, composed of mill hands or former collegians, were organized by western Pennsylvania and Midwestern industrialists to alleviate labor tensions. In 1900, Carnegie executives organized professional teams in the mill towns of Homestead and Braddock. The latter's club consisted mainly of steelworkers who received a bonus to play and were excused from mill work during the season. In 1902 the first professional football league was organized, purportedly to reduce strains caused by an anthracite coal strike. Thereafter the center of professional football shifted to small industrial Ohio towns such as Canton and Massillon, where most spectators were rubber or steel workers. By the mid-1910s there were about eighty-six professional and semiprofessional teams sponsored by social clubs, ethnic fraternities, and especially the labor relations departments of industrial companies. As Harry A. March recounts in *Pro Football: Its Ups and Downs* (1934) that boilermakers playing for the Columbus Panhandles, a division of the Pennsylvania Railroad, "worked in the shop until four Saturday afternoon, got their suppers at home, grabbed the rattlers to any point within twelve hours' ride of Columbus, played the Sunday game, took another train to Columbus, and punched the time clock at seven Monday morning." Several original National Football League teams were company-sponsored squads established to deflect labor unrest. They included the Dayton Triangles, financed by Delco and other local firms, the Packers of Green Bay's Indian-Acme Packing Company, the Hammond Pros, funded by an Indiana steel magnate after the 1919 industry-wide strike, and the Decatur Staleys (the future Chicago Bears), backed by a starch manufacturer, object of a 1919 strike and the brainchild of labor relations director George Halas.

Working-Class Women's Sport

Working-class sport was all but completely a male sphere because of restrictive social norms and lack of access. Lower-class sportswomen were looked down upon, and their femininity was questioned. A handful of professional sportswomen dated back to rowing contests in 1867 and, in the 1870s, boxing matches and pedestrianism. These sports were covered with relish by the *National Police Gazette* because of their incongruity with the cult of domesticity. Lib Kelly, who fought in 1878 at Hill's Dance Hall, was the first outstanding female boxer. One year later Bertha Von Berg covered 372 miles in a six-day marathon. Women also competed in feats of strength such as weight lifting, endurance contests such as walking a narrow plank for time (a popular saloon sport), and both strength and endurance such as wrestling and exhibitions of bodybuilding. An 1898 charity exhibition of women wrestlers at the Polo Grounds drew 12,000 spectators.

Baseball also attracted young working-class women. There were numerous female teams of touring baseball players, such as Harry H. Freeman's "buxom beauties." These women's clubs had a bad public image and their members were occasionally presumed to be prostitutes. Probably the best female ballplayer of the nineteenth century was Lizzie Arlington, a coal miner's daughter from Pottsville, Pennsylvania. Arlington was considered such a good pitcher and gate attraction that she was paid $100 a week to play in exhibition games against professional teams. Arlington even appeared in a minor-league game in 1899, when she pitched one inning for the Reading, Pennsylvania, team of the Atlantic League.

Conclusion

Between 1850 and 1920 the sporting options of American men and women were heavily shaped by their status in society. The rich enjoyed the greatest options, and they used sport to escape from urban problems and withdraw into their own private world. Sport provided a means to certify one's social prestige and boundaries to identify people of similar status. Sport offered young men an opportunity to prove their manliness and women to display their independence. Middle-class people found in modern sports a new and socially approved form of recreation that fit in with their value system. They had the necessary free time, discretionary income, and easy access to sporting facilities to participate in sports or watch events, and they used sports to have a good time while improving their health, teaching children morality, and making new friends and business contacts. On the other hand, working-class participation in sport was hindered by urbanization, industrialization, and a civilizing process that tried to eliminate traditional sports that emphasized gambling and violence. The decline of the independent artisan and the rise of the factory (with its time and work discipline) curtailed leisure time and discretionary income, and the rapid growth of cities supplanted traditional playing sites. Sport remained a vital part of lower-class culture, but it was largely limited to the neighborhood tavern and billiard hall.

By the 1920s working-class sport participation would become commonplace among male old-stock Americans and second-generation immigrants. It had limited appeal to their sisters, who wanted to retain an image of femininity and respectability. Blue-collar workers enjoyed a significant boost in their standard of living after World War I, when industrial workers earned $1,400 a year, approximately the same as clerical workers. Furthermore, working hours declined to forty-eight hours for skilled workers and fifty-four for unskilled, and Sunday blue laws outside the Bible Belt were becoming less restrictive. In addition, the working class had greater access to participatory sports with the completion of small public parks and spectator sports with the expansion of cheap mass transit. By the 1920s, the working class had become full-fledged members of the consumer society.

CHAPTER THREE

Sport, Ethnicity, and Race

The sporting culture of the industrial era was in large measure a product of ethnic and racial variables. Mid-nineteenth-century sport was significantly influenced by the athletic practices and values that western European immigrants from Great Britain, Ireland, German-speaking nations, and Scandinavia brought with them to America in the period between 1840 and 1880. These newcomers established voluntary sports organizations to maintain their athletic heritage and ethnic identity. The immigrants from eastern and southern Europe who flocked to America primarily between 1882 and 1914 came with little if any sporting background and they were uninterested in physical culture. Yet their sons became ardent sports fans, idolizing noted athletes, especially men from their own ethnic group. Second-generation Poles, Italians, and Jews used sport to prove they were real Americans and not green-horns, becoming particularly prominent in sports that fit in with their socio-economic conditions. The African American experience was quite different from that of immigrants. They were American born and reared, and they had participated in American sports at a high level of accomplishment. They encountered enormous dis-crimination, however, when they competed in or attended sporting events and were even forced out of several professional sports, a reflection of America's pervasive racism.

Athletes from ethnic and racial minorities were prominent heroes who were idolized by fellow group members for their accomplishments. Ethnic folklore, particularly among the most downtrodden groups, recounted the accomplishments and legends of their champions to promote group pride and teach valuable lessons. Some of the earliest sports legends were Irish superstars such as boxer John L. Sullivan and the fabled baseball player Mike "King" Kelly, or African American icons such as heavyweight champion Jack Johnson.

The Old Immigrants

British Americans

The English, who comprised the largest number of colonists, brought with them many traditional rural sporting pastimes such as cricket, animal baiting, cock fighting, and field and equestrian sports, and indoor games such as billiards. Then, in the early nineteenth century, English, Scottish, and Welsh immigrants arrived, bringing their sporting culture, the most prominent in the western world. About 353,000 Englishmen arrived between 1830 and 1850. Their interest in sports became a focal point for voluntary organizations that sustained distinct ethnic heritages and promoted a sense of community for the newcomers. In addition, by the 1840s professional British athletes were coming to America to compete for money, particularly boxers (one-fifth of antebellum New York boxers were English immigrants) and long-distance runners. Pedestrian matches at Hoboken's Beacon Race Course reputedly drew up to 30,000 spectators. Publicists for these races built up interest by emphasizing the ethnic factor: "It was the trial of the peculiar American *physique* against the long held supremacy of the English muscular endurance."

The first British sports organizations in the United States were rowing and cricket clubs. Early cricket elevens were "steak and ale" clubs, organized by textile workers or wealthy English merchants. They mainly played on Saturday afternoons, as in England, where a Saturday half-holiday was becoming customary. New York's St. George Cricket Club (SGCC), organized in 1840, was the most famous of many northeastern clubs, arranging high-level competition, including an international match against a Toronto St. George team. Members were virtually all high-status, English-born businessmen, although as late as 1848 one-fifth of them were artisans. The St. George Cricket Club increasingly became more of a status than an ethnic association, however, and by 1865 merely 5.7 percent of its members were artisans. While New York cricketers were predominantly English, the sport became so popular that by midcentury it was considered the leading American ball sport. The number of American players grew, especially among the more prosperous folk in Brooklyn and Philadelphia. Even in heavily industrialized Newark, the number of American cricketers equaled the English representation.

Englishmen established sports societies wherever they went, recreating the atmosphere of a traditional county fair. After the Civil War, Englishmen frequently organized "Albion" (an archaic name for Great Britain) societies to promote familiar pastimes, particularly picnic games with running contests and dances. British settlers in rural southern Minnesota raced horses, organized a boat club, played rugby, and hunted foxes, while their urban counterparts formed curling and cricket clubs. British weavers in Fall River, Massachusetts, were so sports oriented that upon striking in 1889, they set aside space in the union hall to exercise with union-supplied athletic equipment.

Soccer was the most popular sport among late-nineteenth-century British immigrants. Soccer in the 1870s was mainly played by sandlot teams or loosely organized clubs of English and Scottish workers in industrial cities such as Paterson, New Jersey, Newark, Philadelphia, and New York. Elsewhere British and Irish miners, steelworkers, and stonecutters organized clubs and leagues. In 1884, British soccer fans organized the forerunner of the American Football Association, and by 1886, St. Louis and Fall River set up their own leagues. Fall River alone had twenty-five teams that averaged about two thousand fans per match. In the early 1880s, northeastern and Midwestern companies began sponsoring teams comprised of men recruited from the British Isles. Chicago industrialist George Pullman hired several athletic British artisans to work at his sleeping-car factory and compete for the Pullman Athletic Associations renowned cricket and crew teams.

Scottish newcomers also used sport as a focal point for ethnic organizations that sought to sustain their traditional culture. The most important were the Caledonians, a Scottish association initially founded in Boston in 1853, described by historian Benjamin Rader as possibly "the single most significant ethnic community in encouraging the growth of nineteenth-century American sport." Its goal was to provide Scotsmen with a sense of community by maintaining "the manners and customs, literature, the Highland costume and the athletic games of Scotland." Eventually over one hundred Caledonian clubs sponsored athletic meets as well as various Scottish social functions. Athletic contests emphasized such traditional Scottish events as throwing the caber (a pine tree over nineteen feet long, and weighing 175 lbs.) and pitching the heavy stone. The Caledonians dominated American track-and-field until the rise of track-and-field clubs and national amateur championships in the mid-1870s.

Caledonian competitions drew people from all ethnic backgrounds, and by 1870 admission-paying crowds surpassed twenty thousand. Besides the traditional Scottish games, there would be sprint races and field events such as the hammer throw, shot put, and pole vault. In 1886 New York Caledonians added a 220-yard women's race. Caledonian contests for cash prizes ranging from $100 to $200 were opened up to all comers, but the stars remained Scotsmen such as Duncan Ross and Donald Dinnie, who used his stature as a major gate attraction to force meet sponsors to pay him appearance fees in addition to his purses. The Caledonians faltered in the late nineteenth century because of a decline in Scottish immigration, the rapid assimilation of the immigrants into mainstream American culture, and the emergence of high-status athletic clubs that supplanted them as the leading track-and-field sponsors.

Irish Americans

The 1.7 million Irish who immigrated to the United States in the decade following the Great Famine of 1845–46 were mainly impoverished, uneducated, and unskilled Catholic peasants. They brought a traditional male bachelor subculture that included a lively sporting heritage. Single as well as married Irishmen spent their leisure time with their "mates" in pubs and other exclusively male surroundings where self-image and prestige were defined by their athletic, gambling, drinking, or sexual prowess. Once in America, the Irish readily moved into a similar subculture where they befriended men of comparable backgrounds, values, and behavior.

The Irish newcomers immediately distinguished themselves in boxing, a violent, bloody, and illegal sport that required courage, strength, and skill, which offered tough Irish immigrants a possible escape from poverty. Boxing was most prominent in such cities as New York, Boston, Philadelphia, and New Orleans, where there were a lot of Irish residents. As historian Melvin Adelman discovered, most New York prizefighters active between 1840 and 1860 were Irishmen (56.3 percent), many of whom had boxed in the Old Country, or Irish Americans (15.6 percent). Midcentury matches were mainly impromptu or secret events staged in neighborhood groggeries.

Second-generation Irish American boxers who grew up in New York were typically alumni of tough street gangs or fire companies closely tied to Tammany Hall. They fought for side bets and to combat anti-Catholic and anti-Irish nativism which was very strong and widespread. Americans saw the Irish as coming to their country to take their jobs, engage in crime, and gain control of the nation on behalf of the Pope and political reactionaries. Boxers also battled to defend their personal honor, Irish pride, or the Democratic Party. Irish pugilists preferred to fight Englishmen or native-born white Americans. The latter composed just 6.25 percent of the prizefighters. These pugilists were typically ex-apprentice mechanics or butchers who supported WASP gangs such as the Bowery Boys, who lived just north of the infamous Five Points District, the worst slum in the United States, and nativist political parties such as the Whigs in the 1840s and early 1850s, and the Know-Nothings of the mid-1850s.

Fighters in the 1850s could not earn a living from boxing because there were few formal matches. They generally depended on political sponsors for patronage jobs or work that required physical prowess, often becoming "shoulder hitters," or political intimidators. The most renowned antebellum Irish fighter was John Morrissey, who was born in Ireland but grew up in Troy, New York. Morrissey went to New York City as a young man seeking fame and fortune. He first gained recognition as a barroom brawler at Captain Isaiah Rynders's Empire Club and as an intimidator for the Democratic Party. Morrissey lacked technique, but he was courageous and determined. In 1853, in only his second formal bout, he defeated the American champion and fellow Irishman Yankee Sullivan for the title. Sullivan dominated the match until a free-for-all broke out after the thirty-seventh round, and he spent some of the thirty-second rest period punching Morrissey's corner man. When the timekeeper called the fighters to "scratch" for the thirty-eighth round, Sullivan failed to meet his opponent in the center of the ring, and the referee awarded the fight to Morrissey. "Old Smoke" won his only defense in 1858 against Irish American John C. Heenan in Long Point, Ontario, Canada, and retired one year later. The champion was a hero to most Irish Americans for his boxing prowess and impromptu brawls with nativists such as Butcher Bill Poole, and Morrissey used his fame to become New York City's most successful gambling-hall proprietor. He also played a crucial role in revitalizing northern racing at the upstate resort town of Saratoga Springs, where he set up the "Club House," a gambling hall in 1862, and the Saratoga Racetrack one year later. Morrissey became a prominent Tammany Hall politician, serving two terms (1867–70) in the U.S. Congress. He broke with the crooked Tweed Ring, the machine that ran New York City politics, before its downfall in 1871, a move that salvaged his political career. Morrissey was elected to the state senate in 1876. He died two years later, and, having achieved a measure of respectability and enormous renown, had one of the largest funerals in the history of nineteenth-century New York.

Considerable interest emerged in the Irish community after the Civil War in traditional Hibernian games such as hurling, a game similar to field hockey but much wilder, and Gaelic football, first played in New York in 1858, although the rules were not formalized until 1887. Both sports employ fifteen-man teams, are very rough, and score by sending the ball through an H-shaped crossbar. In hurling, players are allowed to catch the ball and run down the playing field with it for four steps, all the while carrying a stick called a *hurley* with which to dribble the ball or bat it forward. Short hand passes are also permitted. A point is made by hitting the *scolar* (ball) over the crossbar between two goal posts, and a three-point goal is scored by propelling it past the goalie and under the bar. Gaelic football is currently the most popular sport in the Republic of Ireland. Players can carry the ball, hand-pass it to a teammate, or kick it forward. A player scores a point by kicking or fisting the ball over "H" shaped goalposts; three-point goals are earned when a player kicks the ball past a goalie and under the crossbar.

Nationalists in Ireland in the last third of the nineteenth century advocated a rebirth of historic Irish sports at home and abroad to promote Irish independence and ethnic consciousness, especially among the Irish overseas. Perhaps the first organization to sponsor traditional sports was the Clan-na-Gael, also known as the United Brotherhood, a notorious, secretive revolutionary society established in 1867 in Manchester, England. Three years later, the Clan began sponsoring annual track-and-field games to promote Irish nationalism, recruit members, and improve its public image. By the late 1870s, independent Irish sports clubs were created in Boston, Brooklyn, New York, and other heavily Irish locales. They provided members with a community of like-minded men, encouraged ethnic pride and Irish nationalism, and enhanced members' status and dignity. In 1879, Boston's Irish Athletic Club had its inaugural athletic meet, featuring traditional contests such as goaling, trapping, and stone throwing. In 1884 the Gaelic Athletic Association (GAA) was founded in Ireland to promote historic Hibernian games. An American tour followed four years later, which helped to stimulate the movement in the United States. Its American units became well known for organizing Sunday hurling, Gaelic football, and track-and-field contests in Irish neighborhoods. A Hibernian spirit permeated New York's Irish football teams that played at Gaelic Park, and the teams named themselves for Irish heroes.

The Irish were recognized as outstanding boxers in the antebellum era, and they continued their dominance in that sport. But in addition, they became a major force in the late nineteenth century in most mainstream American working-class sports. Irish immigrants and second-generation Irish Americans achieved considerable success in track-and-field, a sport largely dominated by wealthier WASPS who could afford the cost of training, admission into the more prestigious clubs, and time lost from work. Certain working-class Irishmen were recruited by elite athletic clubs because of their outstanding ability, which gave them a chance to parlay their physical dexterity into jobs or business opportunities. In 1888, Tommy Conneff, a promising distance runner and future mile-record holder, came to America to better himself. He joined the prestigious Manhattan Athletic Club after the club's secretary hired him to work as a clerk in his company. There were some limited opportunities for Irish professional track-and-field stars, most notably the six-day marathons popular in the late 1870s and early 1880s. One of the most successful was Irish-born Patrick Fitzgerald, a future Long Island City alderman, who won an 1884 Madison Square Garden marathon, completing 610 miles, and earning over $18,000.

New York's Irish American Athletic Club provided training facilities at Celtic Park, a stadium in the Borough of Queens opened in 1901 for world-class Irish (and selected non-Irish) athletes who were not welcomed at the more prestigious clubs because of their heritage. Its impressive roster produced nineteen of seventy-seven American Olympic track-and-field competitors at the 1908 Olympics in London. Quite a few Irish club members won Olympic medals in the years 1900–12, including five muscular policemen who starred in field events. They included Irish-born John Flanagan, who won three gold medals in the hammer throw (1900, 1904, and 1908) and Irish-born Martin Sheridan, who won five gold and one silver medal in the shot put and discus (1904, 1906, 1908). Irish American Johnny Hayes, winner of the marathon in 1908, was ostensibly a shipping clerk at Bloomingdales, but the job was a sinecure, which enabled him to train full-time.

Sport was a major preoccupation for second- and third-generation Irish Americans such as Danny O'Neill and Studs Lonigan, protagonists in James T. Farrell's novels about Chicago's Irish youth in the early twentieth century. They joined community baseball and football teams that played lads from different streets or neighborhoods. These teams were often based on turn-of-the-century formalized gangs, known as social and athletic clubs (SACs). These organizations typically had about one hundred members, mainly in their late teens. They had constitutions, rented street-front clubhouses, and were often sponsored by a local machine politician who expected the club to work on his behalf on Election Day. These clubs promoted camaraderie and organized social events, including dances and sports, supplying uniforms and arranging contests. The SACs could be either uplifting or destructive. Chicago's most famous such club was the Ragen Colts, located in the Southwest Side, at the Back of the Yards district adjacent to the Stockyards. Frank Ragen was a Democratic Cook County Commissioner, and his brother James became a prominent bootlegger, labor intimidator, and gambler. The Colts, who had as many as 2,000 members, first gained renown for their athletic prowess, and a team sponsored by the club eventually evolved into the Chicago Cardinals, a charter member of the National Football League. However, but by the late 1910s, the Colts were mainly known as sluggers and political intimidators who terrorized the Southwest Side and the emerging Black Belt to the east. The Irish were frightened by the growing African American presence as stockyard workers and by African American support of a Republican mayor, William H. Thompson, archenemy of Chicago Democrats. The Colts felt it was their duty to protect the Southwest Side Irish, just as they protected Washington Park, a large public park in their neighborhood ("their turf") from the infiltration of the black newcomers. When the Chicago Race Riot broke out in 1919, the Colts were second to none in their attacks against African Americans.

Irish Americans were particularly avid about professional sports as spectators and as participants, seeing sport as a potential vehicle for social mobility. Irish immigrants and their families struggled throughout the nineteenth century to earn a living in America. As historian Stephan Thernstrom explained in his seminal book, *The Other Bostonians: Poverty and Progress in the American Metropolis, 1890–1970* (1973), as late as the 1890s just 10 percent of Boston's first-generation Irish had white-collar jobs, compared to half of native-born white Americans. The sons of immigrants fared much better. One-third of Irish Bostonians born between 1860 and 1879 ended up in white-collar jobs. However, they were less successful than second-generation western Europeans, who were 52 percent white-collar workers. Ambitious but poor, uneducated, and unskilled Irish Americans sought success in such alternate areas of employment as the church, politics, crime, and sports.

The Irish dominated prizefighting well into the twentieth century, when they were among the poorest and least educated Americans living in the mean streets of the inner city. In the 1890s, eight of fourteen American-born world prizefighting champions were of Irish descent, including John L. Sullivan, the last bare-knuckle heavyweight champion and the greatest sports hero of the nineteenth century. The Boston Strong Boy won the American heavyweight title in 1882 from Paddy Ryan, who admitted that "when Sullivan struck me, I thought that a telegraph pole had been shoved against me endways." Recognized as world champion in 1885, Sullivan kept the crown until knocked out in 1892 by fellow Irishman James J. Corbett, an ex-bank clerk and boxing instructor in San Francisco. This was the first and only loss for Sullivan in forty-two fights. It was both the first legal heavyweight championship and the first contested under the Marquis of Queensberry rules, published in 1867, and adopted in the United States in 1889. The new rules, replacing the London Prize Ring Rules of 1838, barred wrestling and required three-minute rounds and the use of gloves, which was supposed to lessen the brutality of the sport. Yet, as historian Elliott Gorn points out, these rules sped up fights and actually made the sport more dangerous because fighters could hit harder and throw more punches with their hands protected. The Queensberry rules also stipulated that a fighter knocked to the canvas had to regain his feet in ten seconds, or was ruled knocked out.

Pugilism provided the working-class ("shanty") Irish with heroes and promoted ethnic solidarity. Every Irish saloon, as did most taverns in America, proudly displayed a picture of Sullivan. However, the "Great John L." was not idolized by the well-to-do ("lace-curtain") Irish, who were embarrassed by his profession and racy lifestyle. He reputedly earned, and spent, more than $1 million during his career, mostly from national and European excursions known as "knocking-out tours," in which he would offer $1,000 to anyone who could last four rounds with him. He also became the first renowned athlete to use his fame for a stage career, mainly in vaudeville.

Irish boxers were prominent members of the sporting fraternity and served as role models to indigent Irish Americans growing up in rough neighborhoods such as New York's Hell's Kitchen on the Lower West Side. These communities were breeding grounds for future fighters, like heavyweight-champion Gene Tunney, who held the title from 1926 to 1930. These Irish Americans learned to fight on the street, usually against newer immigrants whom they intimidated, to prove their manhood and gain the respect of their peers. Youths interested in cultivating their roughhousing and learning the manly art of boxing could train at neighborhood athletic clubs, gymnasiums, and settlement houses. They started out fighting as amateurs, and the best usually went on to the professional ranks. The Irish retained preeminence in prizefighting in the period 1900–19, with eleven out of thirty-one world champions, a record far superior to any other ethnic group. The relative decline resulted from improving job opportunities for the Irish and the growing competition from impoverished second-generation southern and eastern European immigrants.

The Irish were also extremely visible in professional baseball, both as spectators and as players. Certain sections of ballparks in the early 1900s were popularly known by Irish names like "Burkeville," a part of the bleachers at New York's Polo Grounds, because so many of the fans were thought to be Irish. In Chicago in 1900, Irishman Charles Comiskey, owner of the White Sox purposely built his American League ballpark a few blocks from the heavily Irish section of town known as Bridgeport. Comiskey expected to draw many Irish fans, especially with Sunday ball games and cheap twenty-five-cent bleacher seats. Watching baseball appealed to the Irish, affording enthusiasts a lot of time to socialize and drink beer with their buddies. It also provided Irish American boys a rite of passage into young manhood and something to talk about with their fathers.

Irish Americans were disproportionately represented on the diamond. One expert in the late 1890s estimated that one-third of the major leaguers were Irishmen. This may have been an exaggeration, but at the turn of the century, only native-born white Americans exceeded them on the diamond. Their numbers were indicative of their sporting heritage and high degree of Americanization. Irish families whose breadwinner was a city worker mainly lived in the zone of emergence, near baseball fields where sons could play baseball and develop their skills. Irish boys hoped to follow in the footsteps of such Hall of Famers as Chicago White Stockings catcher Mike "King" Kelly, the most famous ballplayer of the nineteenth-century; slugger Ed Delahanty, who hit four home runs in one game and had a lifetime batting average of .346, fifth highest in history; and Willie Keeler, who "hit 'em where they ain't." The Irish success was hardly limited to the playing field; in 1915, eleven of sixteen major league managers were Irish. They included John J. McGraw of the New York Giants (1902–32), the leading proponent of "inside" or "scientific" baseball, which emphasized intelligence, mastery of fundamentals, and scrappiness, and Philadelphia Athletics owner Connie Mack, who managed his club from 1901 to 1950, longer than anyone in history. McGraw won ten National League pennants and three World Series, while Mack captured five World Series and won 3,731 games—more than anyone ever—and lost 3,948 games—also the most ever.

Irishmen became very active in the business of sports as bookmakers, boxing promoters, and baseball-team owners, reflecting the close nexus that existed between urban politics, organized crime, and sports. Several major-league owners such as Mack, Comiskey, and James Gaffney of the Boston Braves were Irishmen. Gaffney was a member of New York's Tammany Hall, whose members were known as "Braves," hence the name of the ball club. Irishmen dominated the commercial side of boxing as promoters, operators of arenas, managers, and trainers. Perhaps the most important Irishman in the business side of pugilism was publisher Richard K. Fox of the *National Police Gazette*, the leading boxing periodical. He gave over $1 million for prizes in sports competition, but he was best known for the diamond-studded belts he gave to boxing champions.

The Irish controlled sports betting, which was a very popular pastime among their fellow Irishmen. Bookmakers and poolroom operators in the late nineteenth century were overwhelmingly Irish, and they continued to dominate long into the next century. New

York's poolrooms were controlled by the so-called Gambling Trust, which included Tammany's number-two man, state senator Tim Sullivan, and gamblers Frank Farrell and Jere Mahoney. Chicago's poolrooms were divided up among Irishmen James O'Leary, a professional gambler (for years everyone incorrectly thought his mother's cow started the Chicago Fire), aldermen Jimmy Rogers, Bathhouse John Coughlin, and Hinky Dink Kenna, and the German gambler Mont Tennes.

German Americans

In the mid-1850s, Germans replaced the Irish as the leading immigrant group. Germany did not yet exist, though there were thirty-nine German speaking states, most notably Prussia, Bavaria, and Austria. By 1860 there were 1.3 million German immigrants in America, rising to 2.8 million in 1890. They were primarily Protestant, mainly Lutherans; about one-third were Roman Catholic, and 250,000 were Jewish. Several factors set off the mid-nineteenth-century German migration, including potato blights and unprofitable small land holdings on which farmers gave up, the loss of skilled jobs resulting from the Industrial Revolution, and political oppression, particularly following the defeat of the 1848 Revolution in Frankfort. The latter group of immigrants, who included journalists, businessmen, doctors, and lawyers, became known as the "Forty-Eighters." Overall, the German migrants were skilled, literate immigrants with some money who were far better prepared for life in the United States than were the Irish, and they encountered less prejudice. Unlike the Irish, who overwhelmingly ended up in cities, about half of the German immigrants ended up in farming communities. The main destinations for German urbanites were Chicago, Cincinnati, Milwaukee, New York, and St. Louis, where they set up German villages. In Milwaukee, about 80 percent of them lived in German neighborhoods. Germans were very proud of their culture, and they worked hard to maintain their ethnic identity in both their rural communities and urban neighborhoods. They established German-language newspapers, theaters, choral societies, and other old-world cultural institutions, including the *turnverein*, which were gymnastic societies founded in 1811 in by Friedrich Jahn.

Jahn's goal was to promote German nationalism and physical fitness to prepare soldiers for future wars with France. As early as the 1820s a number of his students immigrated to the United States to teach gymnastics at prominent colleges. Members of the turnverein, known as turners, were typically students, artisans, and intellectuals. In 1848 the movement was brought to America by radical refugees escaping the defeated democratic revolutions. The first clubs were organized in Louisville, Cincinnati, and Newark, and in the next few years, other societies were organized in cities and even rural areas such as New Ulm, Minnesota.

In 1851 socialist turners established the North American Socialist Turner Association to promote their political, social, and athletic interests. Most turners, however, joined the progressive new Republican Party, which was organized in 1854 in opposition to slavery, nativism, and laws curtailing personal freedom. The majority of turners were skilled workers, although the first societies in the booming Midwestern cities of Chicago and Milwaukee were founded by conservative or apolitical businessmen, and the members were mainly white-collar workers.

Turner societies promoted gymnastics, liberal politics, German culture, and working-class interests. Turner halls, often the largest building in German neighborhoods, became important community centers. The finest ones had gymnasiums, billiard rooms, a library, dining room, club room, dance halls, and an auditorium. Turners frequently established militia units and sharpshooting companies to prepare for the day they would return home to Germany to fight for liberty. The militia in the mid-1850s actually had a more practical value because they defended the community against violent nativists who resented the German presence. When the Civil War broke out, turners enlisted en masse into the Union Army. The Seventeenth Missouri was popularly known as the Western Turner Regiment because nearly all of its members were turners. The widespread German participation in the Union Army significantly bolstered their public image.

The number of turners grew substantially in the late nineteenth century, from about five thousand members in 1859 to nearly forty thousand by 1890. It was primarily a male institution, although women could join social auxiliary units. In 1865 the North American Turner Association (NATA) was established as a national organization for all turners. Membership in the post–Civil War era remained predominantly hard-working, respectable blue-collar men (55.5 percent), chiefly craftsmen. Cities with large German communities, such as Chicago, had several turner units, some almost exclusively working class, which were the most politically radical.

Turners in the late nineteenth century continued to foster physical fitness, ethnic pride, and improved working-class conditions. They were a political pressure group that focused on such ethnopolitical issues as Sunday blue laws, prohibition, and foreign-language education. The turners were also leading advocates of professionally supervised physical education and parks for vigorous exercise. As early as 1866, Chicago turners convinced the board of education to introduce exercise programs for elementary schools. In 1889 the program was expanded into the high schools, often with turner instructors. Athletic competition was not stressed, but in 1881 a group of Milwaukee turners competed in a gymnastic festival in Frankfurt, Germany, winning several medals. Annual national turnfests had limited appeal and became quadrennial events in 1885, though interest increased following the introduction of competitive gymnastics.

Turner membership in the late nineteenth century became increasingly bourgeois as Germans and their American-born children fared well economically. Nonetheless, many local units, as well as the national organization, still supported traditional socialist demands for worker control over the means of production, justice for all, factory inspection laws, restricted child labor, and the eight-hour day. Turner halls were used for union meetings and public debates on labor issues. Left-wing politics heated up in 1877 following the violent nationwide railroad strikes. Nine years later, eight anarchists, including journalist August Spies, a Chicago turner, were sentenced to death for allegedly fomenting a conspiracy that led to the Haymarket Riot. Tensions erupted in Chicago between the bourgeois and socialist turners based on their positions on anarchism and the guilt of the anarchists. When radicals took over the national association, the middle-class societies temporarily dropped out.

Even after the middle-class turners returned to the association, the society remained active in left-wing politics. In the early 1900s members helped organize the Socialist Party of America, assisted socialist turner Victor Berger in his election as mayor of Milwaukee, and repeatedly supported socialist Eugene V. Debs for president. All clubs, however, gave greater emphasis to nonpolitical social activities such as picnics, socials, balls, and theater. In the summer of 1906, for instance, the turnverein of Chicago's working-class-suburb of Aurora sponsored a sports outing to Indiana that drew over five thousand people in five chartered trains.

Declining German immigration hurt the turners. The declining German-speaking membership led the turners in 1908 to use English as an official language at meetings. Nonetheless, the society's main problem was its weak appeal to second-generation German Americans, who preferred American sports to gymnastics. The viability of all German institutions in America was badly shaken after the United States entered World War I. Anti-German sentiment encouraged many Teutonic organizations to rename themselves to avoid public disapproval. Membership in the German sports clubs, like Chicago's Germania Club, sharply declined after the war, and the turnvereins became less prominent institutions.

While the turners dominated German physical culture in America, Germans were also active in other sports such as target shooting and bowling. Bowling in the second half of the nineteenth century was considered primarily a German sport. Bowlers laid out lanes in their clubhouse basements, churches, beer gardens, and saloons, and bowled outdoors at picnic grounds. German immigrants brought a legacy of target-shooting companies, or *schutzencorps*, to America. These clubs comprised merchants and other "respectable" people, who held *schutzenfests* that became annual affairs after the Civil War. There were also plebeian target companies, such as the *Lehr und Wehrverein* (Educational and Defense Society), which were more politically (socialist) oriented. German sharpshooting organizations were briefly banned in Chicago in 1877 at the time of the nationwide railroad strike for fear they would protect workers against the police or the National Guard.

The New Immigrants

Unlike the old immigrants who brought a sporting heritage to America, the new immigrants from eastern and southern Europe, who came in the late nineteenth and early twentieth centuries, had little if any sporting background. These impoverished newcomers hailed largely from premodern societies. They included about 4.5 million Italians, and over 2 million Poles and Russian Jews. The Italians and Poles were unskilled, uneducated, Catholic peasants. Over one-half of Italians and nearly 40 percent of Poles traveled back and forth between the United States and their homelands, not settling permanently in America. These newcomers ended up working at dangerous, low-paying jobs and living in slums. Ninety percent of the Polish and Italian immigrants ended up in blue-collar jobs, mainly unskilled, compared to 75 percent of the Jews, who had more experience in business, often as peddlers. They established ethnic villages where they coped with culture shock and alienation by speaking their own languages and relying on old-world institutions, such as the parish church or synagogue, saloons, choral groups, and theatrical clubs, and starting new ones such as mutual aid societies and foreign-language newspapers. They were seldom interested in sport, which for most of them was a strange American institution.

The Bohemians, who came from the westernmost province of the present-day Czech Republic, in what was then the Austrian Empire, were among the first of the new immigrants. They adjusted better to American life than most other groups because many were artisans and came from a relatively modern part of east central Europe. Unlike the other new immigrants, Bohemians brought an emerging sporting culture based on the *Sokol*, a voluntary society organized in 1862 by M. Tyrs and J. Fuegner to promote resistance to the Austrians who controlled their homeland. The Sokol philosophy was modeled on the romantic nationalism of the turnverein. Its goal was to develop strong bodies and minds to lead the fight for liberation. The first American Sokol was established in St. Louis in 1865, and by 1900 there were 184 American Sokols. The organization promoted physical culture by establishing gymnasiums that emphasized calisthenics and championed Bohemian culture by supporting libraries, choral societies, and theatrical groups. Most members were freethinkers (religious skeptics) and got along poorly with devout Catholics, who established their own Sokols.

The Sokol hall, typically one of the tallest buildings in Bohemian neighborhoods, was a community center that housed the immigrants' major institutions. Sokols sponsored annual gymnastic shows and family outings involving gymnastic drills and folk dancing. Its physical culture program did not appeal to the second-generation Bohemians, however. Consequently, in the 1890s Sokols organized Sunday baseball leagues to attract the American-born and to sustain their ethnic identity. Chicago's Bohemian League performed at a very high level, and by 1910, several graduates had made the major leagues. Their achievements were a source of pride to the entire community, even to those who were not baseball fans.

Sport had a similar purpose among contemporary French-Canadian immigrants in New England. They also used sports programs to maintain ethnic identification and separation from other groups. Historian Richard Sorrell found that Francophone St. Ann's Church in Woonsocket, Rhode Island, built a gymnasium in the early 1890s "to keep the church as the center of social activities for youths and to prevent them from mixing with Irish Catholic and Protestant children at other recreational areas."

The new immigrants who came after the Bohemians had little if any athletic tradition. Sport was largely unknown among the oppressed Polish people whose homeland was divided between Russia, Prussia, and Austria, all of which sought to assimilate the Poles into their culture. The Poles' one important sporting organization was the Falcons, organized in 1867 by nationalists in Austrian-controlled Galicia on the model of the Sokols, following the failed uprising of 1863 against Czarist Russia. They soon established hundreds of "nests" in Galicia and Poznan (German Poland). The first American nest was established in Chicago in 1887, followed by others in Polish mining communities in Pennsylvania and industrial cities of the Great Lakes. The Falcons encouraged ethnic pride, Polish independence, and strict morals, and they sought to promote a positive public image. The Falcons and Sokols both had paramilitaristic aspects. They wore uniforms, marched in parades, and organized military schools to train freedom fighters. By 1914 there were 25,000 Falcons in the U.S. compared to 44,000 in all of Galicia and Poznan. Three years later, when the United States entered World War I, about five thousand Falcons ineligible for the draft joined Polish military forces to fight for their homeland.

Jewish Americans

The impoverished 2 million Jewish newcomers pushed out of Russia were better prepared for life in America than other new immigrants. They were more likely to come from cities, were often skilled workers or had entrepreneurial experience, and had a keen respect for education. They had not been allowed to own farms in Russia, and they were stereotyped as weak, physically unfit, and unaccustomed to strenuous physical labor that Americans considered as manly. These newcomers had no familiarity with sports. The rare Jewish immigrant who became a sports fan would be ridiculed by his peers as a fool. The game of baseball made no sense to them. What were grown men doing, running around in short pants, and hitting a ball with a stick?

Americanized German Jews whose families had migrated to the United States a generation or two earlier were embarrassed by the customs, odd clothing, and physical appearance of their devout eastern European brethren. Nonetheless, they accepted the responsibility of helping them adjust to modern American life. Philanthropic German-Jews established settlement houses such as the Educational Alliance (1893) in New York's Lower East Side and the Jewish Peoples Institute (1908) in Chicago's West Side. These institutions, along with secular settlements, offered a wide variety of activities to help newcomers adjust, including civics classes, employment bureaus, and sports programs. Athletics provided bait to attract young people inside, where they could become acculturated. In addition, participation in sports could teach them American values and behavior and destroy negative stereotypes about Jewish manliness and fitness.

Settlement houses were supplemented by the Young Men's Hebrew Association (YMHA), a German-Jewish organization dating back to 1854. Based on the model of the YMCA, the association promoted physical fitness, learning, sociability, spirituality, and "muscular Judaism." German-Jewish immigrants had originally participated in turner societies along with other Germans, but their sons preferred American sports. Furthermore, rising anti-Semitism in the late nineteenth century resulting from the new wave of immigration meant that German Jews were barred from top colleges, resorts, and sports clubs, such as the New York Athletic Club. Consequently, the YMHA gained prominence in the 1890s, originally serving the German-Jewish middle class. The YMHA broadened its appeal in the 1910s to become a Jewish community center, becoming more accessible to inner-city youth by constructing new facilities in slums such as Brooklyn's Brownsville.

Second-generation Jews became fanatical sports fans. Playing and talking about sports proved they were becoming real Americans. Success in sports gave them an opportunity to display prowess and gain status. However, their sporting options were limited by a variety of factors, including negative parental attitudes and Sabbath restrictions. Parents from southern and eastern Europe often saw sports such as baseball as a child's game and a waste of time. Their foreign-language newspapers rarely covered baseball, although the Yiddish *Forward* did publish an article in 1903 that sought to explain baseball. In addition, like other poor youth, their opportunities were limited by their amount of leisure time, costs, and accessibility.

The limited available public space in inner-city neighborhoods often became ethnic battle-grounds. During the early 1900s, ethnic groups did not mix in the new small parks, but they divided them up to play with their own kind. Because of this practice, parks reinforced, rather than broke down, ethnic and racial barriers. The more established ethnic groups, such as the Irish, intimidated youngsters of the newest and least numerous groups who moved into their neighborhoods. Parks located between ethnic adversaries became focal points for Irish, Italian, Jewish, or Polish gangs. If no one group gained control, then the park became a no-man's land entered only at great peril.

Second-generation youths were big baseball fans who followed their favorite players and teams in the daily press. Progressive reformers supported the second-generation interest in baseball because they considered the national pastime second only to public education as an agent of Americanization. The youths seldom attended games, however, because ballparks were located far from their inner-city neighborhoods and tickets were expensive. Occasionally they might see a game through a knothole in the fence or by returning a ball hit out of the park for a seat. In addition, the odds were stacked against them actually playing a lot of baseball. Besides encountering parental opposition to playing baseball because they should be working (or maybe studying if they were Jewish), there was often insufficient space to play baseball in their crowded neighborhoods, unless it was an adapted version of the game like stickball in an alley or softball on a small field. Furthermore, they had no chance to play secondary-school sports because they rarely attended high school; either due to lack of academic interest, or because they had to work to help support the family. Consequently they missed out on improving themselves under experienced coaches, and they had few opportunities to compete against highly skilled opponents.

If the youths did play baseball, there was no guarantee doing so would lead to acceptance by the core society, or loosen ethnic ties. Ethnic teams and leagues existed throughout urban America to keep boys with their own kind. There were not only Jewish leagues in New York and Polish leagues in Chicago (sponsored by the Polish National Alliance), but Chinese and Japanese leagues on the West Coast. Furthermore, playing members of another ethnic group on a mixed team was just as likely to promote ethnic pride and cultural pluralism as much as it did mutual respect and Americanization. French Canadians in Woonsocket, Rhode Island, became ardent baseball fans in the 1890s without losing their ethnic identity. They read baseball scores and followed the major league career of their hero, star second baseman Napoleon Lajoie, in the French-language press. The players used their linguistic skills to signal plays in French when they played Anglo teams.

The barriers faced by second-generation immigrants in baseball resulted in their underrepresentation on major-league rosters until the mid-1930s. In 1910, for instance, there was not a single major league rookie of southern or eastern European ancestry. In 1920, there were just two Italians, two Bohemians, and no Jews or Poles out of 133 first-year men. Among the few Poles to make it to the big leagues were pitchers Harry and Stanislaus Coveleski. Stan, a future Hall of Famer for the Cleveland Indians, won three games in the 1920 World Series, and 215 in his career. He started out as a miner in Shamokin, Pennsylvania, working seventy-two hours a week for $3.60. Stan felt it was a miracle he became a ballplayer because he had no time to play during the week and "Never saw the sunlight." As recounted in Lawrence Ritter's *The Glory of Their Times*: "Most of the year I went to work in the dark and came home in the dark. . . . Never knew the sun came up any day but Sunday."

Those few new immigrants who became professional ballplayers encountered a lot of discrimination. For example, the first five Cohens to appear in the major leagues all played under an alias to hide their Jewish identity. Sammy Cohen became Sammy Bohne and Phil Cohen became Phil Cooney. Most Jews who made the majors in the early 1900s were not from New York, where half of all American Jews lived, but from other communities like Hamburg, Arkansas, or Metropolis, Illinois, where Jews were much more assimilated.

While Jews were underrepresented on the diamond, German Jews were overrepresented among major league executives as they tried to demonstrate their civic mindedness, and make money. As early as the 1880s, German-Jewish entrepreneurs were involved with the Cincinnati Red Stockings of the American Association. The Jewish owners of National League teams at the turn of the century were Barney Dreyfuss of the Pittsburgh Pirates, Andrew Freedman of the New York Giants, and Julius Fleischmann of the Cincinnati Reds. The baseball business at the time was very similar to the fledgling film industry, a business completely dominated by recent eastern European Jewish immigrants. These entertainment industries were new and open to aggressive entrepreneurs, regardless of their social backgrounds, willing to take risks. Neither venture encountered much competition from the more-established WASP businessmen, who preferred more conservative and higher-status investments.

Second-generation new immigrants were most successful at cheap indoor sports that did not require much space, namely track, boxing, basketball, billiards, and bowling, the latter a particularly popular sport in Polish neighborhoods. Although they were not welcomed at the most prestigious track clubs because of their religion or social class, Jewish youths had an excellent role model to emulate, Lon Myers, the greatest American sprinter/middle-distance runner of the nineteenth century, who held the world record for the quarter mile and every American record from 50 yards to one mile. The first great Jewish track-and-field star of the twentieth century was Meyer Prinstein, the son of Russian Poles, who won four Olympic gold medals in the long jump (1904, 1906) and triple jump (1900, 1904). After college, Prinstein, along with a few other Jews, competed for New York's Irish American Athletic Club because more prestigious clubs would not admit them.

Second-generation Russian-Jewish youths living in urban slums achieved considerable proficiency in track, a popular sport that did not require sophisticated equipment or highly experienced coaching. Jewish boys had lots of opportunities to gain experience in the sport through the YMHA, intersettlement competition, and the Public Schools Athletic League, whose Manhattan meets were dominated by Lower East Side elementary schools. The Jewish American press applauded the PSAL for improving the health of inner-city children and giving Jewish youth a chance to gain the respect of the Gentile community.

Track provided an early opportunity for southern Europeans to use sport to demonstrate pride and affirmation of an Italian rather than a regional identity in 1908–10 through Italian Olympic star Dorando Pietri's professional marathon races in the United States following his stunning collapse at the end of the 1908 Olympic marathon in London. Italians then were largely absent from mainstream American sports. Historian Matthew Llewellyn argues that it also paradoxically enabled them to become more acculturated, getting involved in the broader society's sporting culture, moving from immigrant to ethnic American.

The contests began on November 25, 1908, at New York's Madison Square Garden in a match race against Irish American Johnny Hayes, the Olympic champion. The race pitted representatives of two hostile ethnic groups who fought over unskilled jobs, neighborhoods, and their own versions of Catholicism, and promoters recognized that the ethnic conflict hyped public interest. Spectators carried in Irish and Italian national flags, sang ethnic songs, and were entertained by Italian and Irish brass bands. The Italian community celebrated Pietri's resounding victory in 2:44.20, parading in the streets with his trophy. America's leading Italian newspaper, *Il Progresso Italo-Americano*, hailed Pietri as the "glorious victor," who initiated a new page in sport history. As historian Pamela Cooper noted, Pietri "personified the agenda of invented ethnicity. He was a symbol that unified the group, defined the group culture, presented its claims to power and status, and even demonstrated the compatibility of the ethnic group with American ideals."

Another inner-city sport in which Jews excelled was basketball, which was invented in 1891 by Dr. James Naismith at the International YMCA Training School in Springfield, Massachusetts. The sport had two important advantages. It was cheap to play and required little space. Second-generation Irishmen, Jews, and other ethnic groups played basketball in school yards, settlement houses, and church gymnasiums, and by 1898 there was a professional league in Philadelphia. As one former New York University All-American remembered, "We played basketball in the streets with a rag ball and used ash cans for baskets. We stressed team play rather than shooting because rag balls didn't bounce." Top-level basketball was a bruising game that required a lot of padding. The playing floor was surrounded by wire mesh to prevent players from fighting over loose balls off the court and to protect them from spectators. This is why basketball players became known as "cagers." Nonetheless, it was not considered a game of "brutality and brute strength," and the *American Hebrew*, an important middle-class periodical, endorsed basketball for its "quick thinking, lightning-like rapidity of movement, and endurance." Two of the first great pros were Barney Sedran and Marty Friedman, "the heavenly twins," who starred in the 1910s and 1920s. By the 1920s, Jewish high school stars were highly recruited by top colleges for their basketball teams.

Jewish and Italian youth were primarily identified in the public mind with prizefighting. Boxing was a very useful skill for inner-city schoolboys and young men to learn since they often got into fights with youths from other groups, particularly the Irish. Brawls occurred on the way to school, in the park, or when rivals encroached into one's neighborhood. As Benny Leonard, world lightweight champion from 1917 to 1925, remembered, "You had to fight or stay in the house when the Italian and Irish kids came through on their way to the [public] baths." Street fighters such as Chicago's Nails Morton became neighborhood heroes who protected youngsters and elderly Jews from rival ethnic toughs. Such experiences prepared rough inner-city youths, such as Chicago's Miller brothers, for future careers as boxers, hoodlums, or policemen. Rugged second-generation young men who learned to discipline their street fighting under the intense tutelage of experienced trainers at settlement houses or neighborhood gymnasiums often aspired to become professional boxers. They anticipated that success in the ring would lead to wealth and fame.

There was a long history of Jewish pugilists, going back to English heavyweight champion Daniel Mendoza (1792–95), and Anglo-American Young Barney Aaron, who won the American lightweight title in 1857. The most famous Jewish boxer in the late nineteenth century was heavyweight Joe Choynski, a member of the Hall of Fame who fought five future world champions. Unlike most fighters, he did not come up from poverty but was the son of a San Francisco magazine publisher.

Professional fighters reared in the slums became ethnic heroes. Tough Jews, such as featherweight Joe Bernstein, "The Pride of the Ghetto," countered stereotypical images of physically weak Jews. Their parents, however, considered them an embarrassment to the family and their ethnic group; Jews, they thought, should be scholars, not fighters. Novices took pseudonyms to prevent parents from discovering what they were doing, avoid discrimination, and advance their careers. Benjamin Leiner fought as Benny Leonard to hide his career from his parents. He only gained paternal approval when he brought his winnings home. At first, ethnic fighters chose Irish aliases (Mushy Callahan was Jewish; Hugo Kelly was Italian) because the Irish were considered the toughest fighters. By the late 1910s, once Jews had been recognized as outstanding fighters, non-Jewish pugilists also took Jewish names (Italian Samuel Mandella fought as Sammy Mandell). Promoters tried to match men from different ethnic groups to heighten interest, such as the Leonard–"Irish"

Eddie Finnegan match in a western coal-mining town. Finnegan took a bad beating, and in a clinch asked Leonard in Yiddish to take it easy on him because he was really Seymour Rosenbaum.

Second-generation Russian Jews were the first new immigrants to gain success in the ring, followed by Italian Americans. For ambitious, uneducated, unskilled, and poorly connected second-generation newcomers who had little chance of succeeding through business or other traditional routes, boxing, along with politics, entertainment, and crime, was an alternative. Historian Stephan Thernstrom found that in Boston one-fourth of second generation Russian Jews and three-fourths of other second-generation new immigrants ended up in blue-collar occupations. More than a few of the poor tough Jews chose to become boxers and follow in the footsteps of their role models. The first Jewish American champions were bantamweight Harry Harris, who won the crown in 1900, and featherweight Abe Attell, who held the title from 1904 to 1912. In the 1910s there were four Jewish champions, most notably Benny Leonard, probably the second-greatest lightweight in history. By World War I, there were more Jewish contenders than any other ethnic group. They were mainly in the lighter-weight classes, reflecting the slight stature of many new immigrants. The first Polish champion was middleweight Stanley Ketchell (Stanislaw Kiecał) from 1908 to 1910, one of the all-time great fighters, while the first Italian was featherweight Pete Herman (Peter Gulotta) from 1917 to 1920. They gained their crowns about a generation before their groups produced a major-league batting champion.

Native Americans

By the early 1900s, just a decade after the Wounded Knee Massacre at the Pine Ridge Oglala Sioux reservation in South Dakota, Native Americans had achieved a high degree of prominence in baseball and football. The first full-blooded Native American major leaguer was Lou Sockalexis, who played for Cleveland from 1897 to 1899. Contrary to popular belief, the team was not named the "Indians" in 1915 in his honor, but after the "Miracle" Boston Braves, who went from last place on July 4, 1914, to win the World Series. About twenty Native Americans played in the majors in the early 1900s, finding the baseball world less discriminatory than other segments of American society. A few had distinguished careers, particularly Hall of Fame pitcher Charles "Chief" Bender of the Philadelphia Athletics, who had a record of 210–128 and appeared in five World Series during his sixteen-year career.

There were more Native Americans in the majors than any of the new immigrant groups, and their presence was pointed out by baseball publicists as proof of the sport's assimilative power and the game's democratic recruitment policies. The general public, too, saw it as evidence of the democratic character of American life. Since there was a relatively small number of Native Americans in the total population (237,196 in 1900), they were not perceived as a threat to the livelihoods of white American baseball players like African Americans. That did not mean that Native American ballplayers did not encounter prejudice, as reflected by Bender's nickname of "Chief."

National attention on Native American athletics focused on the Carlisle Indian Industrial School, founded in 1879 as a boarding school, and its superstar, Jim Thorpe. Although not really a collegiate institution, Carlisle, beginning in the late 1890s, played all the top football powers, virtually always on the road. The public attitude toward Native American football players was originally racist and demeaning (in 1896 the *New York Journal* published nude photographs of Native American football players), but in time they were treated with more regard. Several Carlisle players earned All-American status, and their team became renowned for remarkable sportsmanship, which the school hoped would gain respect for Native Americans. The football program compiled a record of 167-88-13 between 1893 until 1917, when discontinued.

Jim Thorpe was a two-time All-American football player who led Carlisle to an 11–1 record in 1911 that included a victory over Harvard. He set a national scoring record the following season with twenty-five touchdowns and 198 points. Thorpe won gold medals at the 1912 Olympics in both the pentathlon and decathlon, and was proclaimed "the greatest athlete in the world." In 1913, however, it was discovered that he had played professional baseball for Rocky Mount and Fayetteville, North Carolina (Eastern Carolina League), from 1909 to 1910, and was stripped of his Olympic medals. Thorpe played in the majors from 1913 to 1915 and from 1917 to 1919. He also played professional football from 1915 through 1926, with a final appearance as a placekicker in 1928, at the age of forty-one. He was the founding president in 1920, albeit mainly a figurehead, of the American Professional Football Association, the forerunner of the National Football League. In 1950 Thorpe was named the outstanding American athlete of the first half of the twentieth century.

African Americans

The African American sporting experience differed dramatically from that of European immigrants because 90 percent of them were slaves in 1850, and even after Emancipation, they encountered enormous racial prejudice that totally surpassed any discrimination encountered by European immigrants, even those like the Italians who were not considered white. During the first years of the Reconstruction Era (1865–77), Republican governments ran southern states with the support of the federal government, especially the U.S. Army, enfranchising African Americans and helping the former Confederate states return to the Union fold. However, by the end of the era, the Democrats, led by former Confederate leaders, were back in charge, and had free rein to run local affairs. Conditions for African Americans in the post-Reconstruction South were abysmal, often limited economically to farm tenancy or peonage, their legal rights circumscribed by Jim Crow customs and laws, and their safety restricted by lynch law.

African Americans had a great deal of familiarity with sport, which was foreign to the experience of the new immigrants. In the pre–Civil War South, slaves swam, hunted, and fished. They were employed as cock trainers, raced in crews at regattas, rode thoroughbreds at racetracks, and boxed in matches arranged by their owners. During the antebellum period, free people of color participated in working-class sports, particularly professional boxing and pedestrianism contests, to gain recognition and make money. In antebellum New Orleans, which had the largest free black population in the United States, African Americans participated in various mainstream sports and also organized raquette clubs (a team sport similar to lacrosse) that played on Sundays before racially mixed crowds of up to four thousand spectators. New Orleans was a uniquely cosmopolitan city with relatively liberal racial traditions.

Southern sport outside of New Orleans was largely segregated well before the legalization of Jim Crow. African Americans participated in sports sponsored by their own fraternal, church, and political groups, which organized picnic games at black sections of municipal parks and "Colored Fairgrounds," while African American sports clubs organized baseball games. These events promoted a sense of community, and, it was hoped, recognition by the white society. By 1876, African Americans had established YMCAs in Richmond and Nashville to promote sound morality and provide an uplifting substitute for "the sporting life." In the post–Reconstruction Era, blacks had limited access to public parks, even in New Orleans, because of custom, inaccessibility, or police harassment. Following the enactment of segregation laws in the 1890s, a few separate and inferior parks were set aside for African Americans. In 1896 the Supreme Court ruled on the question of discrimination in the case of *Plessey* v. *Ferguson*, ruling that separate but equal was the law of the land. However, southern governments failed to adhere to this standard. Blacks in Birmingham, Alabama, did not get their first municipal park until 1908, after seventeen white parks had been constructed.

As historian Dale Somers has pointed out, interracial sporting competition existed in New Orleans until the mid-1880s. African Americans were permitted in general admission sections of local racetracks until 1871, when the Metairie Course erected a separate seating area. Local African Americans responded with a boycott, and management was compelled to restore integrated seating in the public stand. New Orleans' lakefront facilities were segregated, however, and African Americans were barred from white athletic clubs. In the 1880s the color line was tightened. Game laws were passed to protect wildlife from black hunters, and white baseball clubs that had played African American teams were boycotted. In the early 1890s, local cyclists dropped out of the League of American Wheelmen (LAW) because northern clubs had African American members, and by 1894, southern pressure compelled the league to ban African Americans.

The last sport in New Orleans to draw the color line was boxing because fighters were regarded as entertainers and lowlifes, hardly the equal of spectators. In September 1892, with boxing recently legalized in the Crescent City, the Olympic Arena over three days hosted the featherweight, lightweight, and heavyweight championships. On September 6, Afro-Canadian featherweight champion George Dixon successfully defended his crown against Jack Skelly with an eighth-round knockout. It was the first time that African Americans had been admitted into the arena. The outcome so shocked local whites that no more mixed bouts were held in New Orleans until the 1950s.

About 10 percent of African Americans at the turn of the century lived in the North, where public discrimination was banned. However, prejudice still occurred at semipublic and public places ranging from restaurants and theaters to parks, beaches, playgrounds, and YMCAs. The cities of Boston, Brooklyn, New York, and Philadelphia all had separate black YMCAs. Chicago's YMCA was integrated until the turn of the century, and in Detroit, only the black elite could use the white YMCA. In 1913, white Chicago philanthropists, and meatpackers trying to gain the loyalty of their black workers, constructed an impressive $190,000 African American YMCA in the city's South Side ghetto.

African American demography was significantly altered by the Great Migration (1916–19) during which about 500,000 blacks left the South to escape sharecropping and lynch law for better economic opportunity and social freedom. The new arrivals mainly settled in black neighborhoods that swiftly became overcrowded ghettoes. White northerners perceived the newcomers as potential threats to their own job security or the value of their property, and discrimination increased. Recreational sites that bordered white and black neighborhoods became disputed territory where African Americans were afraid to venture. Racial clashes in Chicago became more common at public facilities, particularly parks considered Irish turf, and Lake Michigan beaches. The Chicago Race Riot of 1919 was precipitated by the death of Eugene Williams, a black youth killed by rocks thrown by whites when he swam away from the "black beach" at 26th Street and came near a "white beach" at 29th Street.

The extent of black participation in high-level northern sport was limited by social convention. African Americans living in the North occasionally played on high school and college teams, but seldom more than one or two on any squad. Forty blacks played on white college football teams prior to 1915, including three All-Americans, starting with William H. Lewis of Harvard in 1892.

African Americans were important participants in track-and-field, and in 1900, one of the trainers for the Olympic team was Mace Montgomery of Georgetown University. Most African American track-and-field athletes ran for all-black clubs, such as New York's Smart Set Athletic Club, and competed against white athletes. In 1904 two African American Olympians won medals in sprint events, and four years later, John Taylor, a veterinarian who ran for the IAAC, won a gold medal in the medley relay (2 x 200 m.; 1 x 400 m.; and 1 x 800 m.), running the 400 meter leg.

African American sports clubs, like their white counterparts, sorted individuals by interest, class, or birthplace. Historian Stephen Hardy found that in turn-of-the-century Boston, long-term, upwardly mobile African American residents copied the city's white elite by forming tennis clubs, while natives of the West Indies organized cricket clubs, and newly arrived black southerners preferred boxing at neighborhood gymnasiums.

African Americans were particularly proficient in professional sports, where ability would presumably overcome prejudice, and where they could make money. Frank Hart was a star in the grueling six-day marathon races of the 1880s and 1890s, with a best distance exceeding 550 miles. However, other star athletes encountered a lot of discrimination as whites tried to push them out of their sport. Cyclist Marshall Taylor, the world (1899) and American (1900) sprint champion, had to overcome jealous white competitors who ganged up to defeat him by blocking his path or boxing him into a poor position. African Americans such as Willie Simms were among the finest jockeys of the late nineteenth century, and Isaac Murphy, who won three Kentucky Derbies and earned up to $20,000 a year, may have been the greatest of them all. For most of the nineteenth century, racing aficionados expected the best horses to win regardless of the rider. However, toward the end of the century, experts began to recognize that the rider's skill played a big role in the outcome of races. Consequently, jockeys' income and status rose steadily. White jockeys who were jealous of the success of their black peers, conspired with horse owners to push African Americans off American tracks in the early 1900s. A few of the best black jockeys, like Jimmy Winkfield, winner of the Kentucky Derby in 1901 and 1902, raced overseas. Despite top performances, African American jockeys were quickly forced out of the sport by prejudice.

African Americans were not pushed out of prizefighting as they were in more respectable sports. Those who participated in boxing were desperate young men, recruited from the bottom layers of society, seeking to escape poverty, who ran the risk of having their brains bashed in. Fighters of color encountered considerable racism and discrimination during their careers, and had a difficult time getting matches against white contenders and champions. Black spectators preferred mixed bouts in which their idols could win symbolic racial victories over white opponents, but local customs and laws, even in New York State in the mid-1910s, barred such matches. Thus a great fighter such as Sam Langford, who fought men from lightweights to heavyweights in a twenty-one-year career, was rarely matched with white boxers. Top pugilists were afraid to fight him, so Langford never got a championship fight. The first black world champion was the aforementioned George Dixon, bantamweight champion in 1890, and then featherweight champion from 1891 to 1900. There were five black champions in the early 1900s, including Joe Gans (1902–08), the greatest lightweight of all time, who occasionally had to fix fights just to get a match, and heavyweight champion Jack Johnson (1908–15).

The heavyweight division was the most glamorous and prestigious championship, and the one with which fans and nonfans were most familiar. The color line was first drawn by John L. Sullivan in 1887 because he did not want to fight contender Peter Jackson, a native of the Danish West Indies, the Australian heavyweight champion, who would have been a very difficult opponent. Four years later Jackson fought a 61-round draw with Jim Corbett, who would defeat Sullivan in 1892.

No African American got a title shot until 1908, when Jack Johnson fought heavyweight champion Canadian Jack Burns in Australia.

Johnson's knockout victory jolted white feelings of superiority and raised fears that his championship would encourage black pride. Cartoonists drew demeaning racist caricatures of him, and journalists rationalized his victory as indicative of the lower evolution of the African American and his greater ability to absorb pain. White rage at Johnson was further exacerbated by his flamboyant personality and threatening behavior. Folklorist William Wiggins, Jr., recounted a tale told by his father about Johnson. "Papa Jack" was speeding through Georgia when he was stopped by a sheriff, "Where do you think you're going, boy, speeding like that? That'll cost you $50!" Johnson gave the officer a $100 bill and gunned his engine. The sheriff shouted, "Don't you want your change?" Jack replied, "Keep it, 'cuse I'm coming back the same way. . . ." Johnson was a "bad nigger" (a term of pride among most African Americans) who flaunted conventional norms and refused to accept an inferior status. He was a bold, lusty man who raced cars at record speeds, had white girlfriends and wives, and disregarded authority. His flaunting of accepted behavior made him a marked man.

Promoters sought a "Great White Hope" who could defeat Johnson and regain the title for the white race. But Johnson dispatched them all with obvious ease. One of his most memorable fights came in 1909 against the much lighter champion middleweight Stanley Ketchell. Johnson promised to go easy on Ketchell so the fight would last long enough to produce a marketable film. In the twelfth round Ketchell surprised Johnson with a flurry and sent him down to the canvas. The stunned champion jumped up and knocked out Ketchell with one blow. Ketchell was unconscious for five minutes and short several teeth that were deposited in Johnson's glove.

Boxing fans were so desperate for a white champion that promoter Tex Rickard brought the corpulent, formerly undefeated champion Jim Jeffries out of retirement for a July 4, 1910, match with Johnson that paid $101,000, then the largest purse in history. Jeffries trained hard, but was well past his prime and was knocked out in the fifteenth round. The outcome led directly to race riots in fifty cities across the United States and twenty-five deaths. There was subsequently a big furor over exhibiting the fight film, which had cost $250,000 to produce (the fighters shared a $117,000 guarantee) because it showed the white man's hero being humiliated. Fearing disorder, most major cities barred the film. In 1912, following Johnson's overwhelming defeat of "Fireman" Jim Flynn, a federal law was passed banning interstate commerce in boxing movies.

Unable to dislodge Johnson in the ring, white America went after the champion in court. The federal government hounded Johnson for his sexual escapades, and in 1913 convicted him of violating the recently passed Mann Act that banned transporting a woman across state lines for immoral purposes. Papa Jack chose to flee the country and spent the rest of his championship reign abroad. In 1915, when Johnson was thirty-eight, he lost his title in Havana to six-foot-six, 250-pound, Jess Willard in the twenty-sixth round on an extremely hot summer day. Johnson later claimed that he had thrown the fight in return for amnesty. He was an old fighter, however, untested in several years, and he probably lost fair and square. He returned to the United States in 1919 and served a year in jail. The color line in the heavyweight division was immediately redrawn, and no black man got a title fight until Joe Louis in 1937.

The most popular sport in the African American community was baseball. The absence of African Americans from major-league rosters was purely a product of racism, not lack of experience. As early as 1862, African Americans were playing baseball in Brooklyn, and four years later there were middle-class black teams in Philadelphia. However, in 1867 the National Association of Base Ball Players drew the color line. In 1872 Bud Fowler became the first African American professional when he played for New Castle, Pennsylvania. By 1899, more than seventy blacks had played professional baseball, including Moses Walker, a college-educated minister's son who was the first acknowledged black major leaguer. Walker caught for Toledo (American Association) in 1884 and had a batting average of .251. Recent research indicates the nineteen-year-old William Edward White, a Brown University student, who played one game for the Providence Grays (AA) in 1879, was likely the son of a former Georgia slave owner and one of his slaves. The best African American ballplayers in the late nineteenth century were probably International Leaguers George Stovey, who won 33 games for Newark in 1887, an all-time league record, and Buffalo's second baseman Frank Grant, whose .366 batting average led the league, plus he had forty stolen bases. Prejudice kept Stovey and Grant out of the major leagues, however.

Black players were insulted and threatened by fans, poorly coached, shunned by teammates, and spiked and thrown at by opponents. Second-baseman Grant reputedly invented shin guards for self-protection. Owners did not want to use black players because of their own prejudice and pressure from racist spectators and ballplayers, especially Cap Anson, the great player-manager of the Chicago White Stockings. Professional ballplayers were also afraid that if African Americans got into the Major Leagues there would be additional job competition, diminished salaries, and lowered occupational prestige. Despite the excellent performances of men like Stovey and Grant, club owners in the high minor leagues agreed in 1888 to stop signing black players. By 1890 the International League was all white, and thereafter nearly all the remaining African Americans in organized baseball were on all-black teams. Following the 1899 season, there were no black players in the minors until Jackie Robinson played for Montreal in 1946.

African Americans responded to white prejudice by organizing their own touring professional teams beginning with the Philadelphia Orions in 1882. However, the first prominent African American pro team was the Cuban Giants, established in 1885 by Frank Thompson, a head waiter. He named them "Cubans" to lessen racial prejudice. The club was so good that within two years they were playing exhibition games against major-league teams. The press usually referred to these outfits as semiprofessional teams, but men on the best independent clubs were full-time ballplayers. By the early 1900s, certain independent clubs were playing up to two hundred games a year. The Chicago Leland Giants, for instance, played at home on Sundays, the day African Americans were off from work, and then toured the Midwest playing town teams during the week. They spent the winter playing ball in California. The Leland Giants were among the few black-owned clubs. The club had its own ballpark and played in Chicago's prestigious semipro City League from 1907 to 1909, against white teams that included former major leaguers and young men bound for the big leagues. The Leland Giants may have been the only black team in the country playing in an otherwise all-white association. The team was so highly regarded that in 1909 they played a post-season series against the Chicago Cubs. In 1910 star pitcher Andrew "Rube" Foster gained control of the club, renaming them the American Giants the following season when it moved to the former White Sox field a few blocks from the growing Black Belt. In 1920 Foster organized the Negro National League to promote black capitalism, employ black athletes, coaches, and secretaries, and encourage racial pride. Seven of the eight teams in the Negro National League (the exception was the Kansas City Monarchs) were owned and operated by African Americans. Neither the players nor the community felt this was a substitute for the major leagues, however, and integration remained the ultimate goal.

Asian Americans

The first wave of Chinese emigrated to the United States mainly between 1849 and 1882, by which time there were about 100,000 in California, about one-tenth of the state's population. They encountered enormous prejudice because of their race, the threat they seemed to pose to white workers as cheap labor, and because many native-born Americans perceived them as unwilling and incapable of assimilating. There were many negative stereotypes that depicted Chinese as opium smokers, devious, and unmanly because some of the men wore long braided hair and dressed in gowns. As a result, in 1882 the federal government passed the Chinese Exclusion Act that banned future migration. Nonetheless, young Chinese males wanted to play American sports. They played baseball in Hawaii prior to annexation, where the game promoted ethnic pride. Chinese Americans dominated ethnic competition at first, and by the turn of the century Chinese American teams were touring Asia and the United States shortly thereafter. In late 1914 Chinese Hawaiian Lang Akena signed with the Portland Beavers of the Pacific Coast League (an AA league, the highest minor league level) but a threatened boycott led to his release. Chinese YMCAs in Hawaii and California provided opportunities in the early 1900s to participate in soccer, track-and-field, softball, and table tennis tournaments. After World War I, Chinese American youth became more active in sport in Chinese ethnic organizations, hoping to prove their American identity and gain respect from the white society, and Chinese sports heroes were often celebrated in the ethnic and local presses. However, the interest of Chinese youth in sport often led to intergenerational conflict, as parents feared the athletes were losing their cultural identity.

Significant Japanese migration to Hawaii and the United States began in 1885. Japanese soon comprised a substantial portion of the island's workforce, mainly at sugar and pineapple plantations. On the mainland they replaced the excluded Chinese, working on railroads, canneries, and farms. The Japanese encountered a lot of prejudice, even though they comprised just 1 percent of California's population. This culminated in the 1907 "Gentleman's Agreement" between the United States and Japan that effectively limited the importation of laborers from Japan. The Japanese farm workers came with a sporting heritage, and held sumo wrestling tournaments in Hawaii and California to celebrate their culture and promote ties between nearby Japanese communities. The Japanese *issei* (first generation) also had some familiarity with baseball back home. The Rev. Takie Okumura encouraged baseball among young Japanese plantation workers in the mid-1890s, and in 1899 he organized the first baseball team comprised entirely of the children of Japanese sugarcane workers. Six years later, the teenagers formed the preeminent Japanese squad, *Asahi* (Rising Sun). Another source of sponsorship came from the Hawaiian Sugar Plantation Association following the 1909 sugarcane plantation strike. The managers formed company leagues with ethnic teams as part of their paternalistic welfare capitalism program to squash labor unrest. Japanese ballplayers in Hawaii were soon playing other islander ethnic groups, while mainland Japanese Americans who started a team in San Francisco in 1903 played games against ballplayers in Japan. They hoped to use baseball to gain recognition from the host society, but that was not forthcoming.

Conclusion

The ethnic sporting experience was a product of cultural heritage, social class, and racism. European immigrants were deeply influenced by their backgrounds. The old immigrants who brought a sporting tradition to America kept it alive, while many new immigrants had no such legacy, and had little if any interest in sports. However, virtually all second-generation sons were interested in sport, although their options were shaped by ethnic traditions, parental attitudes, and the neighborhoods in which they lived. Sport offered a means to disprove negative ethnic stereotypes, develop ethnic pride, bond with peers, become Americanized, and gain respect from the broader community. The most-gifted white ethnic athletes used sport as a potential route for social mobility. African Americans, on the other hand, regardless of generation, were familiar with the American sporting culture. Yet their participation was limited by *de jure* and *de facto* racism, as well as by poverty. Nonetheless, African Americans achieved a high level of proficiency in sports, which they employed to advance racial pride and develop a sense of community. They sought, but did not always achieve, a begrudging respect from the broader society, and were limited in efforts to get ahead through their athletic prowess.

CHAPTER FOUR

Sport and the Educational Process

The leading sponsors of sport for children, adolescents, and young adults were formal and informal educational institutions that sought to implement the positive sports creed and thereby up-lift, instruct, and socialize American youth. Intercollegiate male sport emerged in the mid-nineteenth century at elite eastern colleges. Athletic leaders at these schools were self-proclaimed defenders of amateurism, yet their win-at-all-costs attitude paradoxically led to professionalization. As historian Ronald Smith points out, by 1900 sport at institutions such as Yale had become rationalized, commercialized, and professionalized, and furnished a model for colleges across the nation. Collegiate sport also gave women the opportunity to contest conventional perceptions of femininity. The collegiate athletic experience served as an important role model for secondary school students, who in the late nineteenth century emulated their elders and organized their own sports programs. By the turn of the century, organized athletics were introduced by educators and youth workers into elementary schools, settlement houses, YMCAs, and playgrounds to acculturate and socialize immigrant children.

125

Sport and Higher Education

Men's Intercollegiate Athletics

In the antebellum era the principal collegiate sporting events were annual interclass contests. These matches promoted class loyalty, supplied a vehicle for hazing or initiation rites, and enabled students to work out excess energy. These amusements were not necessarily endorsed by parents, teachers, or administrators, but were preferred to harassing the faculty or rioting in town. The main game was the football rush, a soccer-style game played on "Bloody Monday," the first Monday of the fall term, by fifty to one hundred freshmen and sophomores. The game gave the latter an opportunity to kick first-year students into submission. Other popular antebellum college sports included handball, fencing, boxing, running, quoits (a game in which flat iron rings are tossed at a stake), horseback riding, and swimming.

College faculties in the second half of the nineteenth century originally tolerated, if they did not ardently support, emerging sports programs. Professors believed athletics kept students busy, taught proper social habits, developed manly traits and character, and advanced American civilization. Furthermore, sports promoted school spirit and publicized their institution.

The first intercollegiate sport was crew, a sport originally made popular by professional boatmen, upper-middle-class rowing clubs, and the Oxford-Cambridge races in England, which began in 1829. The earliest recorded college race in America took place fifteen years later when a four-man team of Yale seniors raced lower classmen. However, the initial intercollegiate athletic contest did not occur until 1852, when Harvard defeated Yale. Only a few races ensued over the next few years, but in 1858 students from four eastern schools established the College Union Regatta to arrange a championship race. The Regatta attracted considerable public attention, attested by the 15,000 spectators at its inaugural race in 1859. Within five years Yale's crew became dominant in the sport. Student supporters raised money for better sculls and a new boathouse, and they hired the first professional coach, John Ward. He followed rigorous training methods that included a strict diet of raw meat and little milk or water. Through sport, Yale sought to certify its parity with Harvard, the nation's most prestigious college. Winning was less crucial for Harvard, which had less to prove. Yet in 1869 Harvard participated in the most notable match of this era when its eight-man crew rowed against Oxford on the Thames. The match attracted enormous attention, and the results were reported almost instantly via the new trans-Atlantic cable. The two-mile race provided an opportunity to display national pride and to compare the character, physical fitness, and technology of the competing nations. Harvard lost by six seconds, which was considered a marvelous showing. The results demonstrated how far the United States had come in just a few years of racing compared to the English, who had been racing far longer. The outcome was perceived as a positive reflection on American culture, indomitability, and education. The well-publicized match increased interest in crew and led to the formation of the Rowing Association of American Colleges (1871). The organization included not only elite institutions, but also such upstarts as Massachusetts Agricultural College and Cornell. Their victories humiliated the elite schools and brought them national prominence.

Baseball was the second major intercollegiate sport, and by the 1870s it had become the principal game on campus. The first contest was played in conjunction with a regatta in 1859, Amherst defeating Williams, 73 to 32 under Massachusetts rules, although subsequent college games were played by the New York rules. After the Civil War, northern and southern colleges organized baseball clubs. Established in 1865, the Harvard nine was the dominant college team for several years, and they traveled to New York to play top amateur teams. In 1870 Harvard's home games drew up to 10,000 spectators. The team made a forty-four-game western tour that season, playing professionals as well as amateurs, and won two-thirds of its games against the pros. They were not the only college nine to play professional squads. Yale from 1865 to 1875 played twice as many professional clubs as it did college teams.

The College Baseball Association, established in 1879, was the first intercollegiate baseball league. It arranged a championship season and enforced the weak or nonexistent eligibility rules, which allowed students in experimental programs and postgraduate schools to play, along with junior faculty. Brown won the first league championship, led by Lee Richmond, who a week before had pitched a shutout for the Worcester professional team in an exhibition against the Chicago White Stockings. The following year, just before graduation, Richmond pitched the first perfect game in major-league history for the new Worcester Ruby Legs of the National League against the Cleveland Blues. Many top college teams used professionals on their rosters. In 1888 Harvard had four professionals, Yale five, and Princeton six. However, few college men sought major-league careers because of baseball's low social status and modest wages. Only 2 percent of major-league players in the 1880s had college experience, although the proportion quadrupled in the 1890s.

By 1900 it was common for top collegians to play for pay during the summer break and then return to school with their amateur standing intact. Summer ballplayers earned between $30 and $40 a week by playing in outlaw leagues (professional associations that operated outside of organized baseball) or on semipro, resort, and even professional teams, usually under a pseudonym or through some other such subterfuge. Players on hotel teams were on the payroll as waiters or cabana boys in order to protect their amateur standing. Semipro owners compensated players by betting they could not jump over a broom lying on the ground. Eddie Collins of Columbia, a future Hall of Famer, played in 1906 for the Philadelphia Athletics of the American League under a false name to protect his college eligibility.

Summer ball became a major educational issue. Advocates such as President Nicholas Murray Butler of Columbia believed all students had the right to use their talents to pay for their education. Ballplayers had as much right to play summer ball as glee club members did to sing in church choirs. Leading critics such as Capt. Frank Pierce of West Point disagreed, however, castigating summer ball for encouraging cheating and lying and for giving violators an unfair advantage over their genuinely pure collegiate competitors. Most college administrators frowned on summer ball, but they seldom initiated action against violators since they probably had many of them on their own teams. Jim Thorpe was the most famous athlete caught playing summer ball.

Another major college sport was track-and-field, which like baseball started as an adjunct to intercollegiate regattas. The sport's main impetus came from the Caledonian Games, Oxford-Cambridge athletic competitions in the late 1850s, and track-and-field contests at Princeton, whose sport was heavily influenced by its strong Scottish heritage. The first intercollegiate track-and-field meet was held in 1873 in conjunction with the College Regatta in Springfield, Massachusetts, under the sponsorship of Scottish American James G. Bennett, Jr., who donated a $500 silver cup to the winner of a two-mile race. Other events included the 100-yard dash, 120-yard hurdles, one-, two-, and three-mile runs, and a seven-mile walk.

In 1875 ten colleges established the Intercollegiate Association of Amateur Athletes of America (IC4A) to regulate track-and-field. Harvard and Yale completely dominated, winning all the team titles between 1880 and 1897. Competition was so serious that teams employed professional coaches or trainers, and they sought innovative training methods, new techniques (Yaleman Charles Sherrill created the crouch start), and superior equipment. By the mid-1890s collegians achieved international distinction by competing against Cambridge and Oxford and by setting world records. Bernie Wafers of Georgetown held world records in 1894 in the 100- and 220-yard dashes (9.8 and 22.6 seconds, respectively). Two years later, four Princeton juniors, a Harvard undergraduate, and five Harvard alumni comprised the United States track-and-field team at the first modern Olympics in Athens, capturing nine of twelve events.

Football: The Big Game

The most popular college sport was football. The first intercollegiate game in the fall of 1869, won by host Rutgers, six goals to four over Princeton, used rules similar to soccer. Players were permitted to bat the ball, but not to carry or throw it. Different versions of football were played at a small number of colleges over the next few years. In 1874 Harvard played two home games against Montreal's McGill University, one under its soccer-style rules and the second under the visitor's rugby rules. This was the first college rugby game in the United States and had important consequences for the future of American-style football. Harvard's players enjoyed the physical contact and the opportunities to carry the oval ball, and decided to adopt the new game. In 1876, Harvard, Princeton, Columbia, and

Yale formalized common rules that included fifteen men to a team and two forty-minute halves, and a scoring system that emphasized kicking (four touchdowns equaled one kicked goal). Controversies on the field were to be decided by a referee instead of by team captains, as in English rugby. Referees became necessary because Americans lacked a traditional football code to rely upon, were less deferential to a captain to decide disputes, and might have been less comfortable with the letter of a rule than in manipulating rules to gain an advantage. Harvard, Princeton, and Columbia established the Intercollegiate Football Association (IFA) and agreed to an annual Thanksgiving Day championship between the prior season's top two teams.

Yale under the leadership of Walter Camp dominated the early years of intercollegiate football. Camp starred on the varsity from 1876 to 1882 (part of which time he was a medical student) which went 30–1–5. Thereafter he became a watch manufacturer and served as volunteer advisor to the field coach (usually the prior year's captain) or paid coach for nearly thirty years. He helped make all types of athletics popular, and wrote twenty books on sports. But his special love was football, which he promoted as a member of the Rules Committee from 1878 to 1925, and by his annual All-American selections, from 1889 to 1924. Camp was an innovative coach who stressed rational management. Practices consisted of warm-up exercises, repetitive drills to develop machine-like efficiency and precise play, and a rough, hour-long scrimmage. His novel methods included the use of tackling dummies, filming practices, developing strategies, and coding signals to communicate plays. Camp's methods were so successful that between 1883 and 1891 Yale outscored its opposition 4,660 to 92, losing just three games.

Walter Camp was not only a creative coach, but was also responsible for most major rule innovations. The regulations evolved by trial and error, according to football historian Michael Oriard, as much by accident as by design. In 1880 when Yale joined the Intercollegiate Football Association, Camp cut the number of players to eleven and decreased the size of the playing field to 110 by 53 yards. He developed logical standardized written rules to bring order to the sport and provide common understanding of play. Camp wanted to create an exciting spectator entertainment with greater drama and changes in the flow of play.

Camp addressed the problem of initiating play after a ball carrier was downed by having the side with the ball maintain possession. Teams would then line up across an imaginary scrimmage line, resuming play once the ball was heeled back to the quarterback. This innovation brought order to the game, but it also meant the offense did not have to surrender the ball. During the 1880 Thanksgiving Game, Princeton kept the ball the entire second half to preserve a scoreless tie and maintain its championship. These tactics were repeated at the championship game one year later. Consequently in 1882 Camp introduced the "down system" to open up the game. The offense was required to advance the ball five yards in three plays to maintain possession. Camp also revised the scoring system to lessen the emphasis on the kicking game.

The new rules encouraged highly coordinated offensive units featuring wide-open attacks with prearranged plays signaled by a code. Blockers were assigned to run interference for the ball carrier, a technique that was illegal in rugby. In 1884 Pennsylvania introduced the V formation in which blockers wrapped their arms up around each other to form a convoy ahead of the runner. The wide-open offense was hindered in 1888 by a new rule that permitted tackling below the waist. This change made shifty, open-field running more difficult and encouraged the use of heavier players. (In 1883 the average Yale football player weighed 173.5 pounds.) Thereafter, coaches preferred dangerous momentum and mass plays employing closed formations, such as Harvard's fearsome flying wedge, developed in 1892, in which the biggest players grouped themselves twenty-five yards behind the line of scrimmage and then ran full-speed ahead of the runner. Rule changes after the 1894 season banned this hazardous tactic, but they did not end violent mass play

Camp's innovations enabled football, at first primarily a participatory game, to become a more exciting spectacle that fans would pay to watch. Camp recognized the sport's potential profitability if games were moved off-campus where there were larger potential crowds. In 1876 the first Intercollegiate Football Association championship was played in Hoboken, and then moved to New York four years later, where it drew about 5,000 spectators. Attendance thereafter steadily increased, reaching 23,000 by 1887, an audience consisting largely of middle-class nonstudent fans. The game became recognized as the start of the winter social season, and rounds of parties followed. The championship match became so popular that $1 and $2 tickets were soon being scalped for up to forty dollars. The three championship games between 1891 and 1893 drew 35,000 to 40,000 fans each year. The 1891 Yale-Princeton match produced over $28,000 in profits.

Football became a big moneymaker. As late as 1888, the student-run Yale Athletic Association made less money from football ($2,800) than either baseball or crew ($5,000 each). But during the 1890s, Yale's annual football profits surpassed fifty thousand dollars. Thus it was surprising that in 1894 the faculties and trustees decided to move the big game back to campus. The Big Three colleges (Harvard, Yale, and Princeton) left the New York market because their leaders felt the games were getting too much attention and that postgame student riots in less respectable Tenderloin theaters were giving the schools a bad public image. The result was that attendance dropped by one half.

The nineteenth-century intercollegiate sports programs were established and operated by student-run athletic associations that supported as many as twenty different sports. Membership cost fifty cents to one dollar, with additional capital coming from fundraisers, private subscriptions, and gate receipts, which in the late nineteenth century became the primary source of athletic revenue. At first an elected captain arranged training programs and practices, selected line-ups, and supervised play during the game with the assistance of an athletic manager who scheduled games, oversaw finances, and checked player eligibility. By the 1880s captains were inviting alumni back to help prepare the team. As competition became fiercer, athletic associations began to recruit athletes and hire professional coaches to mold winning teams. The employment of expert coaches fit in better with the growing professional orientation of American higher education than with the more elitist model of gentlemanly student control.

Students strongly backed the athletic association because they found sports more exciting than traditional extracurricular activities. Furthermore, the association promoted a feeling of community, provided publicity and prestige for their school, and operated independently of adult supervision. Students at large state universities had limited direct contact with their peers, but all could be sports fans who attended games and participated in the rituals of spectatorship. They cheered ("Eckie, Eckie, Eckie, Break his Little Neckie" roared Michigan fans when their team played against quarterback Walter Eckersall and the University of Chicago in 1905) and sang school songs, enjoying a moment when Victorian decorum could be temporarily forgotten. Furthermore, students found athletic participation more useful preparation for life in the modern, bureaucratic, capitalist society they intended to enter upon graduation than was membership in literary societies or debate clubs. The suave, sophisticated behavior learned in fraternities, and the cooperation, leadership qualities, and hard work taught on the playing field were seen as valuable qualities for getting ahead. Walter Camp agreed. He felt that football developed a personality of leadership and brains that would help bring success after college in corporate America.

By the 1890s, Midwestern and far western universities had growing intercollegiate sports programs, especially public universities that sought statewide, if not regional and national, recognition. Even predominantly female teachers' colleges began football programs to attract more male students. However, sports programs were less developed at urban, working-class commuter colleges and at impoverished southern institutions because of the expense, and, in the South, the less-developed modern sporting culture.

The newer schools had a hard time gaining national recognition because the media had a strong pro-eastern bias. No All-American was selected from a non-eastern school until Clarence Hergensheimer of the University of Chicago in 1898. Three-fourths (76.9 percent) of the All-Americans from 1889 to 1916 came from Yale, Harvard, Princeton, or Pennsylvania.

Faculty members began to take leadership roles in regulating athletics in the late 1880s, following the model of Harvard's three-man Faculty Committee, established in 1882 to protect amateurism.

The committee banned football for the 1885 season because of rough play and fighting, a decision strongly opposed by students and alumni. Dr. Sargent, one of the members, who had hoped to eliminate only the game's worst excesses, lost his professorship in 1889 as a result. The board was restructured in 1888 as a nine-member athletic committee with equal representation from faculty, alumni, and students, and was granted full control over athletics. The mixed committee format was widely emulated, but did not resolve intercollegiate sport's major problems. At Yale, students maintained free rein over the Athletic Association. Its faculty did not even seek control until 1905, when an investigation discovered the association had a slush fund in excess of $100,000 for gifts, vacations, and tutors, and an income one-eighth that of the university's.

Failure to control sports problems at individual schools led to interinstitutional cooperation. The Southern Intercollegiate Association, formed in 1894, the first college conference, was ineffective, but the Inter-Collegiate Conference of Faculty Representatives (or Western Conference, later known as the Big Ten) established one year later by their school's presidents was somewhat successful. The conference banned freshmen eligibility, and limited bona fide students to three years of participation. However, while faculty in the Western Conference and the Brown Conference, an association of Ivy League schools established in 1898, set policy, student organizations still managed the sports programs, and it took about twenty years for the conference model to become widely adopted.

Demands to win led to the practice of hiring a professional coach, who at first was usually employed just for the season. The days of the wealthy amateur such as Walter Camp, for whom coaching was an avocation, were rapidly disappearing. Amateurs were pushed aside, just as gentlemen-scholars were being displaced by highly trained specialists with Ph.D's. Paid coaches were under heavy pressure to win to keep their jobs, and they vigorously promoted the efficient management of college sport. The coach became one of the most visible people, if not the most important, on campus, and coaches were often paid more than top professors. Harvard's Bill Reid, the highest-paid football coach in the early 1900s, had a $7,000 salary,

30 percent more than any instructor, and nearly equal to that of President Charles Eliot. Early football coaches were mainly Yale men (forty-five by the mid-1890s) recruited by schools across the country to elevate the quality of play, win games, and bring new status to their institution.

The most successful and respected football coach was Yale alumnus Amos Alonzo Stagg, a former ace Yale pitcher, who during the late 1880s had led Yale to five championships in six seasons. He also played right end as a graduate divinity student on the 1888 team that outscored the opposition 698-0, and he made the first All-American football team in 1889. Stagg's poor oratorical skills blocked his ministerial aspirations, and instead he studied and coached for two years at the Springfield YMCA Training School, preparing to promote muscular Christianity. In 1892, Stagg was hired by President William Rainey Harper of the new University of Chicago to coach football, basketball, baseball, and track. Although Harper sought a national reputation for his school as a research institution, he understood that success in sports would be a quicker route to recognition. Stagg was appointed chair of the physical culture department with a $6,000 salary, the first coach to receive an academic appointment and tenure. Stagg became the winningest football coach of the day. He coached for fifty-seven years (forty-one years at the University of Chicago), and had a career mark of 294-200-36, second at his retirement in 1946 to "Pop" Warner's 319. Stagg was a superb tactician who helped invent many formations and plays, such as the onside kick, and trained twenty-four future coaches.

A collegiate coach's primary duties were recruiting, evaluating teams' strengths and weaknesses, determining tactics, supervising workouts and diets, and arranging schedules. Stagg so deftly arranged his team's schedule that between 1896 and 1905, 90 percent of its games were in Chicago, where the Maroons had a big home field edge and a large potential gate. Furthermore, he scheduled weak teams early in the season, a strategy that bolstered the team's confidence, built up its record, and encouraged fan interest.

A key to any coach's success was recruiting talented players. In the 1870s, certain athletic associations employed financial inducements to attract top baseball players, and by the late 1890s, colleges throughout the country offered scholarships or other inducements to attract top athletes. Teams often used players attending professional or graduate schools—two-thirds of Harvard's football team in the 1880s were in law school or another professional school—and it was not until 1905 that major colleges changed that policy to eliminate the "perpetual athlete." Top recruiters such as Michigan's Fielding Yost used players who never even enrolled in classes, "special students" who did not meet the normal admission standards, and transfers from other colleges. The transfers included "tramp athletes" who switched from school to school depending on the best offer. Yost's greatest player in the early 1900s was halfback Willie Heston, a future Hall of Famer, who had already played three years for San Jose. Heston enrolled in law school at Michigan, and went on to become a judge.

Stagg originally opposed scholarships as contrary to amateurism, but he changed his mind after a couple of poor seasons. Stagg recruited top prospects by promises of scholarships, easy course loads, tutors, campus jobs, access to a Rockefeller trust for needy athletes, assignment to the best dormitories, their own dining facilities, and special parties and trips. Football junkets to the West Coast and baseball tours to Japan were excellent recruiting tools and superb advertising for the university. Stagg further enhanced the university's visibility by organizing in 1902 an annual interscholastic track meet on campus, and, fifteen years later, a national high school basketball tournament. Such exposure gave Chicago first crack at many top athletes.

Competition for top recruits was fierce. Student athletes might sign up for classes at one school and be in uniform one week later at another. One of the most highly publicized recruits was James Hogan, who entered Yale in 1901 at age twenty-seven after a fabled career at Exeter, the renowned prep school. In 1904, when he captained the Yale football team, the Athletic Association paid his $100 tuition, his board, a luxurious suite at the University Club, and a ten-day vacation to Cuba during the semester. In addition Hogan shared profits from the sale of programs at Yale's baseball games with two teammates, and the American Tobacco Company gave him a commission on all cigarette packs sold in New Haven. Despite his pampered treatment, Hogan was intellectually quite capable, and went on to make *Law Review* at the Columbia University Law School.

Once on campus, it was not difficult to keep players eligible. Lest Chicago fans worry, the *Inter-Ocean* reported, "It seems safe to say that no really valuable man will be lost to the team on account of any little educational deficiencies." Stagg selected easy classes for his players, often in his own department, enrolled them in courses taught by sympathetic instructors, hired tutors, and arranged for special examinations, as late as the morning of a game. Chicago athletes were not required to take a full academic program until 1905. Two years earlier, only three of twenty-three football players were fully registered. These practices seem to prove historian Ronald Smith's point that there never was a golden age of the intercollegiate student athlete.

Playing major college football was a serious matter. The first football "Game of the Century" took place on Thanksgiving Day, 1905, between the undefeated University of Chicago ("Monsters of the Midway") and the University of Michigan, known as the "Point a Minute" team for having averaged fifty points a game over the previous fifty-five contests. The contest for the mythical championship of the Midwest featured outstanding coaches and All-American players. Ticket requests were triple the 27,000-seat capacity of Marshall Field, leading to a scalping frenzy. The game was a defensive struggle, and Coach Stagg, referring to the ill William Rainey Harper, urged his squad to "win for the dying president's sake." The decisive play in the game occurred in the third quarter when a Chicago punt was carried out from behind the goal line by Michigan's Dennison Clark. He was stopped after a few yards and dragged back into the end zone for a safety, the only score of the game. (Players then did not get credit for their forward progress). Clark was despondent after the game, and he talked about suicide. Twenty-seven years later Clark did commit suicide. He left a note hoping that his "final play" might atone for his error on the gridiron.

The Football Crisis of 1905–1906 and the Rise of the NCAA
While there was a lot to admire about football, the sport also had its problems, which led in the late nineteenth century to an important debate about the merits of the game. On the positive side, America

appeared ripe for a virile game that would verify courage and strength of character and foster such qualities as cooperation and obedience. Social Darwinists applauded football as a rough game, a test of the fittest, extolled by President Charles K. Adams of the University of Wisconsin for developing "those characteristics that have made the Anglo-Saxon race pre-eminent." As discussed in Chapter Two, elite and upper-middle-class young men were concerned about their physical fitness because of sedentary lifestyles, their ability to measure up to fathers who had been Civil War heroes, and their virility because of the feminization of culture. Football seemed a perfect test because it put young men under fire but spared them the carnage of warfare.

Criticisms of football focused on its violence—the sport caused more deaths than prizefighting—commercialization, and impact on the educational process. Unsympathetic journalists, such as editor E. L. Godkin of the *Nation*, chastised football for its violence and brutality, poor sportsmanship, and win-at-any-cost mentality. Godkin also admonished the sport's growing commercial nature and harmful influence on educational institutions. Religious periodicals compared football unfavorably to boxing because, unlike boxing, it lowered the morals of the respectable classes.

By the late 1890s, college professors were among the sport's most zealous critics, including the renowned historian Frederick Jackson Turner of the University of Wisconsin, a former football advocate. Academicians were concerned about the growing influence on campus of alumni and local residents who contributed to the athletic association and about the impact of intercollegiate sports on academic integrity and their school's reputation. Disparaging professors felt there was an over emphasis on sport that slighted their school's mission of teaching and scholarship in favor of providing carnivals for the masses. Academics also complained that the commercialization of sport fostered nonexistent or weak eligibility standards, the recruitment of tramp athletes, and unsportsmanlike conduct, along with raucous crowds, bitter rivalries, and gambling.

The issues of football's brutality, professionalism, and commercialism came to a head in 1905. The game had become so violent that eighteen players died that year, although most of them were not collegians. As a result, Columbia and several other colleges dropped football, while Stanford and California replaced it with rugby. In addition, devastating investigative reports appeared in newspapers and popular muckraking periodicals such as *McClure's*. These critical stories emphasized commercialization, recruiting scandals, and a win-at-all-costs ethic that permitted unsportsmanlike tactics such as ganging up on an opponent's star player to put him out of the game. These accounts were illustrated with frightening photographs of injured players, particularly the gruesome picture of Swarthmore star Bob Maxwell after a mauling by University of Pennsylvania players. President Theodore Roosevelt, a football fan and the preeminent advocate of "the strenuous life," invited representatives of Yale, Harvard, and Princeton to the White House to discuss reform of the sport. Little concrete progress was achieved, although the meeting did publicize football's serious problems. At the end of the year Chancellor Henry MacCracken of New York University, which had just dropped football, organized a national conference attended by sixty-eight colleges to consider the game's future. Significantly, neither Harvard nor Yale chose to attend. The delegates decided by a narrow majority to reform the game, establishing the Intercollegiate Athletic Association (IAA) (renamed the National Collegiate Athletic Association [NCAA] in 1910). Only thirty-six schools joined at first. The traditional athletic powers such as Harvard and Yale, unwilling to share power with the less-prestigious colleges, did not. But by 1909 membership was up to sixty-seven, including Harvard and the University of Chicago. The IAA guidelines banned freshman participation, required transfer-student athletes to sit out one year, and allowed students three years of eligibility. However, the association had little enforcement power over its own rules, relying on its members to self-regulate.

Historian Ronald Smith argues that the democratization of the old boys' self-perpetuating rules committee in 1906 was just as important in reforming football as was pressure from the White House and the rise of the Intercollegiate Athletic Association. Harvard's Bill Reid replaced Camp as secretary of the committee and secured significant rule changes to discourage mass play and open up the sport: ten yards for a first down; no tackling below the knees; and legalization of the forward pass, albeit under complicated restrictions that included a fifteen-yard penalty for an incompletion. Yet Smith points out that the so-called "revolution of 1906" barely changed the style of play since coaches were afraid to pass, and the sport remained very dangerous. More rule changes were added over the next three years, however: seven men on the line of scrimmage; no interlocking of arms for blocking; four tries for a first down; touchdowns were raised from five to six points; and the ball was streamlined to make it easier to throw in a faster and more accurate spiral. Coaches thereafter experimented more with the forward pass. In 1913 coach Jess Harper of Notre Dame, a former Stagg student, decided to use the forward pass as a tactic in its game against heavily favored Army. The small Catholic college won 35–13 by capitalizing on the passing of Gus Dorais to Knute Rockne. The stunning outcome of that game helped popularize the forward pass. The use of this new weapon opened up play and made contests more exciting to watch.

The popularity of college football in the 1910s encouraged the construction of new stadiums at private institutions to house growing crowds. The first was Harvard's Soldier's Field, built in 1903 for $250,000. The 38,000-seat, concrete-and-steel structure was the first major athletic field built on a college campus, and it had the largest seating capacity of any American sports field. Named in honor of alumni who had fought in the Civil War, the field symbolized regeneration through sport. Ten years later the 67,000-seat Yale Bowl was constructed for $400,000, and similar edifices were completed at Syracuse, Princeton, and Chicago. Public institutions soon followed suit, including the 66,000-seat Ohio Stadium in 1922 for Ohio State; Michigan Stadium in Ann Arbor, built in 1927 to seat 72,000 for $950,000; and the University of Illinois's Memorial Stadium, built in 1923 in honor of 182 alumni and one alumnae who died in World War I at a cost of $1.7 million. Such large stadiums required top-flight teams, heated conference and intersectional rivalries, and the nationalization of the traditional Thanksgiving Day game to fill them up. Teams now had to reach out beyond student and alumni support to fill their stadiums. Colleges invited the local middle class to become vicarious alumni and demonstrate hometown (or home state) pride by attending games. The "Big Game"—a major rivalry or championship—became popular entertainment, complete with pregame ceremonies such as rallies, parades, and bonfires, and game rituals such as organized rooting led by male cheerleaders. Another way to enhance fan interest started in 1913 when the University of Chicago began numbering players so they could be easily identified. Its students could buy cheap season passes for end-zone tickets, while the higher-priced choice seats were sold to the general public. The best seats at Marshall Field in Chicago cost $3, highest in the Western Conference. Football earned the university about $30,000 a year in the mid-1910s, with profits peaking at $212,000 in 1924, the year of its last Big Ten championship.

Women's Collegiate Athletics

Scholars have recently suggested that as important as sport was for men on campus, women's physical culture may have been more consequential because physical education and sport shaped a woman's self-image, as well as public attitudes about femininity and women's relationship to men. Historian Cindy Himes, author of "The Female Athlete in American Society, 1860–1940" (Ph.D. diss., 1986), further argues that fitness programs protected women's access to higher education by assuring the public that women were healthy enough to stand up to academic rigors.

Physical culture was an important part of the curriculum at late-nineteenth-century women's colleges. Most instructors were trained by Amy Morris Homans, who established the Boston Normal School for Gymnastics in 1889 and directed it for twenty-nine years. Another important mentor was Dr. Dudley Sargent of Harvard, who opened a gymnasium for women in 1881, which a decade later became the Sargent School for Physical Education. Sargent stressed individual programs of "corrective gymnastics" tailored to bolster each student's weaknesses. Sargent, an early anthropometrist, advocated increased muscularity. The professor kept detailed records of his students' weight lifting and calisthenics, which he preferred to games.

Homans' and Sargent's female students, predominantly young, unmarried, middle class, and urban, developed the first woman-centered philosophy of sport that emphasized cooperation and friendship among sportswomen rather than competition. Woman physical educators stressed the feminine potential of sport that helped them gain credibility and advance their careers. They were very active in professional organizations such as the Association for the Advancement of Physical Education (later named the American Physical Education Association), founded in 1885. Historian Susan K. Cahn, author of *Coming on Strong: Gender and Sexuality in Twentieth Century Women's Sports* (1994) argues that these physical education pioneers forged an alliance with physicians by encouraging a middle-class model of sport designed to preserve gender differences, protect women's delicate sexual sensibilities, ensure the health of future mothers, and guard female athletes from male sports promoters.

Women physical educators exercised more control over students than their male colleagues. They supervised expansive athletic programs, required health exams for all students, set posture standards, and organized classes for "defective students." Educators' concerns that physical culture could "unsex" women and their opposition to competition that might harm female camaraderie led to modifications in women's sports to make them less like men's. Professional educators opposed the stress on winning, individual achievement, and professionalism identified with intercollegiate competition. They preferred mass participation, fair play, and health-improving activities. Instead of competitive sports, athletic festivals such as play days were established to celebrate traditional feminine qualities. Play days attracted athletes from several colleges who played on mixed teams so that individual schools would not compete against each other. The athletes played under women's rules for female audiences.

Efforts to improve college women's fitness dated back to at least 1866 when Vassar instituted a mandatory fifty-minute daily walk. Physical education at Bryn Mawr was originally voluntary, but compulsory gymnastics was introduced because students skipped the boring classes. Smith students were required to do calisthenics with dumbbells, Indian clubs, wands, and chest weights while listening to slow music. While exercising, students were compelled to wear blouses and ankle-length skirts, but they preferred more comfortable clothing. In the 1880s they began wearing sensibly divided skirts (bloomers), stockings, and tennis shoes, and swam in sailor dresses worn over tights.

Students preferred sports to calisthenics. At Vassar, women organized two baseball teams in 1866, and subsequently, despite parental opposition, they also participated in recreational archery, croquet, tennis, rowing, and horseback riding. In 1878 Smith College women organized a baseball game, but two players were injured and the game was halted. School officials then banned the sport because they feared violence and broken windows. Baseball was not resumed there until an interclass match in 1892.

Organized women's collegiate sport developed in the 1890s, as female students demanded more control over their extracurricular activities. Bryn Mawr's Women's Athletic Association, formed in 1891, became a model for other campuses. Basketball, track-and-field, and field hockey were introduced between 1892 and 1901, primarily on an interclass basis. Although the athletic associations experimented with intercollegiate competition in basketball and tennis, faculties preferred intramurals, so intercollegiate matches were few and infrequent.

In 1892, Smith's new gymnasium director, twenty-four-year-old Senda Berenson, modified the newly invented rough game of basketball to make it more appropriate for feminine young ladies. Unlike the students, she did not come from a blue-blood background, but was the daughter of Jewish-Lithuanian immigrants. She believed that "carefully supervised games" promoted self-reliance, self-control, and teamwork, which were "so necessary to the modern woman." Her rules prohibited physical play by banning anyone from snatching the ball and promoted teamwork by forbidding a player to hold the ball for more than three seconds or dribble it more than three times. Berenson also redesigned the basketball court, placing three women in the offensive zone, three in the defensive, and two in midcourt to encourage team play, lessen reliance on a dominant player, and reduce fatigue (reflecting contemporary views of women's limited physical capacity). Excellence was recognized with varsity letters, and top ballplayers became campus leaders. Himes claims that sport at women's colleges was a culture-creating activity that promoted camaraderie, class spirit, and school pride. Women's sports also became enormously popular at coed western colleges. Although elite eastern women's colleges played a leading role in encouraging basketball, the first match between institutions occurred in 1892 on the West Coast when the University of California played Miss Head's School. Four years later, Stanford defeated California 2–1 in the first women's intercollegiate contest. Only women were allowed to attend.

Berenson justified college athletics as preparation for the physical strength women would need in their future professions, although these occupations were then just barely open to women. Respected middle-class-women's periodicals such as *Godey's Lady's Magazine* decried women's sports for promoting competition, developing muscles, and spending too much time in the sun, resulting in tanned bodies. But the students sided with Berenson. The 1898 Wellesley yearbook applauded the faculty's acceptance of basketball, asserting, "The grimy and generally disheveled appearance of the players as they emerge from the fray, fills our athletic souls with pride."

The conflict between faculty and students over competitive sport was reflected by a change in preparations for Wellesley's Float Day in 1898. Class crews originally emphasized fashion and beauty rather than ability, and victory was determined by form and grace rather than speed. The students preferred competition, however, and candidates trained ardently during the winter with rowing machines in hopes of being selected to row for their class. The regatta that year drew about 7,000 spectators, including women and men. The athletes were not worried about ridicule from men and wanted them present so the rowers could demonstrate their prowess.

Nonetheless, physical educators in the early 1900s succeeded in downplaying competition in favor of sport for sport's sake. They only supported athletic activities such as play days, which stressed traditional feminine qualities. Participants would enjoy themselves, gain health benefits, and learn teamwork without the taint of masculinity. Their sports would promote friendship and sociability rather than individual accomplishment.

Secondary School Sport

Secondary schools in antebellum America were originally private college preparatory institutions, but after the Civil War growing numbers of communities established public high schools to socialize middle-class youth and train them for college or clerical occupations. In 1890 there were 200,000 high-school students in the United States, mostly girls, whose graduation rate far surpassed boys. Thirty years later the number of high school students had risen by 711 percent. Just one-third of elementary-school students attended high school, however, and one-third of those graduated. High school student populations became more inclusive in the 1920s, when the national standard of living rose and the prevailing educational philosophy shifted from emphasizing academics to promoting life adjustment.

Antebellum academies allotted perhaps fifteen minutes a day to physical education to alleviate health problems caused by a sedentary lifestyle. During the Civil War era health reformers such as Dr. Dio Lewis advocated programs for urban boys that stressed military drill and gymnastics to cultivate the body and develop traits such as courage, perseverance, and self-control. Few schools had physical education programs until the late 1880s, when educators became even more concerned about building manly bodies, a reflection of middle-class concerns over masculinity and race. They wanted to enhance the "natural" body and connect muscular development, stamina, and power, to manliness. Physical culture was intended to produce hard, virile bodies, the opposite of the dreaded soft, limp, effeminized boy, and especially the deviant homosexual. New England schools adopted the Swedish system, which emphasized calisthenics, while the Midwest favored turnerian gymnastics, based on the turn-verein model. A mixed system was implemented in Brooklyn, New York, and Washington, D.C. In 1917, just before the United States joined the Great War, military training was added to physical education. The goal was to enhance the "natural" body through exercise.

Chicago stood in the forefront of promoting physical education in schools, a long-term goal of the local German turners. In 1889, the public schools hired their first physical education instructor, an experienced turner. That year not a single school had a gym, but by 1913 all its twenty-one high schools had gymnasiums. In 1899, Chicago schoolboys from elementary to high school were measured to see how their height, weight, strength, lung capacity, hearing, and overall fitness compared to an ideal norm. The best scores were achieved at schools in middle-class neighborhoods, and the worst in the slums. Experts claimed that the closer a boy was to the model, the more intellectually, socially and physically superior he would be, and the better soldier he would become.

Educators also believed that physical education was important for high school girls, but to promote femininity. They were encouraged to participate in light gymnastics, dance, and exercises to break up the school day, improve their health and posture, prevent mental strain, and prepare for their future. Physical culture would enhance their appearance, grace, and poise so they could better capture a mate, as well as train them to be cooperative for involvement in women's clubs, and make them fit to become healthy, happy mothers.

School administrators preferred exercise programs over team sports because they were cheaper and less time-consuming, and therefore a better fit for the curriculum. Students, however, preferred sports. High school students in the 1870s and 1880s established their own athletic organizations without formal school ties in emulation of collegiate associations, and in the biggest cities, they established intracity leagues in imitation of intercollegiate leagues. Students financed Boston's Interscholastic Football Association (formed in 1888), secured playing sites, and arranged matches, sometimes traveling out of town to play. All students were expected to join the school's athletic association, attend games, and root for the team. Interest in school sports provided a common topic of conversation, a diversion from academics, and a means to encourage school spirit. Sports provided a focal point for developing a shared identity among students and alumni, extremely important for citywide institutions such as Boston Latin, as well as for new schools in neighborhoods that lacked a sense of community and local pride and needed something to rally around.

High school sport suffered many of the same problems as their college counterparts, and by the mid-1890s administrators questioned student control. Headmasters wanted to protect their institution's reputation from such problems as unsportsmanlike-play, lack of attention to schoolwork, and unenforced eligibility requirements. Furthermore, administrators were under parental and student pressure to play star athletes regardless of their academic standing.

Administrative control was generally welcomed by student leaders, however, who recognized their inability to deal with the win-at-all-costs mentality. Students did not regard adult supervision of interscholastic sport as an effort to subvert their independence, but rather to manage sport programs professionally, prevent difficulties from arising, and respond to pervasive problems. The secondary-school community agreed on the need for fair play and control of abuses: they wanted to see the realization of the positive sports creed. Administrative governance did not dampen the competitive spirit; instead, a wide variety of championship matches developed at the local, regional, and state levels. The New York Public Schools Athletic League, founded in 1903, had the most prominent and varied city-wide championships, including basketball, baseball, track-and-field, riflery, soccer, cross-country, swimming, tennis, crew, and lacrosse.

Student interest in sport also worked its way into physical education programs and intramurals as instructors sought to promote sport for all male students. Physical educators taught sports to promote physical fitness and help students adjust to an industrial capitalist society that demanded discipline, punctuality, and teamwork. Instructors contributed to the preparedness movement prior to America's entry into World War I by teaching riflery and military drill.

Adult-Directed Youth Sport

Children in the nineteenth century received little physical education, and their recreational activities were mainly self-designed. Boys played pick-up baseball games in vacant fiends, played stick ball or stoop ball in crowded city streets, and swam off the docks or in local watering holes. They also gambled with dice, played with fire, got into fights, and joined gangs that taught destructive values and encouraged antisocial criminal behavior. Turn-of-the-century progressive reformers who were frightened by life in the slums and wanted to promote order in the cities advocated rational recreation as an alternative to deleterious street amusements. In particular, they recommended adult-supervised sport programs to provide city children with pleasurable, self-improving activities. Reformers believed sport would provide a replacement for the small-town lifestyle of earlier days. Reformers founded boy-workers organizations such as the Public School Athletic League and the Playground Association of America, and supported established societies such as the YMCA to uplift inner-city youth by providing them with wholesome pastimes. Sport would help newcomers adapt to a new culture and strengthen ties to their new home.

The YMCA originally focused on young clerks, but so many youngsters drifted in to use the gym that leaders decided to enroll boys who could pay the $5 membership fee. Junior departments were established in the 1880s to keep ten to sixteen year olds occupied in the afternoon. The YMCA sought to prolong childhood and delay the dangerous years of adolescence, when sexuality and emotions would weaken self-control. Professor Benjamin Rader contends that after the turn of the century the philosophic foundation for YMCA boy-workers shifted from muscular Christianity to G. Stanley Hall's theory of recapitulation. The Clark University psychologist argued in *Adolescence* (1904) that an individual's psychological development (ontogeny) occurred in fixed stages that recapitulated the cultural evolution of mankind (phylogeny). Hall asserted that adolescence was a time of optimism and uncertainty when youths, especially urban boys, were vulnerable to moral degeneration. They often lacked close familial and community ties, the experience of hard work, and the religious influences that had protected rural youth from dissipation.

In 1899, Dr. Luther Gulick, a son of missionaries stationed in China, who was an instructor at the YMCA Training College and editor of the *American Physical Education Review,* employed the recapitulation theory to justify adult-directed boys' sport. Gulick developed the evolutionary theory of play. He believed man had acquired an instinct to play during evolution. Boys aged seven to twelve years enjoyed games like tag and track-and-field sports, which had evolved from the hunting instinct acquired during the presavage stage of evolution, while teenage males preferred team sports, which combined the hunting instinct with a predisposition for cooperation, a trait that emerged in the savage stage of development. These instincts encouraged the modern child's proper physical, mental, and moral growth. Gulick looked to team sports to promote sound morality in youth, particularly inner-city male teenagers. These youths were attracted to gangs, wherein thievery, vandalism, and violence recapitulated a heritage of tribal hunting and warfare. Adult-supervised team sports would provide a substitute, and, by appealing to the cooperation instinct, teach teamwork, obedience, and self-control. Gulick's ideas influenced not only his attitudes toward sport, but also prompted him to help establish the Boy Scouts and, with his wife in 1911, the Camp Fire Girls.

Rader explains that Gulick's biological theory of play provided a scientific rationale for boy-workers. First, the theory justified the creation of special institutions to organize adult-supervised team sports to encourage the development of socially desirable traits. Second, it encouraged boy-workers to deemphasize the promotion of piety, exemplified by the increasing secularization of the YMCA. Third, it encouraged reformers to downplay ethnocultural differences, focusing on boys' shared experience of maturation. And fourth, Gulick's theory justified single-sex play. Boys and girls were believed to prefer play activities based on sex-specific instincts acquired during evolution. Gulick believed girls should not play strenuous competitive sports, but should instead participate in such amusements as folk dancing, cooking, and singing around the campfire, all of which would help prepare them for domesticity.

In 1903, Gulick became director of physical training for the New York City Board of Education, where he implemented his play theories. He sought to replace traditional fitness programs with sports that emphasized gymnastics and calisthenics but at first only reached a small proportion of urban youth. Consequently, Gulick organized the Public Schools Athletic League (PSAL), a private corporation that received no public funding. It did, however, have the backing of the New York school board, progressive educators, the Amateur Athletic Union, and prominent philanthropists such as Andrew Carnegie and Solomon Guggenheim, who helped finance the program.

The new league proposed the most comprehensive and sophisticated sports program ever initiated for schoolboys, offering interscholastic sport for the athletically gifted, sports for all students in New York's 630 public schools, and special events including field days, public exhibitions, and "Safe and Sane" July Fourth Games. The league received instant credibility when it organized the world's largest athletic meet at Madison Square Garden on December 26, 1903, which drew 1,040 competitors, primarily elementary school boys.

Mass participation was encouraged through class competition in the fifth through eighth grades, with the winning team in each grade determined by the highest average performance. Each school held championships in events such as the broad jump, pull-up, and sprint, with top teams advancing to compete for borough-wide titles. In addition, students with adequate grades could also compete for athletic badges. Elementary school students needed a B average in order to participate, while high school students needed to demonstrate "satisfactory progress" toward graduation. Competitors who achieved prescribed age-group standards in running, jumping, and chinning received a bronze or silver certificate. The program had a very beneficial impact on student fitness, reflected by the rise in medals awarded from 1,162 in 1904 to nearly 25,000 eleven years later.

In 1905 a Public Schools Athletic League Girls' Branch was established by wealthy women to provide exercise and activities for girls. Director Elizabeth Burchenal agreed with Gulick's theory of play, and she developed a program that stressed group participation ("Athletics for All Girls"). It comprised fifteen different sports and folk dancing to foster better agility, fun, and good health. Competition in athletics was restricted to interclass contests, and games were modified to prevent rough, unladylike play. For example, basketball fouls for girls were more heavily penalized (a point for the offended team and a foul shot) than in boys' games.

The PSAL organized athletics on the largest scale anywhere in the world, with programs that reached about 100,000 children. It provided a model for other major cities, including Baltimore and Chicago. By 1910 seventeen cities had organized similar programs to promote social control, good health, and traditional American values among the children of new immigrants. These programs were no panacea, however, as not all young athletes quit smoking or other bad habits, and they did not reach youth who were out of school.

Settlement workers who lived and worked in inner-city slums were ardent advocates of adult-directed sports for youth, and they tried to reach those youngsters whom schools did not. Settlement houses were first established in the 1880s to improve living conditions in the worst urban slums. By the 1910s, sixty-eight settlement houses operated in Chicago alone. The volunteers who staffed them were mainly middle-class women whose goals were to identify a community's problems and then try to resolve them. Settlement houses used athletic programs to attract neighborhood youth and draw them away from gangs, poolrooms, and saloons. The settlement workers believed in the power of team sports to Americanize inner-city youth and improve their morals, character, and health. Participation in sports would boost self-confidence, teach athletes to get along with different kinds of people, and prepare them to be team members in their future occupations. Soon after Jane Addams opened the renowned Hull House in 1889 on Chicago's Near West Side, volunteers organized gymnastic and calisthenics classes, recreational clubs for young boys, bowling and billiard tournaments, boxing classes for older boys, and competitions in boxing, wrestling, and basketball for its best athletes. Settlement sports programs were less attractive to second-generation immigrant daughters because of parental opposition and the unfeminine image of athletics among the foreign-born working class. Nonetheless, Hull House's women's basketball team achieved considerable acclaim.

In New York, sports programs at the settlement houses were so popular that by 1902, inter-settlement competition began. One year later, the settlements established the Inter-Settlement Athletic Association, which claimed in 1911 to have reached more working boys than any other sports program. Their contests were held in the evenings to maximize the number of participants and spectators. Saturday night athletic programs followed by a dance were especially popular.

Progressive settlement workers led the movement to develop inner-city public recreational facilities. These neighborhoods desperately needed bathhouses, playgrounds, and gymnasiums, as well as professionally trained youth workers to organize and supervise sports programs. The Progressives helped quadruple to forty-three the number of cities with supervised recreation programs in the period between 1900 and 1906. In the latter year, settlement workers and other Progressives established the Playground Association of

America with Gulick as president and Addams as vice president. The association's philosophy was based on Gulick's biological theory of play, which was expected to help bring street-tough city children under control and promote community pride. The Playground Association focused its efforts on publicizing the needs for supervised municipal recreation facilities, particularly in the inner city. While the precise impact of the association is difficult to measure, the concept of publicly organized leisure for urban youth certainly took hold. By 1917, 504 cities sponsored recreational programs, mostly in emulation of Chicago's small parks. They included such innovative features as New York's evening centers for working people and the use of piers to create additional recreational space.

Conclusion

Advocates of the sports creed overestimated its ability to remake society, in part because most physical educators, coaches, administrators, high school and college players, and spectators were native-born white Americans who already shared the same basic values. In addition, the ability of adult-directed sport to ameliorate inner-city youth was exaggerated. Most inner-city youth were outside of the umbrella of sports reform, and participation would not necessarily transform a bad character into a model citizen. Less than one out of ten urban children regularly used playgrounds, which were mainly enjoyed by middle-class WASP children. Many older youths never participated in adult-directed sports because they worked, had no access to a YMCA or settlement house, or simply preferred the spontaneity, disorder, and defiance of authority that characterized life on the street. Although reformers were often able to overcome the negative features of highly competitive athletics that stressed victory at all costs, they did not anticipate that the toughest youths would take over playgrounds and small parks for their own uses, or that such public space located between rival gangs would become contested turf. At the same time, reformers overlooked the potential of sport for self-directed growth. Boys left alone to play had to create their own field in a street or a narrow alley, make up their own rules ("anything to right field is out"), and respond to unique situations that established conventions could not cover ("do-overs").

CHAPTER FIVE

Baseball and the Rise of Professional Sport

The rise of commercialized professional spectator sport was the most significant development in post–Civil War athletics. Prizefighting, although commonly illegal, had an enormous appeal among the sporting fraternity, who respected the ability of manly men to defend themselves and knock opponents senseless. Horse racing, which had its own legal problems, was very popular with the elite as well as the lower class, who were thrilled by the sight of one-thousand-pound thoroughbreds ridden by one-hundred-pound jockeys spinning around the turn to the finish line and the wagers made on their favorite horses. And when it came to baseball, everyone was excited by the drama of the sport. Unlike today, professional ball games did not take a long time to complete. Something exciting was always happening or anticipated: a hit and run, a Walter Johnson fast ball, or the steal of third base by Ty Cobb. What could top the intensity of a game on the line: two out in the bottom of the ninth, tying and winning runs on base, and a full count on the batter? Baseball was the unchallenged national pastime that symbolized the finest American ideals, like democracy and opportunity, and seemed to provide a means to promote community pride, educate youth, and assimilate newcomers.

Before the 1860s, few sporting events were staged in enclosed semipublic facilities in which spectators were charged admission fees, and only a few athletes made their living as oarsmen, jockeys, pedestrians, or cricket players. In the late nineteenth century, however, the spectator sport business boomed. Some of the factors were external to the world of sport, notably the impact of urbanization, industrialization, and the commercialization of leisure, which had acclimated people to the concept of paying for their entertainment. There were also several factors internal to sport that contributed to its commercialization, such as the modernization of particular sports, the emergence of sports entrepreneurs unaffiliated with taverns, the interest of fee-paying spectators in watching highly skilled athletes perform, and the professionalization of sportsmen. There were a number of minor professional sports, including cycling, rowing, wrestling, track-and-field, and football, but public interest was dominated by baseball, boxing, and horse racing. The three major professional sports were all controlled by politicians and their closest business associates, often streetcar owners or professional gamblers, who employed their political clout to advance and protect their sporting investments. These entrepreneurs recruited top athletes, coaches, and trainers, and promoted championship contests, organized baseball leagues, and established racing circuits. They also constructed or rented boxing gymnasiums, arenas, ballparks, and racetracks to stage their contests in front of paying audiences.

Prizefighting

Prizefighting was first formally banned in New Jersey in 1835, and by 1894 thirty-seven states had criminalized professional boxing. In the 1890s three states (Louisiana, New York, and Nevada) passed laws allowing prizefighting, but it continued to have a shaky existence until the 1920s. Professional boxing was largely shunned because of its brutality and corruption. The people who arranged bouts, participated in matches, and attended contests were viewed as lowlifes. Throughout this period, urban machine politicians were especially prominent in the sport. Many of the leading managers and promoters were professional politicians who used their power to gain influence in the sport. Furthermore, political bosses used their clout to protect illegal bouts and ultimately to make prizefighting legal.

The earliest bouts were arranged personally by fighters or their managers in sporting taverns. The last big antebellum fight was the international match in 1860 between British champion Tom Sayers and his challenger, the younger, taller, and heavier (by 28 lbs.) American champion Tom Heenan. The match went forty-two rounds (140 minutes) and ended in a draw. While the underdog American was disappointed in the outcome, he was treated as a hero back home for his excellent showing against the man presumed to be the greatest fighter in the world.

Pugilism struggled right after the Civil War, with frequent charges that matches were fixed, and increased episodes of violence around the ring. Purses, if any then, were usually small, with most fighters' earnings coming from side bets. Illegal bouts occurred in barns, river barges, or saloon backrooms, with spectators charged as little as twenty-five cents, and even national championships had to be held on the sly

A revival of boxing took place in the 1880s through the sporting press, through which many important bouts were arranged, particularly Richard Fox's *National Police Gazette*, the leading promoter of the decade. Boxing historian Elliott Gorn credits Fox with cleaning up much of the sport's iniquity, such as the fixed bouts. Another factor was the adoption of the Marquis of Queensberry rules in the 1880s that contributed to the legitimization of the sport by making it more humane. A third key to the revitalization of pugilism was the arrival of a great charismatic champion, John L. Sullivan, "the Boston Strong Boy," who won the American heavyweight championship in 1882 when he knocked out Paddy Ryan in the ninth round of a match staged in Mississippi City, Mississippi, to avoid police interference. Afterwards, the fighters returned, along with the spectators, to New Orleans. The *Police Gazette* published a special issue to report the fight that sold 150,000 copies.

In the early 1880s the sport became increasingly popular in New York City, where politically connected promoters arranged boxing matches. Prizefights were against the law, so these bouts were described as "exhibitions," promoted as a demonstration of the art of self-defense, though fans fully expected to see a fighter's body pummeled into a mass of jelly. Several contests were staged in spacious downtown opera houses, theaters, public armories, and multipurpose arenas such as Madison Square Garden, which opened in 1879. The Garden's owner, William K. Vanderbilt, brought in other popular events, including the prestigious National Horse Show and long-distance running races, but he emphasized boxing exhibitions. A few programs featuring champion John L. Sullivan were especially successful. Nevertheless, sometimes the police would stop matches for "outraging decency and tending to corrupt public morals" as when they halted the second Sullivan–Paddy Ryan bout in 1885 in the first round. Thereafter, Vanderbilt discontinued his boxing shows.

In 1890 the state of Louisiana, which had a reputation for political corruption and loose morals (epitomized by the notorious Louisiana Lottery), passed a law enabling New Orleans to permit prizefights if they were staged by established athletic clubs. The city's prestigious sports clubs secured sites, provided purses, and negotiated with managers to arrange bouts. New Orleans' boxing boom peaked in September 1892 with three world-championship fights. The boxing extravaganza climaxed with Gentleman Jim Corbett's defeat of the great John L. Sullivan for a $25,000 purse plus a $10,000 side bet. Two years later, however, following the death in the ring of a local boxing hero, the sport's popularity declined rapidly in New Orleans.

The center of boxing shifted back to metropolitan New York. In 1892, boxing was revived at Coney Island, under the protection of Brooklyn's Democratic bosses, who owned the most notable arenas. Four years later, Democratic state senator Tim Sullivan, who controlled New York City's most important boxing arenas, secured passage of the Horton Act, permitting sparring matches in buildings owned by athletic clubs. Sullivan was the number-two man in the powerful Tammany Hall machine. Over the next few years, hundreds of prizefights, including several championships, were fought in Greater New York (Brooklyn and New York merged in 1898). In 1900, however, conservative upstate Republicans, who controlled the state government, opposed prizefighting on moral and political grounds and repealed the Horton Act. Championship bouts in New

York were halted, although the sport survived under the guise of politically connected "membership clubs," private organizations that were permitted to stage weekly three-round matches between members for the entertainment of other members. This was simply a ploy to evade the law, because anyone who paid a $1 fee could join the club and watch the fight.

Prize fighting struggled in the early 1900s. In Philadelphia and Chicago, the police permitted bouts that went no longer than six rounds. Chicago's reformers worked hard to end all professional boxing, especially after a 1900 match between featherweight champion Terrible Terry McGovern and the rising African American star Joe Gans, who had a hard time getting good fights. Gans blatantly threw the fight which ended in the second round, killing public confidence in boxing in Chicago. In 1905 the city banned prize fighting, which was not resumed until 1926. In the 1900s the national center of boxing shifted west to San Francisco, where machine boss Abe Reuf protected the city's twenty-round championship bouts that he promoted. However, he went to jail in 1907 for corruption stemming from his events.

In 1911 New York regained its preeminence in prizefighting following a Democratic sweep in the state elections. The legislature passed the Frawley Act, legalizing ten-round, no-decision contests supervised by a state athletic commission. This was a big advantage for champions, since they could not lose their crown unless knocked out. Bettors did not like this system because so many fights ended in a draw, so the custom developed for bettors and bookmakers to rely on the judgment of sportswriters to determine winners and losers. Matches between inexperienced and less-well-known pugilists were staged in small gyms located in lower-class residential neighborhoods, but the big bouts headlined by contenders and champions were held in large midtown arenas, such as Madison Square Garden, in the heart of New York City's entertainment district. The second Madison Square Garden was built in 1890 on the site of the old Garden by renowned architect Stanford White at a cost of $3 million. It was the second tallest building in the city and seated 8,000.

Boxing crowds were exclusively male, and often rowdy, particularly in small neighborhood gyms. Spectators there sat close to the action and bet heavily, often on local ethnic heroes with whom they identified. Promoters recognized the value of matching a Jewish fighter against an Irishman or an Italian against either of them. Riots occurred periodically because excited fans brought with them traditional animosities and longstanding rivalries that heated up during interethnic bouts. Fans would throw chairs into the ring, seconds would jump into the ring, and fistfights would break out among spectators. Riots occurred for other reasons as well, even at big arenas, because of unadvertised price increases, inadequate security, and overcrowding, not to mention unpopular decisions by the referee, or an obvious fix.

The boxing revival was short lived. In 1917 the sport was again banned by antiurban, upstate Republicans who sought to regulate the behavior of New York's foreign-stock population. They also hoped to limit the power of those Tammany Hall politicians (and their hoodlum friends) who promoted the sport and controlled prizefighters. In 1917, prizefighting was legal in twenty-three states, but the sport was severely restricted in its major markets. Even San Francisco, a city tolerant of boxing in the early 1900s, only permitted four-round bouts.

During World War I boxing's image improved considerably because it was used for training soldiers. Consequently, a lot of the press after the war, including the reform-minded *New York Times*, supported Democratic state senator James J. Walker's campaign to restore prizefighting as well as lift other restrictions on the personal freedom of returning veterans. In 1920, Governor Al Smith, a liberal member of the Tammany machine, and very supportive of his working-class constituency, signed the Walker Act, which reestablished a boxing commission and permitted twelve-round fights to a decision for the first time. New York immediately regained its position as the national center of boxing. Madison Square Garden, a financial white elephant for years, became the mecca for prizefighting under its new boxing impresario Tex Rickard, promoter of the Johnson-Jeffries fight of 1910. Championship matches at the Garden in the 1920s drew record crowds and were glamorous social events attracting the rich and famous, men in their tuxedos as well as, for the first time, women, who arrived in evening gowns.

Thoroughbred Racing

If prizefighting was the sport of pugs, horse racing was the sport of kings. Thoroughbred racing revived after the Civil War in the North under the leadership of the upper class who enjoyed the social and competitive aspects of racing. They used their political connections to keep the sport operating despite renewed moral opposition. Critical reformers castigated racing and sought to ban it because of the betting that went along with the sport. Furthermore, animals were abused, races were fixed, and, in addition, racing had close connections to machine politicians and syndicate crime organizations that ran illegal off-track betting at downtown poolrooms and provided race results to bookmakers in residential working-class neighborhoods. The political connections of the racing world were especially prominent in New York, the national center of American racing in the late nineteenth century. Its local racing scene was dominated by politically active elites and their associates in Tammany Hall.

The Racetracks
The first major thoroughbred racecourse to open after the war was New York's $530,000 Jerome Park in 1866, operated by the elite American Jockey Club. The club's original members included financier and national Democratic Party chairman August Belmont as well as the notorious William Tweed, the crooked boss of Tammany Hall. The AJC made several important innovations in racing, most notably the dropping of long-distance heat racing for the English dash system that permitted more races each day (facilitating more betting), and enabled horses to run more frequently. The AJC also established handicapping events and the second oldest permanent stakes, the Belmont Stakes in 1867.

Wagering at Jerome Park was originally conducted by auction pools. Pool makers organized several betting pools in which they "auctioned" off the choice of horses in a particular race to the highest bidder. Then they auctioned off the other horses in the race. Pool makers took 5 to 10 percent off the top, and distributed the balance to the winning bettor. This system worked well for rich bettors who could outbid other gamblers for the favorite, which won about 40 percent of the time. Small bettors were at a big disadvantage.

In 1871 Jerome Park introduced the French pari-mutuel system, invented in 1865 by Pierre Oller of Paris. Bettors could wager on any horse in a given race, and the odds were determined by the amount of money wagered on each steed. Bettors holding winning tickets split the pool, less a 5 percent fee to the track or its agent who ran the pool. This system seemed more democratic than the auction, because everyone could bet on the more popular horses. The system did not catch on, however. Heavy bettors disliked it because they lost the advantage they had in the auction pools, plus their big bets would drive odds down, while poorer participants deplored it because major tracks required a minimum $5 bet, and offered no credit. Jerome Park dropped the pari-mutuels in 1878, though it was soon adopted by elite tracks in Louisville, Baltimore, Washington, and Chicago.

In 1877 New York State banned auction pools following the heavy betting on the scandal-ridden Tilden-Hayes presidential election of 1876. The pools were replaced by bookmaking, which by the early 1880s became the dominant form of betting at American racecourses by making the betting more accessible. Bookmakers rented space at the tracks where they set up a stall, posted their own odds on all horses in each race, and recorded the wagers in a notebook. They tried to set the odds at numbers that would create a "balanced book" so that any payout would not exceed the amount bet for that race, in which case they had to personally make up the difference. Bettors preferred this system since they paid little or no commission at first (though it soon rose to 3–5 percent), could bet for just two $2, knew the odds upfront, and could also bet on second-place horses ("place" bets).

The elite tracks were very successful, which encouraged entrepreneurs to establish proprietary tracks such as Brooklyn's Brighton Beach in 1879, which generated a $200,000 profit by its third year, and Gravesend, which opened in 1885. The success of New York racing over the next twenty-five years was a product of the political clout of leading elite Democratic horsemen such as transit magnates William C. Whitney and August Belmont II and such prominent Democratic Irish American sportsmen as Tammany boss Richard Croker and his colleague Tim Sullivan. These men all raced horses and used that common interest to form a coalition that worked together to protect horse racing and on-track betting in New York State.

Their political clout enabled the passage in 1887 of the Ives Act, which legitimized the right of tracks to permit gambling on their races for sixty days, while reinforcing the ban on off-track racing. Seven years later, the opponents of racing took advantage of the state constitutional convention to redraw an article of the Constitution to ban all gambling on racing; this ban would have killed the sport. However, in early 1895, the state legislature passed the Gray-Percy Act that contradicted the gambling ban in the constitution to permit betting exclusively at racetracks, making off-track betting a felony. The act put the sport under the control of the State Racing Commission, the first state agency to regulate any sport, in cooperation with The Jockey Club, a private elite organization established one year earlier to license owners of racing horses, trainers, jockeys, and racetracks, allot racing dates, and blacklist anyone who cheated or did not accept its authority from member tracks. In addition, a 5 percent tax was imposed on the net earnings of all New York tracks.

Racetracks required an enormous amount of space. Racing ovals alone ranged from one-half to one-and-a-half miles, except for the outlaw tracks (courses operated independently of any regulatory agency), which seldom raced more than a few months a year. Racecourses were the least accessible semi-public sporting facilities, located on the urban periphery or in suburbs where land was relatively cheap. The rich might ride out to the racecourse in elegant carriages, but most fans traveled by mass transit or commuter railroads. For most of the nineteenth century, New York's elite tracks were a one-hour train ride from midtown Manhattan, although they were usually closer to midtown in other cities. Two exceptions were Monmouth and Saratoga, located respectively in distant resort areas (Long Branch, New Jersey, and Saratoga Springs, New York), that were several hours away from any major metropolis, which required a long railroad ride to reach. Profit-oriented tracks that sought lower-class crowds were typically located nearer to the heart of population centers than were the high-prestige courses. For example, in the early 1890s, New Jersey's Guttenberg was a short ferry ride from the West Side of Manhattan, and Chicago's Garfield Park was a five-cent, thirty-minute ride from the Loop.

Racetrack ambience varied substantially from lavishly appointed, elegant clubhouses of elite tracks to spartan facilities at the plebeian tracks. Jerome Park set a high standard with its clubhouse that was comparable to a luxury hotel. It had an elegant ballroom and dining room, and bedrooms for overnight stays. The most prestigious tracks, such as Brooklyn's $135,000 Sheepshead Bay, Chicago's $150,000 Washington Park, and New York's $2.4 million Belmont Park, had large grandstands with separate sections for jockey club members, women, and the masses. A grandstand seat was priced at $2 to $3, which discouraged class intermingling. The masses were confined to the seventy-five-cent standing room in the infield. Races with major stakes at elite tracks, such as the Futurity in Brooklyn, the Belmont in New York, and the American Derby in Chicago, were great attractions, drawing as many as 40,000 spectators in the 1890s and 1900s. The single richest race was the Futurity at the Sheepshead Bay Racetrack, with a purse of $77,000 in 1890, of which $60,274 went to the winner, Potomac. By comparison, plebeian tracks charged as little as fifty cents for admission, and outlaw tracks often opened the infield for free to encourage wagering. Crowd control was rarely a problem at the finest tracks, which were patrolled by Pinkerton detectives. Lesser tracks drew rougher crowds, which included petty criminals and prostitutes.

Reformers Close the Tracks
Despite the political clout of racecourse operators, nearly all major tracks were forced to close, briefly in some states, and for decades in others. A broad-based coalition of moral reformers like Anthony Comstock of the Society for the Suppression of Vice, Rev. Howard Crosby and Rev. Charles H. Parkhurst of the Society for the Prevention of Crime, and members of various civic reform groups and antigambling leagues in the late nineteenth century led the way in fighting horse gambling. They were joined by progressive reformers in the early 1900s. The movement was a great success, and it nearly killed thoroughbred racing in the United States.

The reformers made a major breakthrough in the early 1890s against the illegal outlaw tracks. One of the first major lowlife tracks to close was Garfield Park in Chicago. It was located on the West Side of Chicago and owned by the politically connected Mike McDonald, the boss of Chicago's underworld and his fellow Democratic bookmakers. They opened the "bookmaker's track" in 1891, after having forced the prior owner to relocate, and made over $500,000 in two years. Garfield Park attracted a lot of public criticism because it held races nearly year-round—even in snowstorms—which were often of questionable integrity, cruel to the animals, and attracted the demi-monde. In 1892 reform Mayor Hempstead Washburne, a Republican, refused to license the track. When the police arrived to halt operations, a deadly gun fight broke out between the police and stable owner Capt. James Brown, a former Texas Ranger, who was shot to death. Garfield Park never reopened.

New Jersey at this time had one elite track, Monmouth Park, and five proprietary racecourses. The latter were all run by politicians and bookmakers, including the notorious outlaw tracks, Guttenberg, located just across the Hudson River from New York City, and Gloucester, outside of Philadelphia. These tracks ran year-round, rain or shine, and were renowned for fixed races. Their Democrat owners controlled the state legislature in 1893, and were presumed to be omnipotent. However, political reformers made racing a major campaign issue that year, and in a surprising upset the Republicans gained control of the state government and closed the tracks. Racing in New Jersey did not resume until 1942.

Gambling was the lifeblood of racing, and reformers knew that racetracks could not survive without it. In Chicago, the Midwestern center of racing, reformers followed up the closing of Garfield Park in 1892 by going after the prestigious Washington Park, whose jockey club was comprised of many of the city's millionaires. They succeeded in closing the track in 1894 and the other area tracks in 1895. Chicago had no racing until 1897, and one year later Washington Park and Hawthorne reopened. Then, after the 1904 season, a coalition of progressives and evangelical ministers got the authorities to enforce the anti-gambling laws, and there was no more racing until the 1920s.

By 1908, 289 of 314 American tracks had been closed for varying periods of time, including such racing centers as St. Louis and New Orleans. New York's courses were under considerable pressure to shut down, especially from Governor Charles Evans Hughes, a progressive stickler for the laws, who believed that the Percy-Gray legislation was unconstitutional. The upstate Republicans passed a law in 1908 terminating on-course gambling, but the racing men managed to circumvent it for two years because of their political influence. However, once the Agnew-Perkins Act of 1910 made track managers personally liable for gambling at their courses, all the state's tracks closed, and the three courses in Brooklyn never reopened. This left Maryland and Kentucky as the only major racing states, which was when the Kentucky Derby, run since 1875, first became the leading race in the United States. In 1913, the track managers found a way to circumvent the laws, and racing returned to New York.

Racetrack wagering was widely criticized as immoral, but at least bettors attended the races and thereby supported the sport. Virtually no one had a good word for off-track betting. It was an illegal enterprise, but was considered a victimless crime, so there was not the same pressure on the criminal justice system to halt it compared to crimes that victimized individuals, like robbery, burglary, assault, rape, or murder. Moral reformers may have considered bookmakers leeches who preyed on their fellow man, but in their neighborhoods many residents saw "bookies" as providing a valuable service for their customers. In any case, progressive reformers like District Attorney Jerome vigorously tried to halt the gambling.

Downtown poolrooms mainly attracted office workers, although some of the more elegant rooms did have a more upscale clientele, and a few rooms catered to women. Poolrooms in vice districts and residential neighborhood were said to service skilled and semiskilled workmen. Bookmakers in the inner city worked the streets and saloons, focusing on the ethnic working class, who made smaller bets, wanted credit, and accepted less favorable odds than those given at the tracks. Off-track gamblers saved time and money by betting with their local bookmakers instead of attending the races. In addition, they could bet year-round on races all over North America.

The poolrooms and generally the bookmakers were protected by Tammany political bosses and local police who worked with the crime syndicates that controlled the off-track betting business. They provided the underworld with advance warning about raids and protection against harassment, arrests, and convictions. Organized crime made more money from horse-race gambling at the turn of the century than from any other source. Gangsters provided access to the racing wire that provided speedy information about race results, the muscle to collect debts, payoffs to prevent police interference, and attorneys to fight indictments. The poolroom business in New York was particularly closely controlled by the "Gambling Trust" that included Sen. Tim Sullivan, former police chief William Devery, and gambling kingpin Frank Farrell. Their syndicate reportedly made over $3 million a year and nearly monopolized the city's poolroom business. No one could enter the business without their approval and making regular payments. Otherwise, the police *would* raid their rooms.

Thoroughbred racing struggled during the 1910s, but the sport revived dramatically after World War I when peace and prosperity returned. People were earning more than ever during the 1920s while working shorter hours, and they wanted some excitement in their lives. In addition, the public interest was captured by the presence of outstanding thoroughbreds, like Sir Barton, who in 1919 won the Kentucky Derby, the Preakness, and the Belmont Stakes, a feat that subsequently became known as the Triple Crown. He was surpassed by Man o'War, probably the greatest horse of all time, whose only loss came to a stallion ironically named Upset. Furthermore, the looser morality of the 1920s looked less askance at legal gambling than before. Between 1918 and 1920 purses doubled, and they redoubled by 1926, to $13.9 million, which led to a 60 percent increase in the number of thoroughbreds during the 1920s. Among the states that legalized pari-mutuels were Maryland, Louisiana, and Illinois, and also the Dominion of Canada. They made this move due to several factors, most notably the continued clout of Irish machine politicians and the growing political influence of their ethnic constituents, who enjoyed gambling and opposed traditional moral values being imposed upon them. In addition, state legislatures were under greater pressure from jockey clubs, breeders, and organized crime to legitimize the sport. Furthermore, several states saw racing as an untapped source of revenue that promoted tourism and generated taxes on racetrack admissions, winning wagers, and track profits.

Professional Baseball

The commercialization of baseball began in 1862 when Brooklynite William Cammeyer enclosed his skating rink, which became the Union Grounds. He allowed local teams to play for free, charging ten cents admission to spectators. The public was already accustomed to paying for other forms of entertainment, and spectators had paid to attend the 1858 all-star series between New York and Brooklyn players to defray expenses. Cammeyer and other early promoters expected ticket sales would cover the cost of operating the field, provide a profit, and discourage the presence of rowdy fans. Teams were increasingly concerned about winning, and a championship system began in metropolitan New York. Teams competed for top players such as pitcher James Creighton, who in 1860 was recruited by the Brooklyn Excelsiors with financial incentives, making him the first professional baseball player. In the past, cricket clubs had hired bowlers, but the National Association of Base Ball Players (NABBP) opposed professionalism because it was considered unfair to amateurs who did not devote their complete attention to sport.

Historians still debate the impact of the Civil War on baseball, which was set to boom when the conflict started. During the war, baseball on the home front struggled in its main sites, like metropolitan New York as many of the top players went off to war. There was a lot of ball played in military camps and even some in military prisons, as we know from correspondence with the home front. A game in 1862 between two New York units was reportedly attended by 40,000 people, likely a large exaggeration.

There was an enormous postwar boom in baseball, partly a consequence of its increased national exposure in Civil War camps. By the late 1860s, more than two thousand organized clubs existed, mostly in the Northeast, of which thirteen were professional. Crowds approaching fifteen thousand were soon reported at major contests. The professional teams played over fifty games a year, including out-of-town contests. Players were paid in cash, given a political sinecure, or received some other form of compensation. Top teams, such as the Brooklyn Atlantics, raised ticket prices to twenty-five cents in 1867 and fifty cents three years later (one year after announcing themselves as professionals).

The first openly all-salaried team was the Cincinnati Red Stockings of 1869, organized by local boosters to bring fame and prestige to the city. The club became enormously successful under the leadership of manager Harry Wright, a former cricket player. The "father of professional baseball," Wright was a shrewd judge of talent who recruited players, mainly metropolitan New Yorkers, for annual salaries ranging from $600 to $2,000, and molded them into a powerful machine. The club toured the East in 1869, finishing with a remarkable record of 57–0–1, drawing about two hundred thousand spectators, but barely broke even. The tie game came against John Morrissey's Troy (New York) Haymakers in a game on which he and his friends had reportedly bet $60,000. With the score at 17–17, an argument occurred over a foul tip. Morrissey ordered the Troy team off the field, which ended the game and voided the wager.

Cincinnati's success encouraged urban boosters elsewhere, most notably in Chicago, to recruit professionals. In 1870 the Reds won their first twenty-seven games before losing to the Brooklyn Atlantics 8–7 in an extra-inning contest marred by fan interference. But the Red Stockings were not making money, and following a loss to the Chicago White Stockings, a professional squad also backed by hometown boosters, management decided to cut expenses, and went amateur the following season.

By the end of 1870 the NABBP was in disarray. The amateurs split off because of commercialization, professionalization, and fears of gambling and fixed contests. In 1871 a nine-team National Association of Professional Base Ball Players (NA) began play under NABBP rules, charging only $10 for a franchise. Each team arranged its own schedule. Most members were joint-stock companies that paid regular salaries. The weaker teams were generally cooperatives whose players got a share of the gate instead of a salary. The stock clubs charged fifty cents admission, and the coops twenty-five cents. The National Association lasted only five years because it could not resolve several serious weaknesses. Problems included players jumping to other teams, weak competition, rumors of fixes, inept leadership, and minimal admission requirements that permitted too many small cities, such as Keokuk, Iowa, and Troy, New York, into the league.

Most association teams were weak, unstable, and rarely broke even. In 1872, for instance, five of eleven teams did not even complete the season. The only real pennant race was in 1871 when the Philadelphia Athletics (22–7) edged the Boston Red Stockings (22–10). Thereafter Boston completely dominated, taking the next four pennants, including a remarkable 71–8 season in 1875. The team was managed by Harry Wright, who had brought over with him most of his old Cincinnati club. Wright emphasized a spartan training regimen, discipline, fundamentals, pregame batting and fielding practice, teamwork, and strategy. He handled players as individuals and used salary as a motivator. Wright also controlled the club's $35,000 budget, arranged the schedule and transportation, and supervised groundskeeping and advertising.

Association players made $1,300–$1,600, about four times the typical nonagricultural worker, with stars getting up to $2,500. Their social origins were similar to the leading amateur players from whose ranks they were drawn. Virtually all (over 90 percent) were American born, and predominantly of native-born white American ancestry. Over four-fifths (83 percent) came from cities at a time when only one-fourth of the national population was urban. Players were drawn especially from Baltimore, Brooklyn, New York, and Philadelphia, all leading centers of amateur and professional baseball. Three-fifths of New York and Brooklyn professionals were previously artisans, and the rest were lower-level white-collar workers.

The Rise of the National League

In 1876 the National Association of Professional Base Ball Players was supplanted by the more profit-oriented National League of Professional Base Ball Clubs (NL). The National League sought to operate on sounder business principles. As reflected by its title, it was a league of "clubs" rather than of "players." The league's first president was politician Morgan Bulkeley (a future U.S. senator) who owned the Harford Blues franchise, but the main man behind the league was William Hulbert (NL president, 1877–82), a member of the Chicago Board of Trade and owner of the Chicago White Stockings. The eight-team NL sought to avoid its predecessor's weaknesses. A franchise cost $100, instead of $10, and member cities were required to have a minimum of 75,000 inhabitants. The league office arranged schedules so that all teams played each other the same number of times, made rule changes, dealt with disputes, and supervised paid umpires. Each franchise was guaranteed exclusive rights in their hometown. The National League sought to bolster its image by waging a moral crusade to ban gambling, Sunday ball, drunkenness, and rowdy behavior; and encouraging decorum and respectability by attracting women to attend games with ladies' day promotions. Admission cost fifty cents.

The new circuit was not an instant success. Only Chicago made money in 1876, and New York and Philadelphia were expelled for not completing late-season western road trips. A number of teams came and went in the first few years, including Troy, added in 1879 even though the city's population was below the stated minimum. One year later Cincinnati was ousted for refusing to ban Sunday games or liquor sales. There were fifteen different clubs in the first four years of the new league, and by 1881 Boston and Chicago were the only surviving original franchises. The National League was also beset by corruption and competition from professionals outside the league, including the loosely knit International Association. The front-running Louisville Grays lost the pennant in 1877 because four prominent players fixed games. The players were immediately expelled for life. This was not the first time players had been caught throwing games. In 1865, three members of the New York Mutuals, a team sponsored by Tammany Hall, were expelled from the NABBP for having thrown a game against the Eckfords, and in 1876 George Bechtel of the Grays was banned for taking $500 to conspire with teammates to throw a game.

National League owners devoted considerable attention to labor relations because salaries comprised over 60 percent of team budgets. They increased control over employees by introducing the reserve clause in 1879, which gave teams an option to renew, trade, or release a player without any reciprocity on the team's part. The league argued that this policy encouraged fairer competition by preventing richer clubs from hiring all the best players. As a result, ballplayers lost any leverage they might have had negotiating contracts. The new policy helped teams to make money in the 1880s.

Management was also concerned about controlling players' behavior so that they would perform at their best, as well as do no harm to the sport's shaky public image. Ballplayers were young men, often bachelors, who liked to chase women, drink, and gamble, and not all of them had disciplined work habits. Consequently, management tried to impose a strict regimen through the uniform players' contract, which stipulated heavy fines and suspensions for poor play, lost equipment, and disorderly behavior on or off the field. These fines also helped management recoup some expenses. Then in 1881, management began to blacklist players for dissipation or insubordination. During the mid-1880s, White Stockings president Albert G. Spalding fostered respectability by fighting his players' gambling and drinking by giving certain players bonuses to stop drinking and also hiring detectives to spy on them. In 1886, Spalding accused superstar catcher Mike "King" Kelly of drinking lemonade in a saloon after midnight. Kelly did not deny being there, but he took umbrage to the unmanly accusation that he had been imbibing lemonade. Spalding sold him the next season to Boston for the unheard of sum of $10,000.

In 1882 the National League's major-league monopoly was challenged by the American Association (AA), organized mainly by entrepreneurs in the beer business who recognized the growing profit potential of baseball and the opportunities it presented for selling their beverages. The AA started with six clubs in major markets (Baltimore, Cincinnati, Louisville, Philadelphia, Pittsburgh, and St. Louis) of which only St. Louis had a NL franchise. The combined population of the six AA cities was 500,000 more than the combined population of the eight NL ones. The AA structured its operations to draw a massive working-class audience by setting the basic ticket price at twenty-five cents, permitting Sunday ball, and selling liquor at games.

The two leagues fought for control of ballplayers and markets, and a baseball war ensued as the AA hired contract jumpers and blacklisted NL players. The AA became very popular, and five of its six teams outdrew the Chicago White Stockings, whose gate receipts tripled that of any other National League team. In 1883, the AA added teams in New York and Columbus, and the NL responded by dropping Troy and Worcester, Massachusetts, in favor of Philadelphia and New York. This change put the NL head-to-head with the AA in the nation's two largest cities. Nearly all AA teams made money that year, led by Philadelphia's seventy-five thousand dollars, while the National League clubs averaged $20,000 in profits. The leagues made peace after the season by signing a national agreement, and merging in February 1884. They recognized each other's contracts, initiated a postseason championship, or "World Series," and together with the minor Northwestern League, set up an arbitration committee to settle disputes.

The White Stockings, who captured three straight National League pennants between 1880 and 1882 and three more between 1884 and 1886, and the American Association's St. Louis Browns, who won four straight pennants between 1885 and 1888, dominated the 1880s. The Browns were owned by "Der Boss President," Chris Van der Ahe, who went into baseball to sell beer, while Chicago's Spalding, the National League's most influential owner, was becoming a renowned sporting goods manufacturer. The White Stockings continued to draw the largest crowds in its league with such stars as charismatic catcher Mike "King" Kelly, fellow Hall of Famer, manager, and first baseman Adrian "Cap" Anson, who played twenty-seven seasons, batting .334 with 3,435 hits, and Ed Williamson, whose twenty-seven home runs in 1884 was a record until 1919. The White Stockings were the most profitable team, with net returns often surpassing 20 percent. By 1887 they had accumulated a $100,000 surplus, and along with Boston and New York, were grossing nearly $100,000 a year. Overall, the National League made $750,000 in the period between 1885 and 1889, a 300 percent increase over the early 1880s. By contrast, players' salaries rose by just 30 percent.

The modern character of baseball was largely established by the 1880s. Important improvements in equipment were introduced, including the catcher's mask and chest protector, shin guards, and small, lightly padded, pocketless gloves. Tactics stressed "inside baseball" (sacrifices, place hitting, stealing, hit and run, fielders backing up their teammates, and infielders playing off the base) and physically rough play. Most modern regulations were already in place, although rule makers struggled to maintain a balance between offense and defense to keep the sport exciting and entertaining. In prior years the offense had the upper hand. When pitchers had to throw underhand, the batter could request a "high" or "low" ball, and fielding was difficult with poor gloves. In the 1880s new regulations gave the advantage to pitchers, who stood only fifty feet from the batter. Pitchers were now allowed to throw overhand and use deceptive deliveries to confuse the batter. In 1887 the modern strike zone was introduced and foul balls could be counted as strikes (though they usually were not). Walks that season counted as hits, greatly inflating batting averages. Two years later, the modern three-strike, four-ball rule was established. In 1894 the balance shifted back to the offense when the pitcher's mound was pushed back to the present sixty feet, six inches, resulting in a thirty-five point increase in batting averages to .309.

Hall of Famer Mike Kelly, the most colorful, popular, and resourceful ballplayer of his day, would try anything to win. If Kelly caught the lone umpire following a base hit to the outfield, he would run from first base to third across the pitcher's mound, bypassing second, or even from second straight to home. According to legend, Kelly often dropped his catcher's mask along the third-base line to hamper runners coming home. In one game he took advantage of substitution rules that required the replacement to notify the umpire; he leapt off the bench, announced "Kelly now catching," and caught a foul ball for an out. Folklorist Tristram Coffin claimed Kelly's greatest stunt occurred while playing right field in the twelfth inning of a late-afternoon game when it was getting dark. There were two out, the bases were loaded, and a shot was hit over Kelly's head. He raced back, far beyond the vision of the umpire, leaped up, shook his glove in satisfaction, and jogged in to the bench. The batter was called out, and the game was suspended because of darkness. His teammates slapped his back and said "Nice catch, Kell." "Not at all," responded their hero, "Twent a mile above my head."

In 1885, player dissatisfaction with the reserve clause and a new twenty-five hundred dollar salary limit (often broken for stars such as Kelly, who in 1887 signed a contract with Boston for two thousand dollars, plus an additional three thousand dollars as team captain for a photograph he sold the owners) resulted in the formation of the Brotherhood of Professional Base Ball Players. Led by attorney John Montgomery Ward, the Giants shortstop, who had formerly been a great pitcher until an arm injury, it was the first sports union. Following the profitable 1889 season when most teams set attendance records, the underpaid players struck back. The 107-member Brotherhood established a separate league, the Players' League (PL), governed by a committee of players and capitalists who invested in the new teams. The new league had no reserve clause or salary classification and players were guaranteed salaries based on 1888 wages plus a share in any profits that exceeded ten thousand dollars per team. The new league was supported by trade unions and the preeminent baseball weeklies, *Sporting Life* and *The Sporting News*. Ironically the PL did not seek working-class fans, preferring spectators who could afford fifty-cent tickets.

The Players' League was a serious threat to organized baseball. Two hundred major leaguers, including nearly all the best players, jumped to the new league, while the NL only held on to thirty-eight veterans. The National League and American Association established a war committee under Spalding, whose *Baseball Guide* chastised the newcomers as socialists and anarchists. Spalding pressured newspapers by threatening to pull his company's advertisements from papers that supported the interlopers. Organized baseball compiled a $250,000 war chest to bribe PL stars to return, sue contract jumpers, and hire thugs to intimidate Brotherhood fans. Members of the Brotherhood stood fast, including Mike Kelly, who turned down a ten thousand dollar offer out of loyalty to "the boys."

Attendance figures for 1890 were inflated by frequent ladies' days and lots of free passes, not to mention false reports. The best estimate is that the Players' League outdrew the National League, averaging 1,850 per game to 1,500. But it was a Pyrrhic victory. Fans were turned off by the bickering in baseball. The PL ran a $385,000 deficit, mostly to pay for new ballparks, while estimated NL losses ranged from $231,000 to $500,000, and the AA teams in Brooklyn and Philadelphia went bankrupt. The Brotherhood players and their backers were dismayed by the balance sheet, and after the season the National League co-opted their rival's financial angels. Except for Buffalo, where there was no competing major-league team, the other PL stockholders sold out to the local NL team, or else merged with them or bought them out. Spalding outsmarted and outmaneuvered the Brotherhood. The Players' League failed to overcome the disadvantages of starting from scratch, and players put too much trust in the capitalists, who had their own agendas.

The baseball peace was short lived, for in 1891 American Association and National League relations collapsed when the latter reneged on an agreement to return players to their original clubs. After a financially difficult year, the leagues negotiated a dramatic settlement. The National League absorbed four of the American Association teams and bought out the other four clubs for $130,000. The enlarged, reinvigorated National League maintained its fifty-cent ticket price (with a few exceptions) and adopted Sunday ball in cities where it was legal. Players were badly hurt by the consolidation, which eliminated 25 percent of major-league jobs. Furthermore, a new $2,400 salary cap was introduced, and with fewer positions available, it was strictly maintained. By 1893 salaries had dropped between 30 and 40 percent as owners tried to recoup losses from the previous years. Cincinnati's popular pitcher Tony Mullane balked at the cuts and held out for half a season before signing for $2,100, one-half his 1891 salary. This helped make the NL profitable from 1893 to 1895 despite the depression of 1893.

The National League struggled on for the next few years, hurt by the long-term effects of the depression and also by a lack of competition in a twelve-team league. Attendance in the 1890s probably averaged slightly more than two thousand per game, significantly below the National League average for the nineteenth century of about twenty-six hundred per game. Only three teams, Boston, Baltimore, and Brooklyn, all renowned for inside baseball, won pennants between 1891and 1900. On the other side, Louisville and St. Louis always finished in the bottom third, and Washington escaped the low ranks but once.

Another problem that emerged at the end of the decade was syndicate baseball, a situation in which the same owners controlled two different teams. For example, in 1898 the Baltimore Orioles owner secured a major share of the Brooklyn Bridegrooms (today's Dodgers). Orioles' manager Ed Hanlon moved over to the Brooklyn franchise and brought along his star players, who helped the team, renamed the Superbas, win pennants in 1899 and 1900. Another product of syndicate baseball was the Cleveland Spiders, who set an all-time record for futility in 1899 with a dismal 20-134 season. The team collapsed after owner Stanley Robison shipped all his best players to brother Frank's newly purchased St. Louis Browns. Alienated Cleveland fans boycotted the team (attendance through June averaged less than two hundred), and the Spiders responded by rescheduling their late-season games out of town.

The National League tried to cope with its problems after the 1899 season by further consolidation, lopping off Baltimore and three of its weakest teams, Louisville, Washington, and Cleveland. The eight-team league (Boston, Brooklyn, Chicago, Cincinnati, New York, Philadelphia, Pittsburgh, and St. Louis) became extremely stable, and the National League had no more franchise shifts until 1953.

Baseball in the Early Twentieth Century

The small number of franchises, an excess of experienced major leaguers, a lack of cohesion among bickering National League owners, and poor leadership from league headquarters opened the door for a rival major league to emerge. In 1901 the American League (known until 1900 as the minor Western League) proclaimed itself a major league with eight teams, including franchises in three of the recently dropped National League cities (Washington, Cleveland, and Baltimore). Under the strong and aggressive direction of President Ban Johnson, the American League successfully filled its rosters with seasoned ballplayers. Eighty-two veterans jumped from the National League in the first two years; over 60 percent of American League players had major-league experience. The American League immediately went head-to-head in competition with the National League in Boston, Chicago, and Philadelphia. One year later it vied with the National League in St. Louis (replacing Milwaukee), and two years later, in New York (replacing Baltimore). Securing a New York franchise was considered crucial for certifying the American League's major-league status and its financial success. It was a difficult task, however, because Giants owner millionaire Andrew Freedman, a prominent, well connected Tammany realtor, used his substantial clout to keep out competition even after he sold his club in 1902 to John Brush. No suitable site for a ball field could be found until President Johnson awarded a franchise to influential local Tammanyites, ex-police chief William Devery and gambler Frank Farrell for $18,000.

Competition for players between the leagues raised salaries, cut profits, and brought the National League to the bargaining table. The leagues signed a new National Agreement in 1903 that recognized the American League and its contracts. The National Commission was established to control organized baseball (which consisted of the major and minor leagues), and the minor leagues were classified for the purpose of drafting players. The Commission consisted of the two league presidents (Ban Johnson and Harry Pulliam of the NL) and a third party they selected, President August Herrmann of the Cincinnati Reds, who served as chairman (1903–1920). The commission's main achievements included the creation of the World Series in 1903, resolving conflicts over players' contracts, disciplining players, and supporting the authority of umpires.

The rise of the American League symbolized baseball's booming popularity, which surpassed that of all other sports at the turn of the century. America's fascination with the game was reflected and promoted by extensive coverage in the daily press, popular magazines, sporting weeklies, and specialized monthlies such as *Baseball Magazine* (1908). The press provided extensive game reports, in-season and postseason gossip, and feature stories analyzing everything from the business of baseball to the physics of the curve ball. Baseball became a staple of fiction, ranging from Burt Standish's juvenile Frank Merriwell series (he starred in five sports in high school and Yale, always winning the game at a last moment, and always the perfect Christian gentlemen, who does not smoke or drink and always protects the weak) to Ring Lardner's humorous short stories such as *Alibi Ike* (1915) about a Chicago White Sox who always finds excuses for his errant play. Baseball's popularity was also evidenced by the doubling of major-league attendance between 1901 and 1909 and the national expansion of professional baseball. The minor leagues grew from thirteen leagues in 1900 to forty-six in 1912, leaving few cities without professional baseball. Even Saugerties, New York, population seven thousand, had a team in the Class D Hudson River League.

Professional baseball's unsurpassed popularity was a result of several factors. It begins with the fact that the game was widely played and was fun to play and watch. Spectators who had grown up playing baseball could watch high drama in well-played competitive contests that only took about two hours. Fans at the ballpark participated in the rituals of spectatorship, which included rooting for the home team, yelling at the umpire and the opposition, eating hot dogs, and drinking beer. Even fans who seldom or never attended ball games could follow the day-by-day achievements of their heroes and favorite teams through the daily press.

Baseball's popularity was also a consequence of how well it fit in with prevailing American values and beliefs. Native-born white Americans in the Progressive Era worried that the growth of industries, cities, bureaucracies, and the immigrant population was creating a distended society whose future was in doubt. The popular press, baseball guides, and juvenile literature conveyed a new baseball ideology which characterized baseball as a game of pastoral American origins that improved health, character, and morality. Furthermore, the baseball creed asserted that baseball fostered the American myths of agrarianism, social democracy, and social integration.

The baseball creed also coincided with the prevailing broad-based progressive ethos that promoted order, traditional values, efficiency, and Americanization by looking back to an idealized past. The game's history and folklore expressed some of society's main values and goals. Baseball fostered social integration by promoting acculturation and hometown pride, teaching respect for authority, and giving factory workers much-needed outdoor exercise and diversion.

The game was said to exemplify democracy because people from different social backgrounds sat together at the ballpark, which would reduce class tensions, promote democratic feelings, and provide plebeians a model of proper behavior to emulate. Baseball was also believed to epitomize democracy since player recruitment and retention was based solely on merit. Because only talent, not social origins, counted, observers assumed that professional baseball was a route of social mobility.

Identified as a rural game, baseball supposedly built character and developed such traditional qualities as fair play, discipline, and rugged individualism. It extended small-town life into cities, where playing and watching the game helped indoctrinate newcomers. Yet at the same time baseball was also perceived as a means to teach boys modern values such as teamwork and self-sacrifice, as exemplified by a crisp double play or a sacrifice bunt. Such traits were considered essential for future bureaucrats and factory workers. Youngsters supposedly learned such behavior by playing and watching baseball and emulating heroes such as Christy Mathewson, a college-educated muscular Christian who abstained from playing Sunday games. He had 373 wins, the most in National League history, and pitched three shutouts in the 1905 World Series. After retirement he managed the Cincinnati Reds for two and a half years, resigning during World War I to become an army captain. Mathewson was severely injured after the Armistice when he breathed poison gas while inspecting German trenches. He subsequently contracted tuberculosis and died in 1925. Matty was eulogized across the country. As *Commonweal*, an independent Catholic journal of opinion wrote:

> No other pitcher ever loomed so majestically in young minds, quite overshadowing George Washington and his cherry tree or even that transcendent model of boyhood, Frank Merriwell. Such men have very real value about and beyond the achievements of brawn and sporting skill. They realize and typify in a fashion the ideal of sport—clean power in the hands of a clean and vigorous personality.

The arcadian, integrative, and democratic attributes ascribed to professional baseball were largely myths. In reality, baseball was not a democratic game of rural American origins, a promoter of social integration, or a builder of character. Baseball was actually an urban sport that had evolved over time from the English game of rounders, and its finest players were raised in the city. Professional baseball was more democratic than most sports, but not all social classes and ethnic groups were equally represented in the audiences nor on the playing field. Until the 1920s, ticket and transportation costs, inconvenient starting times, and the absence of Sunday ball prevented many people from attending games, while fans from different social backgrounds did not sit together in the ballpark; different-priced sections effectively separated the classes. Furthermore, professional ballplayers did not represent a cross-section of the national population; virtually all were white and the overwhelming majority were from native-born American, Irish, or German stock.

Baseball's capacity to integrate as exemplified by hometown pride and hero worship was substantially exaggerated. To begin with, not all Americans participated in the rituals of spectatorship, since they did not all attend games. In addition, baseball idols such as Ty Cobb were often poor role models. Cobb was respected for his work ethic, aggressive style of play, and statistical accomplishments, yet at the same time he was hated by his peers and was a notorious racist and misanthrope. Furthermore, social psychologists like Leonard Berkowitz discount the cathartic potential of sports. In the early 1960s, his students who watched the boxing film *Champion* (1949) afterwards became more aggressive rather than less. A few years later, social psychologists Thomas Tutko and Bruce Ogilvie reported research findings demonstrating that participation in sport did not build character.

Although the realities of baseball had little in common with its myths, the public accepted the ideology as truth, and even mistaken assumptions influenced the way people behaved and thought. Middle-class WASPs believed that traditional values still counted in a fast-paced, urban society. They believed that attending a ball game provided a way to recapture the essence of life in rural and small town America and promoted a sense of community. They uncritically held up baseball players as role models for their children. Social workers in the early 1900s considered playing baseball second only to the public schools as a means to acculturate immigrant children into the American way of life, and they stressed baseball and other team games in their recreational programs.

Another popular myth was that team owners were selfless, civic-minded men who sponsored teams as a public service and to promote hometown pride. In reality they were hard-headed middle-class businessmen trying to make money in an untapped field that well-to-do WASPs disdained. Owners were typically professional politicians, business allies of politicians, or streetcar executives deeply involved in urban politics. Ted Vincent found that nearly one-half of the 1,263 nineteenth-century baseball stockholders and officials he studied were politicians, including fifty-six mayors and 102 state legislators. Their ball clubs, especially in the minors, were shaky small businesses. Vincent reported that only three-fourths of the nineteenth-century teams lasted more than two years. For example, from its formation in 1885 to 1899, the Southern League completed only four seasons and did not play at all during three.

In the early 1900s all major-league clubs had political connections. Political ties were especially strong in cities with powerful citywide machines, such as New York, where Tammanyites owned the Giants and Highlanders (renamed the Yankees in 1913), but such connections also existed in most other cities. Politically connected owners used clout to benefit their baseball business just as they did any other investment. Political influence assured lower tax assessments and minimal license fees, cheap or free police protection, and security against interlopers. Friends at city hall also supplied inside information about property values, anticipated land uses, and mass-transit plans, invaluable knowledge for teams selecting a playing field. On the other hand, owners without protection were vulnerable to political pressure for passes or payoffs. Such owners might encounter repeated inspections by fire marshals or even the construction of city streets through the field. In 1902 John Brush sold the Cincinnati Reds to a coalition of local Republican politicians that included boss George B. Cox and Mayor Julius Fleischmann after he was warned that streets would otherwise be cut through his ballpark.

Major-league teams in the early 1900s were very profitable. They achieved substantial annual earnings, and franchise values, worth $50,000–$100,000 early in the decade, increased by about five times in little more than ten years. The teams in Chicago and New York had the greatest profit potential because of the size of their cities. The Chicago Cubs (the former White Stockings) were sold by Spalding for $105,000 in 1905 to Charles Francis Murphy, a former sportswriter who had borrowed the money from his former boss Cincinnati publisher Charles P. Taft, brother of the future president. Murphy made so much money that he paid off the loan in one year. The Cubs earned $1.2 million between 1906 and 1915. One year later, the Cubs were sold for $500,000.

The New York Giants were even more valuable than the Cubs. In 1902 Andrew Freedman sold the club to John Brush, former owner of the Cincinnati Reds, for $200,000, which was about four times more than he had paid in 1895 for his majority share in the team. Brush made a great investment because the team earned about $100,000 a year from 1906 to 1910. In 1919 Brush's heirs sold the franchise for $1 million to Charles Stoneham, a Tammany curb-market broker. This was a great buy for Stoneham, whose family owned the team until 1976. In 1920, following the advent of Sunday baseball the year before, the Giants made $296,803, a National League record. An important component of the profit was the $65,000 in rent the team received from the Yankees, their tenants at the Polo Grounds. Stoneham was distressed, however, that the Yankees outdid him at his park, taking in a major-league record $373,862. That season, the Yankees featured a new star, Babe Ruth, the greatest player of all time.

The Ballparks

The early baseball parks were cheap wooden structures, which reflected the sport's financial weakness, the state of building technology, the frequent mobility of teams, and the high failure rate of teams. Nineteenth-century clubs moved frequently, exemplified by the Chicago White Stockings, who played at six different sites between 1870 and 1894. Teams shifted locations because of high rents, burned-down ballparks, declining neighborhoods, streetcar subsidies, or political pressure. In 1889, for example, the Giants had to move from the original Polo Grounds (just north of Central Park) to a new site two miles farther north because prominent aldermen, disgruntled at the low number of passes they received, opened a street through the old park.

The best sites were accessible by inexpensive rapid transit, were cheap to rent or purchase, and were located in safe middle-class neighborhoods near their fans. They were rarely located in working-class neighborhoods and almost never downtown, where real estate was prohibitively expensive. The exception was Chicago's beautiful 10,000-seat Lake Front Park, a model facility built in 1883 for just $10,000. The team had to relocate two years later, however, because it was occupying public land that the federal government had given Chicago for public use and not for a private business.

Construction costs in the late nineteenth century for ballparks escalated to between thirty thousand and sixty thousand dollars. New York's Hilltop Park, built in 1903 for $75,000 (plus another $125,000 to excavate the rocky land), was the last wooden major league park. These wooden fields had serious disadvantages. Their seating capacities had become inadequate, the ambience was plain, and they were dangerous buildings, often built cheaply by politically connected contractors who sometimes used substandard materials. Furthermore, the wooden parks were highly inflammable. Five fires occurred in major-league parks in 1894; St. Louis alone had six in a ten-year period. Five major conflagrations in ballparks occurred between 1900 and 1911, and in 1903 an overcrowded railing broke at Philadelphia's Baker Bowl, killing twelve people.

The era of the dangerous wooden ballparks ended in 1909 with the construction of the first fully modern, fire-resistant edifices. This major innovation occurred because of baseball's increased popularity and profitability, its growing stability as a business, the need to compete with other popular entertainments, and the dangers posed by wooden structures. Municipalities in the Progressive Era were extremely concerned about the threat of fires in public places, such as the 1902 Iroquois Theater blaze in Chicago that killed 603 people, and they compiled strict new building codes. Chicago's revised regulations of 1909 specifically barred future construction of large wooden ballparks. The construction of new playing fields was also stimulated by the existence of the necessary technology, decreasing labor and material costs, and growing competition from other popular entertainments, such as vaudeville, movies, and amusement parks.

The first of the modern ballparks was Philadelphia's 20,000-seat Shibe Park, opened in 1909 at a cost of $500,000. It was the first fully fire-resistant ballpark, soon followed by Pittsburgh's 23,000 triple-decked Forbes Field, which featured elevators, inclined ramps, electric lights, and telephones. The first in the American League was the $500,000 Comiskey Park that seated 28,800. Between 1909 and 1916, ten new major-league parks were built at an average cost of $500,000, and nearly all the rest were modernized using fire-resistant materials. Fenway Park, built in 1912, and Wrigley Field, built in 1914, are still in use. Nearly all the teams took advantage of the new parks to charge higher ticket prices that largely killed the custom of twenty-five-cent bleacher seats except at Comiskey Park, whose 8,000 cheap seats catered to the Irish fans who lived in the surrounding community.

The new modern ballparks were designed in a classical style by professional architects with greatly increased seating capacities, and the use of exposed steel, brick, and stone. The Polo Grounds was designed with a decorative frieze on the grandstand below the balustrade with figures of men and women. Ebbets Field in Brooklyn had a fabulous foyer highlighted by a massive chandelier with twelve arms shaped like bats and suspended globes designed to look like baseballs. It had enlarged curved seats and parking lots for fans who drove to games. Its outfield walls were painted deep olive green, and ivy seeds were planted at the base of the walls so vines would grow up them. This provided a good background for batters and, along with the lush green grass in the outfield, also promoted the rustic atmosphere of the field.

Several grounds had two-tiered grandstands held up by steel pillars that obstructed the view from many seats, but enabled more fans to sit near the playing field. In 1923 the Yankees built the 58,000-seat, three-tier Yankee Stadium to facilitate the huge crowds they were drawing. The outfield dimensions of the classic parks were often highly asymmetrical, and unique, to conform to the size of the lots on which the parks were built. Center field at the Polo

Grounds was 483 feet from home plate compared to 279 for left field and 258 for right field.

These privately constructed civic monuments were located on the urban periphery in middle-class or underdeveloped areas; the relatively cheap sites had been either purchased or leased on a long-term basis. Although the fields made a strong impact on the neighborhoods in the immediate vicinity of their entrances, where parking lots, restaurants, and taverns sprang up, they did not significantly harm peaceful residential locales. Named for an owner (Ebbets Field), team (Braves Field) or location (Fenway Park), these rustic, green oases were referred to as a "park " "field," or "grounds," rural metaphors that reinforced the pastoral imagery of the national pastime. An important change in nomenclature occurred with the opening of Yankee Stadium (1923), a more modern and urbane name. Constructed at a cost of $2.5 million (plus $675,000 for the land), the "House that Sunday Baseball Built" was by far the most expensive and biggest ballpark of this era.

Most historians believe that spectators were mainly lower-middle to upper-lower class, and of WASP or old-immigrant stock. Historian James Sullivan's study of Cincinnati (AA) crowds in the 1880s suggests that blue-collar fans were even under-represented at American Association games, despite its working-class orientation. He found that, except on Sunday, fans in the more expensive sections surpassed those in the cheap twenty-five-cent seats. The National League originally sought a middle-class audience by setting high prices for admission, dividing seating areas by price, using security guards, and banning Sunday baseball and liquor sales. Games began at convenient times for white-collar workers (Chicago games began at 2:30 because the Board of Trade closed at 2:00 P.M.; Washington games at 4:30, reflecting the closing time of government offices). Blue-collar spectators were mainly artisans with half-holidays on Saturday; workers with unusual shifts like bakers, butchers, and policemen; men taking an unpaid holiday; or the occasional unemployed fan. High ticket prices, the absence of Sunday ball in eastern and southern cities, and the cost of transportation curtailed working-class attendance. A round-trip on mass transit cost at least ten cents, which was more than low-income workers, who rarely rode streetcars at the turn of the century, could afford.

The behavior of nineteenth-century fans was occasionally unruly. Disorder was usually caused by overcrowding, drunkenness, and the misconduct of rowdy players who carried on vitriolic exchanges with umpires and fans. If the umpire's ruling "robbed" the home team, cries of "kill the umpire" would come from fans and team members. Fans might throw food or bottles at or physically attack the umpire. In the early 1900s Ban Johnson's strong support of umpires helped discourage egregious umpire baiting, and the dimensions of modern ballparks eliminated overcrowding and placed fans farther away from umpires and ballplayers. Furthermore, spectators were not primarily from the sporting fraternity, whose members had a greater proclivity for the kind of antisocial behavior witnessed at boxing matches. Rather the audiences were more "civilized" and acted in a more acceptable manner at the ballpark. Middle-class women comprised a small but visible segment of audiences since the earliest days of baseball; clubs encouraged their attendance with ladies' days, starting in 1883 at the Polo Grounds, on which women were admitted free or for a nominal fee. Their interest was reflected in the popular song of 1908, "Take Me Out to the Ball Game," sung by a girl who tells her date she prefers an afternoon at the ballpark eating peanuts and Cracker Jacks and rooting for the home team to the theater or any other alternative he would fancy.

Baseball crowds were less disorderly than soccer fans today in many parts of the world, whose identity and worldview is wrapped up in the success of the home or national team. Baseball spectators have always had an easier time than soccer fans accepting unfavorable decisions and defeats, partly due to baseball's long season, which meant that most single contests were not crucial. Furthermore, there was no intracity competition in baseball (except for exhibitions and the World Series, the closest was the Brooklyn Superbas v. the New York Giants, whose cities merged in 1898 when New York was the largest city, and Brooklyn, the fourth largest city in the United States), as there was for decades in Glasgow, Scotland, between the Celtic Football Club (Irish) and Rangers (Scottish), which raised the level of fan excitement to dangerous levels.

The Ballplayers

The social origins of major leaguers changed substantially around the turn of the century. A slight majority of nineteenth-century ballplayers were from blue-collar backgrounds, about three in ten were white collar, and the rest were sons of farmers. They were not well educated, saved little money, and often lacked marketable skills. These social characteristics combined with the low status of their occupation resulted in over one-third of players active between 1871 and 1882 sliding down into blue-collar occupations after retirement. Their short-lived fame had little impact on their future careers except for the 10 percent of retirees who went into the saloon business as an owner or employee.

By comparison, major-league players in the period from 1900 to 1919 were drawn from higher socio-economic backgrounds, attracted by professional baseball's enhanced status and higher wages, which averaged about $2,000 in 1901, $3,000 in 1910, and $5,000 in 1923. They were mostly white-collar sons, 44.6 percent, a figure more than double the proportion of nonmanual workers in the American labor force in 1910. One-fifth of ballplayers were sons of farmers, and one-third were blue-collar sons. One-fourth had attended college, five times the rate of other men their age. Their social backgrounds, education, and the increased number of baseball-related jobs resulted in a much smaller number (14.1 percent) falling into blue-collar work upon retirement compared to earlier ballplayers. The less successful retirees were typically poorly educated blue-collar sons who had lived for instant gratification and ended up unprepared for life after baseball.

The Game in the Dead Ball Era

Early-twentieth-century baseball was known as the "dead-ball era." Pitching dominated, and runs were hard to come by, averaging fewer than seven a game for both teams. Teams played for runs one at a time, stressing "inside baseball." The entire National League had only 101 homers in 1907, and in the following season major-league batting averages were the lowest ever until 1968. That year the entire Chicago White Sox team hit a record low three home runs. Pitchers had several advantages, beginning with the modern home plate, introduced in 1900, which was five inches larger than its predecessor. One year later foul balls were counted as strikes for the first time. Games were played with just one or two balls that would become softened and discolored and thus harder to hit. Hurlers used foreign substances like spit, sandpaper (emery ball), or talcum powder (shine ball) to roughen a ball's cover, making it move through the air unnaturally and befuddle batters. Rader argues, however, that even more important than trick pitchers (whose earned-run averages were similar to other hurlers) was the use of bigger and stronger pitchers, the introduction of relief pitching, and improved fielding. The introduction in 1910 of a livelier cork-centered ball increased home runs by 30 percent, but they were still rare. Frank "Home Run" Baker of the Philadelphia Athletics hit the most home runs in the American league for four years (1911–14), yet his yearly total of homers never topped twelve.

Intraleague competition remained unbalanced, with four National League teams winning seventeen pennants, and four American League teams winning nineteen from 1901 to 1920. The Pirates, led by eight-time batting champion, shortstop Honus Wagner, won the first three NL titles, while the McGraw-managed Giants took the next two, plus four more in the 1910s. The Cubs took pennants in 1906, 1907, 1908, and 1910. They won 116 games in 1906, an all-time record, yet lost the "El[evated] World Series" to the Chicago White Sox, known as the "Hitless Wonders" with a dismal team batting average of .230.

The American League's biggest winners were Philadelphia and Boston with six pennants each. Between 1910 and 1914 the Athletics won four pennants and three World Series, led by a brilliant pitching staff and the "$100,000 infield." In 1915, however, owner-manager Connie Mack dismantled the team rather than meet spiraling salary demands, and the team ended the decade mired in last place. The A's were supplanted by the Red Sox, who won pennants in 1912, 1915, 1916, and 1918. The Sox had an extraordinary outfield and a stellar pitching staff, which included Babe Ruth. As a twenty-one year old in 1916, Ruth went 23–12, with nine shutouts (an all-time AL record for a left-hander) and a league-leading 1.75 earned run average. Ruth went 65–33 with a 2.02 earned run average in his first three complete years in the majors, and was spectacular in the World Series, going 3–0 and establishing a record of twenty-nine and two-thirds consecutive scoreless innings that lasted until 1961. Then, in 1919, he focused on his batting and set a major league record with twenty-nine homers. Ruth sought to have his salary doubled to $20,000, which was rejected by Red Sox owner Harry Frazee, a Broadway producer, who had overextended himself when he bought the franchise for $1 million in 1916 and could not service his debt. Frazee sold his troublesome star to the Yankees one year later for $25,000 in cash and three promissory notes, also for $25,000, plus a $300,000 loan, which mostly went to pay off his mortgage on Fenway Park.

Ruth became the Yankees right fielder, and immediately smashed his own home-run record with an astounding fifty-four in 1920, more than every *team* except the Philadelphia Phillies. This marked the end of the dead-ball era as other players sought to emulate his power. Ruth eventually played twenty-one years in the major leagues with a lifetime .342 batting average and a record 714 home runs. He was a self-made man who demonstrated that America was still the land of opportunity. Idolized for his natural prowess, with his large income and insatiable appetite for women, food, and fame, Ruth symbolized the consumer ethic of the 1920s.

Organized baseball's monopoly was severely tested in 1914 when the year-old Federal League proclaimed itself a major league. Its owners included several extremely wealthy men who wanted to own a big-time sports franchise, and they concluded that baseball was popular enough to support a third major league. The Federal League did not recognize the reserve clause, and owners openly vied for top players, such as Ty Cobb and Walter Johnson, who used the opportunity for leverage to negotiate lucrative new contracts with their old clubs. Cobb resigned with the Tigers for $20,000. Twenty stars who remained with their clubs secured an average 92 percent increase in pay. Only a few luminaries, such as Chicago Cubs future Hall of Famers Mordecai "Three Finger" Brown and Joe Tinker, on the tail end of their careers, did change leagues. Consequently, the Federal League rosters were composed of players past their prime, journeymen, and minor-league players.

The Federal League challenged organized baseball where the major leagues were strong and well organized, and lacked the outstanding leadership that Ban Johnson provided the American League when it took on the National League in the early 1900s. The Federal League, unlike the American League in 1901, was starting virtually from scratch, and its Brooklyn Tip-Tops and Chicago Whales franchises built expensive $250,000 fireproof ballparks (Washington Park, and Weeghman Park, respectively; the latter was renamed Cubs Park in 1920 and Wrigley Field in 1927)) to comply with their cities' strict new building codes. Following two years of competition during which the new league lost $2.5 million and the major leagues encountered skyrocketing salaries, costly legal action, and rumors that the interlopers were moving into New York, a settlement was negotiated. The intruders received $600,000 to dissolve, and the Chicago and St. Louis Federal League franchises were allowed to buy the Cubs and Browns in their respective cities. The Federal League team in Baltimore balked at the settlement and sued organized baseball under the Sherman Antitrust Act. The case eventually went to the Supreme Court. In 1922 Justice Oliver Wendell Holmes, Jr., wrote the majority opinion, stating that baseball was not trade or commerce because "personal effort . . . is not a subject of commerce," nor was baseball an interstate activity because crossing state lines to play was merely incidental. This crucial ruling exempted organized baseball from antitrust legislation.

The Black Sox Scandal

Baseball's darkest moment came when the Chicago Grand Jury in September 1920 announced indictments against eight White Sox accused of having fixed the 1919 World Series with the Cincinnati Reds. The White Sox, who had won the Series in 1917, were considered the best team in baseball, but they lost the 1919 Series to the underdog Reds five games to three. The news of what became known as the "Black Sox" scandal shook public confidence in the integrity of the national pastime, for Americans had always believed that ballplayers would never cheat, its outcome nearly ruining organized baseball.

Baseball, unlike horse racing and boxing, was not identified in the public mind as a gambling sport but as a pastime enjoyed for its own sake. In reality, however, baseball gambling was very popular, notwithstanding ballpark signs forbidding it. Fans bet confidently because baseball was considered honest, wagering on many aspects of games, including the winner and loser, statistics such as hits and runs, and even the call of a pitch. Baseball's meticulously kept statistics were popularly regarded as data to help management and fans evaluate players, but they also helped gamblers make informed judgments when betting on baseball. Club owners themselves were often avid bettors, and a few of them had connections to horse racing and gambling.

The presumed fixer of the 1919 World Series was the notorious Arnold Rothstein, known as "the Big Bankroll." He was the leading professional gambler in the United States and a partner in the Oriental Racetrack in Havana, Cuba, with Giants owner Charles Stoneham. Several rumored fixes had occurred in the early 1900s, but they had been dismissed or kept quiet "for the good of the game." Actually, the idea of the fix originated with first baseman Chick Gandil, who had friends in the underworld and different groups of bribers including former major leaguer "Sleepy" Bill Burns and his partner, ex-prize fighter Billy Maharg, who had connections with gamblers. Others involved in pushing the fix were Joseph "Sport" Sullivan, a Boston gambler, and former world featherweight champion Abe Attell, known as the "eyes and ears" of Rothstein. They could not finance the players' demand for $100,000, and in the end Rothstein provided the cash, but well below the players' expectations. He reportedly made $350,000 by betting on the Reds. His purported role as the fixer of the Series became part of American lore, reflected by the character of Meyer Wolfsheim in F. Scott's Fitzgerald's *The Great Gatsby* (1925), one of the best novels of the twentieth century.

Gandil convinced six other unsophisticated teammates to fix the series for a $100,000 bribe from gamblers, although they ended up getting only $80,000. The players were well paid as compared to the average American—the average "Black Sox" received $4,300, including $6,000 for Joe Jackson—but were underpaid compared to their peers, as well as to team captain Eddie Collins, a college graduate, who made $14,500. They also had serious grievances against owner Charles Comiskey, particularly his star pitcher Eddie Cicotte, who had been promised a $10,000 bonus in 1917 if he won thirty games, but was benched after winning 28. One of the indicted, third baseman Buck Weaver, played to win, and accepted no money, but did not report the bribery offers, and Jackson, who did receive $5,000, hit a robust .375 in the Series

The Grand Jury was told by starting pitchers Eddie Cicotte and Claude "Lefty" Williams, and the illiterate star outfielder "Shoeless Joe" Jackson (whose lifetime batting average was .356, third highest in baseball history) that eight players had fixed the World Series. As a result, seven of them (save for utility infielder Fred McMullin who barely played) were indicted for participating in a conspiracy to defraud an individual who had bet on them. At the time, fixing a sporting event was not a crime. None of the gamblers involved were indicted.

When the case went to trial, their convictions seemed a foregone conclusion because of the confessions made to the Grand Jury. However, the prosecutor reported that the confessions had been lost. Years later it was revealed they had been stolen by the outgoing state's attorney and ended up in the office of Alfred Austrian, Comiskey's attorney. The absence of this key evidence destroyed the state's case, and the players were acquitted. Nonetheless, all of them were banned from the sport in 1921 by baseball's first commissioner, Judge Kenesaw Mountain Landis. Landis had absolute power, became the arbiter of last resort in all baseball disputes, and employed broad investigative and punitive powers to protect the owners' interests.

The Black Sox scandal was an important symbolic event at a time when many old-stock Americans were worried about the future of their country. People were disillusioned by the nature of the peace that followed World War I. The Treaty of Versailles, which featured a League of Nations, was rejected by the Senate. Economic discontent resulted in major strikes in the steel and railroad industries, a general strike in Seattle, and a police strike in Boston. Growing fears of Bolshevism and radicalism at home led to the nation's first Red Scare and a resurgence of nativism that resulted in the passage of the National Origins Act of 1924 to curtail immigration, and racial antagonisms such as those that erupted in the Chicago Race Riot of 1919. The country seemed to be coming apart at the seams. If baseball—the finest American institution that epitomized and taught the nation's traditional values—was corrupt, what hope was there for the future? The acquittal fortuitously redeemed baseball (the jurors carried the players out of the courtroom on their shoulders), restored national self-confidence, and paved the way for the golden age of sports of the 1920s. During that decade, the stern leadership of Judge Landis and the slugging of Babe Ruth helped the country forget the Black Sox and restored baseball to its pedestal.

Conclusion

The rise of commercialized professional spectator sport in the industrial era strongly reflected the spirit of industrial capitalism. Entrepreneurs sold consumers entertainment that was provided by highly trained and skilled athletes. Businessmen in horse racing and especially baseball, like their contemporary oligopolists and monopolists, tried to limit entry into their business by creating organizations such as state racing boards and leagues to control access to their sport and thereby assure greater revenues for themselves.

Sport in the industrial era was mainly controlled by urban politicians and their close associates, who used their power and influence to aid their sports businesses. Sports promotion offered a means to make money, gain prestige and fame, create patronage opportunities, and provide a service for sports-minded constituents. A strong nexus between ethnic machine bosses and organized crime developed in the gambling sports of horse racing and boxing. While the elite remained a vital force on the racecourse, off-track betting provided a major source of underworld revenue. During the 1920s, horse racing experienced a dramatic resurgence, and the sport became more legitimate, a trend that accelerated during the Great Depression. By the mid-1930s, professional gamblers and organized-crime figures gained control of several racetracks, cash-rich businesses in which they could make legitimate profits, skim off money, secure jobs for syndicate members, shake down unions that represented their workers, launder their ill-gotten gains, supply races to promote off-track gambling, and even facilitate fixed races.

In the case of prizefighting during the 1920s, it became widely legalized during the Golden Age of Sports, and boxing suddenly became a glamorous and profitable sport. In years past, politicians had played a big role in managing fighters and promoting bouts, but in the 1920s the underworld began to supplant them. Gangsters were highly attracted to boxing, having grown up in tough neighborhoods with people who became hoodlums or pugilists, and they enjoyed the glamour of being associated with a contender or champion. In the 1920s they were on their way to becoming a dominant force in the ring, and were prepared to use violence to get their way. Since men with criminal records could not get a license to work as a manager or promoter, underworld figures acted as secret managers, putting up some stooge to act as the manager of record. They used their position to influence which fighters got the best bouts or even to fix fights. The biggest fight of the era was the Dempsey-Tunney heavyweight championship held in Chicago's new Soldier Field in 1927 that attracted over one hundred thousand fans and brought in $2.7 million in live gate receipts (over $33 million in current money), a record that lasted for over fifty years. In this famous fight, the scheduled referee was replaced at the last minute because he had taken a car ride with Al Capone, a big backer of Dempsey, supposedly to make sure the fight was honest. The bout is remembered as the "long count fight" because when Dempsey knocked down Tunney in the seventh round, referee Dave Barry did not begin counting Tunney out for about five seconds until Dempsey moved to a neutral corner. Tunney arose when the referee's count reached nine, and went on to retain his title by decision.

During the 1920s, other professional sports vied for public attention. The National Football League was founded in 1920, the National Hockey League, in 1917, though it did not secure an American franchise until 1924, and the American Basketball League in 1925. The main individual professional sports included automobile racing, six-day bicycle races, and golf. These sports, however, as well as boxing and horse racing, were dwarfed by professional baseball, even if major-league baseball's attendance did not keep pace with population growth. Baseball overcame the Black Sox scandal, and maintained its image as the clean, all-American game that stood for all that was good endured. It had the preeminent sports hero in Babe Ruth and the most-famous sports facility in Yankee Stadium, and while movie-going may have supplanted it as the real national pastime, baseball was still the sport of choice for Americans. Organized baseball had achieved near-monopoly status; it was a national sport with minor league teams all across the country (although the major leagues were at the time only in the North and Midwest), and appealed to all social classes. African Americans were banned from playing in organized baseball, although they could attend games, and they established their own major leagues with their own heroes. Baseball was the only major professional sport whose allure was primarily the game rather than the potential gambling gain. Only the most jaded observers saw it as the crass business that it was, owned by politically connected entrepreneurs looking to make as much money as they could. The typical fan saw it as a game that epitomized the finest qualities of American society, reminded one of one's youth, promoted traditional and modern values as well as hometown pride, provided role models for youth, and assimilated newcomers. These perceptions were cultural fictions that encouraged the public to act as if these ideas were true, even though they were not.

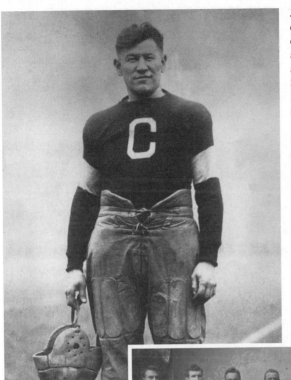

Jim Thorpe is widely considered the greatest athlete of the twentieth century. Raised as a Sac and Fox, and educated at the Carlisle Indian Industrial School, he was All-American in football (1911–1912), scoring 198 points in 1911. In 1912 he won Olympic gold medals in the pentathlon and decathlon. Thereafter he played professional football for twelve years, and six years in the Major Leagues. *Courtesy Jim Thorpe Foundation/Oklahoma Historical Society*

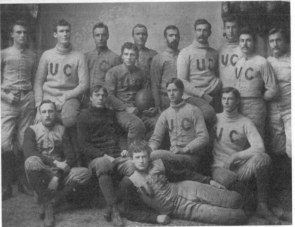

Manly Men: The First University of Chicago Football team, 1892. Coach Amos Alonzo Stagg (holding a rounded football) recruited this team to bring instant prestige and recognition to the brand new University of Chicago, whose goal was to promote scholarship and research. Stagg, the first coach to have tenure, worked at the University of Chicago from 1892–1933, capturing two "mythical" national championships in 1905 and 1913. *Special Collections Research Center, University of Chicago Library, (apf4-00669)*

Boys playing basketball in 1911 at the Carnegie Playground, 5th Ave., New York City. Despite the presence of a playground supervisor, the players are behaving like a mob, hardly the behavior intended by sports reformers trying to elevate these boys' conduct. *Library of Congress Prints and Photographs Division, (LC-USZ62-71329)*

The Girls' Branch of the Public Schools Athletic League (PSAL) folk dancing at New York's Central Park. The Girls' Branch was founded in 1905 by philanthropists to provide exercise and activity programs for school girls. The PSAL supported recreation for all girls that promoted fun, health, and happiness, including basketball, track, and folk dancing, but barred competition which was thought to promote masculine values. *Library of Congress Prints and Photographs Division, (LC-DIG-ggbain-00493)*

Young Women Exercising with Ropes and Rings, YMCA Central Branch, Philadelphia, PA, 1918. Women exercising at a YMCA gym, wearing the typical outfit that included bloomers and stockings. The YMCA movement's main focus was protecting single women's morals and welfare, and emphasizing educational and career programs rather than physical fitness. *Credit: Courtesy of the Historical Society of Pennsylvania, Central Branch (DAMS 682), Philadelphia Record morgue photo collection [V07], call# V7:3242*

Senda Berenson (1868–1954) was a Jewish Lithuanian immigrant who in 1892 introduced basketball at Smith College. Berenson (middle, in long dress) modified the rules to make the game more feminine and less manly. *Smith College Archives*

Saratoga Racecourse. The current track was built in 1864 in Saratoga Springs, New York. Once considered an elite resort, this track is the oldest sporting site in the United States. The first event was the Travers Stakes, which is still contested today. *"A Finish at the Celebrated Saratoga Course,"* Harper's Weekly *50 (2 April 1892): 1218*

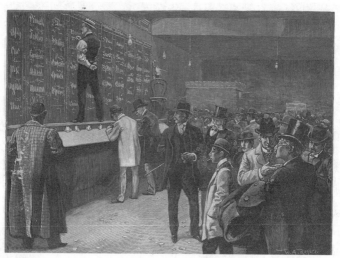

This downtown New York betting parlor in 1892 drew a well-off clientele, reflected by the clothing and features of the gentlemen present. Note the ethnic-looking youths in the forefront smoking and looking "tough." Engraving by W.A. Rogers. *A New York Pool-Room,"* Harper's Weekly *31 (2 April 1892):324.*

Paddy Ryan v. John L. Sullivan, American Championship 1882. The fight was staged bare-knuckled under the London Prize Ring Rules and each side put up $2,500 for the winner. The fight crowd met in New Orleans, and moved to Mississippi City, near Gulfport, Mississippi on February 7, 1882. After nine rounds, Sullivan knocked out Paddy Ryan to claim the American title. *Courtesy of National Police Gazette Enterprises, LLC. Used by permission.*

Jim Jeffries v. Jack Johnson, Havana, Cuba 1910. Jack Johnson, heavyweight champion of the world, 1908–1915. The "Galveston Giant" was the first African American heavyweight champion of the world. His success threatened prevailing racist attitudes, and enflamed racism in the United States, leading the search for a "Great White Hope" to defeat him and put blacks back in their place. Race riots followed his knockout of former champion Jim Jeffries (left), seen as the last best hope of White America. *Library of Congress, Prints & Photographs Division, (LC-DIG-ppmsca-31943)*

"Slide, Kelly, Slide." Michael Joseph "King" Kelly, is shown sliding into second base in this famous painting by Frank O. Small. Copies were often proudly displayed on the walls of Irish saloons. The renowned base-stealing catcher and outfielder of the Chicago White Stockings and the Boston Beaneaters (1878–1893) was the most popular baseball player of the late nineteenth century, who twice led the National League in batting and three times in runs scored. His exploits on the basepaths led to the popular cheer, which later became a poem and a famous song. *Boston Public Library, Print Department*

The third Polo Grounds opened in 1890 in the Washington Heights neighborhood of New York for the Brotherhood team. A year later it became the home of the Giants, who played there until it burned down in 1911. This 1905 photo of an overflow crowd shows fans and carriages in the outfield. Coogan's Bluff overlooks the double-decked grandstand. *Library of Congress, Prints & Photographs Division, (LC-USZ62-119636)*

Christy Mathewson (left, with teammate Jeff Tesreau) of the New York Giants won 373 games (1900–1916), the most in National League history, and was one of the first five men elected to the Baseball Hall of Fame. He was idolized as a Christian gentleman who never pitched on Sunday and always exemplified the highest standards of sportsmanship. *Library of Congress Prints and Photographs Division, George Grantham Bain Collection, (LC-DIG-ggbain-13904)*

Detroit Tigers Star Ty Cobb Stealing Third Base, 1909. Ty Cobb played 24 years in the majors (1905–1928), the highest in Major League History. He set 90 Major League records, and was the outstanding player in the early 1900s. Cobb was a fierce competitor who intimidated opposing players, sliding into bases with sharpened spikes raised high. *Library of Congress, Prints & Photographs Division, (LC-DIG-bbc-2061f)*

Philadelphia's Shibe Park was the first modern major league ballpark, with a seating capacity of 20,000. The home of the Philadelphia Athletics was completed in 1909 using concrete and steel materials, setting a standard for other teams to emulate. Named for principal owner Ben Shibe, a sporting goods manufacturer, it cost $457,167.61 ($141,918.92 for the land, $315,248.69 for the stadium). *Library of Congress, Prints & Photographs Division, (LC-B2- 689-5)*

Keio University baseball players with ballplayers from the Chicago White Sox and New York Giants, World Tour of 1913–14. The Japanese collegians were one of the finest teams in Japan, and regularly played American college nines in Japan and the United States in the early 1900s. *Library of Congress, Prints & Photographs Division, (LC-DIG-ggbain-16209)*

Grèce, Jeux Olympiques à Athènes Ἀθῆναι, Ὀλυμπιακοὶ Ἀγῶνες

The start of the 100 meter race at the First Modern Olympic Games in Athens, 1896. In the early days of track and field, short distances were often raced in roped-off lanes to help keep runners in their lanes and facilitate the work of judges to insure fair racing. As late as 1924, short ropes ("strings") were used in certain races at the Olympic Games in Paris. © 1896 / Comité International Olympique (CIO)

In 1920, the U.S. sent its first women's team to the Olympics in Antwerp, Belgium to compete in aquatic sports. Riggin, just fourteen, and merely 4′7″ and 65 pounds, competed despite criticisms about her youth and innocence. She captured the women's springboard diving, the youngest American Olympic champion until 1936. She competed at the Paris Olympics four years later, and became the only woman to win medals in both diving (silver) and swimming (bronze in the 100 meter backstroke). © 1920 / Comité International Olympique (CIO).

Ray Ewry, 1906 Intercalated Olympics High Jump Gold Medalist. An alumnus of Purdue University, Ewry competed for the New York Athletic Club and won a remarkable ten gold medals in individual Olympic events, the most ever until 2012. He won the the standing high jump, long jump and triple jump in 1900 and 1904, and the standing high jump and long jump in 1906 and 1908. The standing triple jump was discontinued as an Olympic event in 1906 and the others after 1912. © 1904 / Comité International Olympique (CIO)

CHAPTER SIX

American Sport
in the International Arena

The emergence of early American sport owed, as we have seen, an enormous debt to the sporting cultures of the English, Scottish, Irish, and Germans. After the Civil War, new sports continued to arrive from Great Britain, including golf, tennis, polo, and soccer, while Scandinavian immigrants brought their love of cross-country skiing and ski jumping. It was in this era, however, that the United States became an important exporter of sports, notably baseball, basketball, volleyball, and boxing, to promote its national prestige and image, expand its power overseas, and make money. Americans were convinced their sporting culture was a positive reflection of the American way of life, and that sports could effectively bring American values to less developed parts of the world, whose residents could be raised up by assimilating to American culture.

The American involvement in the globalization of sport was not limited to exporting its sports around the world, but included competing in international events like the America's Cup. The New York Yacht Club first successfully defended the cup in 1870, followed by eleven more victories by 1903. The next defense did not occur until 1920. The opponents were from England (5), Ireland (3), Scotland (2) and Canada (2). In 1879, James Lord Bryce, the great

English historian, believed that the America's Cup races contributed positively to promoting international community and mutual respect, and hoped international competition would expand, resulting in positive diplomatic consequences.

The United States became a leading participant in the modern Olympic Games, first staged in 1896 in Athens. The quadrennial games, inspired and organized by French Baron Pierre de Coubertin, began modestly, with limited American involvement at first, but the games quickly became an important venue for American amateur athletes to demonstrate their prowess on the world stage, where they could prove to themselves and their foreign hosts, the superiority of American civilization, American manliness, and, by 1920, the athleticism of American women.

The Cultural Diffusion of Sport

The process of cultural diffusion largely began at America's borderlands, and then extended overseas. This process was primarily achieved by the private sector, not by formal government decisions to promote imperialism, which did not develop into a full-blown policy until the early 1900s. The exporting of sport was primarily done by individuals, including businessmen, teachers, sailors, and missionaries who were in the third world to make money, uplift the population, or proselytize for Protestantism, promoting hard work, health, and welfare for the benighted people of the world. There was little formal support for the exporting of sports, although the military, especially the U.S. Navy in Japan and Hawaii in the 1890s, did spread baseball. This became more prominent in the early 1900s in the new U.S. colony in the Philippines. Thereafter, it was not until after World War I that governmental backing for the globalization of American sport notably expanded.

The prevailing diffusion model, advocated by such scholars as Allen Guttmann and Joseph Arbena, argues that the sporting culture of highly developed nations spread beyond their borders, entering host cultures among the elite, and then filtered down to the lower classes on a voluntary basis. The diffusion of sport was an instance of cultural hegemony, a concept developed by Italian Marxist Antonio

Gramsci. Thus, a sport popular in the dominant country is introduced into the subordinate nation, possibly by colonial officials, soldiers, merchants, or even workers, where it is willingly accepted and adopted by the subordinate nation's cultural leaders as enjoyable and socially functional. The receiving society adopts the sport as its own, fulfilling its own cultural needs. When baseball was introduced overseas to Cuba and Japan, it did not symbolize oppression, but rather it represented modernization, anti-imperialism, liberation, and national identity.

Sports systems were typically not imposed on the receiving nation. The exporting of sports was not an incident of cultural imperialism, a process in which a powerful nation imposes its culture on a weaker country. Such an imposition occurred in nineteenth-century Poland, which was divided up between Prussia, Austria, and Russia. The foreign powers all tried to impose their own language and civilization on their section of Poland and suppress Polish culture. If the United States did force sports on Filipinos, it was probably through compulsory physical education programs like those in the United States required for children in Filipino schools.

Great Britain was the most successful nation exporting sport in the nineteenth century, relying on a government that purposely employed sport to integrate people and states within the British Empire and promote social control. Cricket, in particular, was employed overseas among its civil servants, officers (both of whom were often former athletes and graduates of elite English public schools whose well developed games ethic indoctrinated students to become courageous leaders), enlisted men, and ex-patriots residing in the colonies to tighten ties with the homeland and boost morale. These exemplars of British culture used the expensive and exclusive game of cricket, which fit in better than more vigorous sports with the culture and warm climates of South Asia and the Caribbean, to capture the attention of colonial elites, whom they hoped to co-opt, train, educate, and acculturate into an elite British lifestyle, providing a cultural bridge to enable the Raj to operate on good terms with local rulers. The subalterns enjoyed the games, the emphasis on merit, and the opportunity to gain honor and respect if they beat the teacher at his game. The British believed the colonial elites would thereby assimilate such values as service, solidarity, duty, self-control, discipline, teamwork, pluck, energy, perseverance, and common sense, while building character and learning British ways of getting things done.

The British also used sports to promote loyalty among those subjects whose ancestors had migrated to distant lands in the Empire, including Australia and New Zealand, and especially in areas where they were linguistically different from hostile white minorities, like the Boers in South Africa and the French Canadians in Quebec. Cricket achieved popularity among British settlers in all of these lands, except for Canada, where baseball supplanted it early on, just as it had in the United States. Rugby, an amateur kicking and ball playing sport also became very popular with British settlers. The working-class professional game of soccer, however, did not gain widespread support within the British Empire (or in the United States), and the colonials never could compete with the mother country in soccer, although they eventually did with cricket and rugby, which bolstered their self-esteem and national identity.

While the British did not do well in exporting soccer throughout the Empire, they did globalize the game they called football. British subjects in the late nineteenth century brought their game to Europe, the United States, Latin America, and elsewhere, due not to government policy but to the voluntary efforts of British merchants and workers who took their inexpensive game around the world as they looked for business or employment.

Sports and the Borderlands

The two nations closest to the United States were Canada to the north and Mexico to the south. The United States and Canada shared the world's longest demilitarized border, which was extremely permeable by people, their culture, and their values. Canada's principal sporting contribution to its southern neighbor was ice hockey, which developed in the 1860s and 1870s from various stick, ball, and goal games. In 1886, the Amateur Hockey Association of Canada was formed and just seven years later the first intercollegiate hockey game was played in the United States between Yale and Johns Hopkins, followed in 1896 by the creation of the U.S. Amateur Hockey League in New York. In 1903, while amateurism was firmly entrenched in Canadian hockey, Canadian Jack Gibson formed the first professional hockey team, the Portage Lakers of Houghton, Michigan, which led one year later to the creation of the International Professional Hockey League. Four of the five league's teams played in the United States, staffed by Canadians, paid $15–$40 a week.

Baseball has a somewhat longer history in Canada, where a variety of ball games were played before the Civil War. Canadians, many of whom were sons of American immigrants, played town ball at least as early as 1838 in the isolated town of Beachville, Ontario; and in 1854 Hamilton, Ontario, hosted a version of the Massachusetts game. Five years later, teams from Hamilton and Toronto competed in the New York game. Canadians, like Americans, preferred baseball to cricket because it was more adaptable to local customs, was more exciting (with frequent shifts between offense and defense) used younger, less skilled players, and games took less time. In 1864, the Canadian Association of Base Ball Players was founded in southern Ontario. Thirteen years later, the Guelph Maple Leafs and the London Tecumsehs played in the International Association, one of the very first professional leagues, whose teams competed well against National Leaguers. In the late 1880s both played in the prestigious International League, one of the top-level minor leagues. According to historian Alan Metcalfe, baseball was Canada's national sport by 1914, although its professional structure was largely intertwined with Organized Baseball in the United States.

The southern borderlands were often seen as a site where American sports crossed into Mexico, but the border operated both ways there, too. The sport of rodeo emerged out of the working practices of cattle herding in Mexican haciendas and the Northern provinces from *Tejas* (Texas) to California, by vaqueros who participated in ranch work competition between rival haciendas. American cowboys often learned their craft from vaqueros. In 1852, the Texas State Fair began with such events as bullfighting, bull riding, and horsemen picking up gold coins while riding full speed. The first actual American rodeo took place in Cheyenne, Wyoming, in 1872, and the initial professional rodeo held in Prescott, Arizona, in 1888. Entrepreneurs like Buffalo Bill Cody popularized shows that displayed the skills and athleticism of cowboys in the 1880s and 1890s, leading by the early 1910s to such major rodeos as the Calgary Stampede, the Pendleton Round-Up, and the Cheyenne Frontier Days. Rodeo evolved into a series of events involving horses and cattle to test the skills of cowboys in such events as tie-down roping, steer wrestling, saddle and bareback bronco riding, and bull riding.

Mexico's modern sporting heritage actually began under British influence, starting with cricket, first played there by British businessmen and mine owners in 1827, and horse racing, which began in the early 1840s. However, few Mexicans played cricket, and the game was supplanted by baseball in the 1880s, which reflected the declining influence of the British business community and the booming American economic influence in the north. The precise date of the first ball game is not certain, though U.S. marines played a game in 1877 in Guaymas. Baseball gained a foothold in the southwestern borderlands during the 1880s at a time when Hispanic and Indian peoples confronted an expanding Anglo culture that included commercial agriculture, land speculation, mineral exploitation, and railway development. The arrival of America's national pastime, according to borderland historian Colin Howell, symbolized a value system that emphasized entrepreneurialism, capitalism, and whiteness as a privileged status.

The popularity of the game was bolstered in northern Mexico in the 1880s after Mexicans working for American-owned railroads began playing ball. Mexican historian William Beezley argues that the game took hold in 1887 with the establishment of a three-team league. One year later, sporting goods manufacturer A. G. Spalding began exporting baseballs, tennis balls, bicycles, and hunting gear to Mexico. By 1890, baseball was played in such Texas border sites as Brownsville/Matamoros, Laredo/Nuevo Laredo, and El Paso/Juarez on the Texas-Mexican border, and as far west as San Diego/Tijuana. Baseball was also played in the Yucatan, popularized there by Cuban émigrés.

The middle and upper classes in late-nineteenth-century Porfirian Mexico saw the adoption of modern sports, notably baseball, boxing, cycling, and horse racing, as a measure of national economic and cultural progress, along with paved roads, good sidewalks, a modern sewage system, a new city hall, and an opera house This was partly a result of the growing American influence, but also choices made by Mexicans who had a sense of boosterism and civic pride, and scorned sports that contradicted their own value system, like bull fighting, a sport brought over by the conquistadores in the sixteenth century. Bull fighting represented their Spanish heritage, of which Mexicans were proud, but it also symbolized submission to autocratic rule.

Baseball became more commonplace in early 1900s with more cross-border games. Nonetheless, the southwestern border maintained a division between the American baseball culture characterized by Anglo exclusivity and a commitment to the ideology of white superiority, and a separate emerging Mexican baseball community. The coming of the Mexican Revolution in 1911 killed a lot of the interest in baseball. When the game later reemerged, the nation had its own entirely Mexican baseball structure—something that never happened in Canada.

The Baseball Tours

Between 1874 and 1914, there were three major-league baseball tours overseas as well as trips by collegians like the University of Chicago to Japan and African American professional teams to Cuba. The major-league tours promoted the national pastime overseas to certify the high level of American sports and the prowess of our ballplayers, popularize our national game overseas, and make money.

In 1874, Harry Wright, manager of the Boston Red Stockings of the National Association, organized baseball's first international tour. The son of a professional cricket player, Wright wanted to return to his native England and promote baseball, even though the English were already totally absorbed by cricket, their own bat and ball game. The tour included his Red Stockings and their chief rival, the Philadelphia Athletics. His stockholders criticized the project, worried the trip would hurt the club's standing in the pennant race, and end up losing money.

Twenty-three ballplayers left on July 16 aboard the *Ohio*, and while on the sea, Wright provided lessons in cricket. Their games were poorly promoted and underpublicized in the British press. The

Americans also played some cricket matches against local teams, employing 18–22 a side instead of the normal 11. The tour failed to popularize baseball in England, and incurred a debt of about $2,500.

Fourteen years later, in 1888, a more ambitious venture was organized by sports entrepreneur Albert G. Spalding, a participant in the 1874 tour and current owner of the Chicago White Stockings. The junket, originally called Spalding's Australian Baseball Tour but more widely known now as Spalding's World Tour, was comprised of the White Stockings and a second team of National Leaguers called the All-Americas. Spalding's primary goals were to spread the national pastime around the world, and expand his sporting goods empire by marketing his bats, balls, gloves, and uniforms to untapped markets, primarily Australia. Spalding also had an ulterior motive, which was to facilitate implementation of the Brush Classification Plan that set up a salary scale for major leagues by bringing on his trip New York Giants shortstop Montgomery Ward, president of the Brotherhood, the ballplayers' union, so he would be out of the country when the plan was unveiled. John Brush, owner of the Indianapolis Hoosiers, unveiled a pay scale that ranged from $2,500 for Class A rated players down to $1,500 for Class E men. Ranking was done by management based on performance on the field and conduct on and off the diamond.

The tour began in Chicago on October 20, and then moved west across the United States with a series of exhibitions, bound for San Francisco, accompanied by wives, journalists, servants, entertainers, and mascot Clarence Duvall, a short black teenage performer. The entourage then sailed to Australia via Hawaii; while en route, Spalding announced they would continue their journey around the world. The tourists were well received in the land down under, where they played eleven games. The initial contest drew some 10,000 spectators.

The tour departed for Europe via the Indian Ocean, playing a game at Colombo, Ceylon (Sri Lanka), and one in Cairo. The European leg of the tour included stops in Rome, Paris, London, Glasgow, Belfast, and Dublin. The English warmly received the travelers who met the Prince of Wales, and were recognized by the House of Commons. Nonetheless, their game was not well regarded, striking many spectators as boring, confusing, and inferior to cricket and its unique subculture.

Despite the poor reviews, and a $5,000 financial loss, the ballplayers were treated as heroes on their return to America. They were feted at a lavish dinner at New York's Delmonico's, where the guests included Brooklyn Mayor Albert C. Chapin, author Mark Twain, and U.S. Civil Service Commissioner Theodore Roosevelt. Twain gave a lecture in which he employed baseball as a metaphor for the raging spirit and drive of Americans, which he compared to the laziness of Hawaiians and Europeans. The tour concluded back in Chicago after several more exhibition games. The journey covered 32,000 miles, with fifty-six games in thirteen different countries, drawing some 200,000 people. In addition, the team played two games of rounders, two of cricket, and one ball game in Australia against expatriates.

Historian Thomas Zeiler regards the tour as an antecedent of American imperialism, foreshadowing historic forces that were making the United States an international force, such as the search for overseas markets. This is a bit of a stretch, although the members of the entourage did believe they were members of a superior civilization, exemplified by high-quality games, well-manufactured sporting goods, as well as superior values and practices. The national pastime had become integral to national identity, and the tour was heavily laden with chauvinistic underpinnings, reflecting America's stature as a rising world power. The tourists did not hide their feelings of superiority over many other peoples, often acting as boorish, racist, ugly Americans, proud of their game that represented a progressive, democratic, and culturally and materially advanced nation.

The American public applauded the players and the concept of the tour, despite its lack of success selling the game abroad. Spalding himself described the players as "representative of the great Western Republic." Two decades later, Spalding, in *Baseball: America's National Game* (1911) emphasized alliteratively how the sport was integral to national identity, promoting such values as "courage, confidence, combativeness; dash, discipline determination . . , energy, eagerness, and enthusiasm; not to mention "spirit, sagacity, success;" and "vim, vigor and virility." He always saw baseball as a reflection of American manliness, fair play, and entrepreneurship.

A third major league tour occurred in 1913, the 25th anniversary of the Spalding World Tour, comprised of the New York Giants, managed by the renowned John McGraw, and the Chicago White Sox, owned by Charles Comiskey. The teams traveled 30,000 miles through thirteen countries to promote baseball, make money (which it did), demonstrate American manliness, elevate national prestige abroad, and encourage people elsewhere to participate in competitive sport. Stops included Japan, China, the Philippines, Australia, Ceylon, Egypt, Italy, France, and England, where King George V attended a game.

The Diffusion of American Sport in the Pacific

The United States long had an interest in the Pacific, going back to 1784 when the *Empress of China* reached Canton, China (Guangzhou today), beginning many years of profitable trade. The United States exported gold, ginseng, and furs to China, and imported tea, cotton, silk, and porcelain, which made millions for merchants. Commercial interest in the Pacific led to Commodore Matthew C. Perry's 1853 mission to Japan to open that nation to the West. Hawaii first drew the attention of missionaries seeking converts, but its excellent harbors had enormous commercial and naval potential. In 1898, the United States began developing a Pacific empire with the annexation of Hawaii, and one year later acquired the Philippines under the Treaty of Paris that ended the Spanish-American War. The United States initiated the Open Door Policy in China in 1900 to protect American commercial interests there.

The expanding American presence in the Pacific was accompanied, like British imperialism, by efforts to export its presumed superior culture and values. Americans going overseas were proving their manliness by building both a formal and informal empire, and by carrying the "white man's burden," as they sought to uplift inferior people. These hardy folk brought with them American religion, education, health care, and elements of popular culture, like sports. Competitive sports were expected to elevate the morals, character and health of third world peoples, while demonstrating the manliness of American athletes.

Hawaii

The first overseas nation introduced to American sports was the Kingdom of Hawaii. Protestant American missionaries first arrived in the island in 1819, seeking to convert the indigenous people and promote higher morality by halting such traditional recreations like hula dancing, gambling, and surf boarding, replacing them with uplifting American pastimes. Missionaries set up schools to Americanize the islanders as well as educate their own children. In the early 1840s, Captain James H. Black, a Boston printer, reportedly introduced the Massachusetts game (see chapter 2) to the islanders. In 1849, Alexander Cartwright, one of the creators of the New York game, settled in Hawaii, becoming a successful businessman and advisor to the royal family. According to local lore, he helped lay out a baseball field in 1852, but there is little concrete evidence to suggest that he promoted the pastime in Hawaii.

The early center of Hawaiian baseball was the Punahou School, founded in 1841 for the children of Hawaiian elite and missionaries. By 1866, Punahou was playing the New York game, and soon thereafter promoted interscholastic games and town leagues. This game fit in well with Protestant virtues, and such American values as competition, progressivism, and capitalism. In the late nineteenth century, baseball spread to foreign plantation laborers, supported after the 1909 strike by the Hawaiian Sugar Plantation Association, as an inexpensive way to Americanize players and fans, improve health, develop time/work discipline, teamwork, and deference to authority. It could also provide an alternative to gambling, drinking, and promiscuity, and, of course, discourage labor unrest. By the turn of the century, racially integrated plantation all-star teams played ball clubs from other farms. An emphasis on winning countered management's traditional policy of dividing workers by ethnicity, since they decided to put the best players, regardless of their social origin, on their teams. This policy inadvertently led to greater worker unity and solidarity.

Hawaii baseball for years maintained a strong ethnic component, promoting ethnic pride as much as assimilation. Chinese teams dominated in the late 1800s, and by the turn of the century, their clubs were touring Asia. The first Japanese players were contract laborers on sugar cane plantations, but the big push for Japanese baseball came at the end of the century led by Rev. Takie Okumura, a Japanese Christian missionary who organized baseball at his boarding school. Asahi Nisei, organized in 1905, was the best-known Japanese nine, and it traveled that year to Japan, the Philippines, and Taiwan.

The diffusion of sport to Hawaii was not a one-way street. The sport of surfing, an integral part of ancient Polynesian culture, one with strong religious overtones, was barred by missionaries in the early 1820s, and nearly disappeared. It revived in the early 1900s at Honolulu's Waikiki Beach, popularized by beach boys like Duke Kahanamoku. In 1907 George Freeth, an Irish Hawaiian, demonstrated surfboard riding on California beaches to publicize the opening of the Los Angeles-Redondo-Huntington railroad. One year later, the Hawaiian Outrigger Canoe Club was established to promote surfing and other commercial amusements at Waikiki.

China

American sports came to China relatively early, although the British influence, according to historian Gerald Gems, may well have originally been greater. Chinese students studying in the United States in the 1850s—Yung Wing, who graduated Yale in 1854, was the first Chinese graduate of an American university—picked up the game of baseball because it was fun. The sport also provided a way to demonstrate manliness at a time when Westerners questioned the masculinity of Chinese men because they wore long gowns, had lengthy braided hair, and kept their finger nails very long. In addition, the Chinese middle and upper classes denigrated physical labor, and the weak emperor and his frail army exercised limited control over China. The Chinese government sought to Westernize after the Second Opium War (1856–60), and reformers began to encourage physicality and sport. The center of the Shanghai Race Course in 1863 was purchased by sports clubs who built a cricket ground, which was home to the Shanghai Base Ball Club, the first in Asia. At the time there were only 372 Americans in Shanghai, and the game was largely a novelty. In 1872 the government sent thirty students to America, and they formed the "Orientals Base Ball Club." Three years later, the Nanking Military Academy introduced physical education.

American Protestant missionaries who went to China to convert the "heathens" by preaching the Gospel and promoting education, good health, and sound morals took an active role in encouraging sport and physical education. Missionary schools introduced calisthenics, games, and sports to promote Christian values, but met with resistance from the upper class, whose clothing interfered with strenuous movement, had distaste for physical activity that seemed like peasant work, and disapproved of recreation tied to Christian proselytizing. The approximately 1,000 American missionaries in China advocated modernization, but they created enemies by upsetting traditional culture, and were perceived as agents of Western imperialism.

The YMCAs, established in China in the 1890s backed up the missionaries, The Y stationed 15–20 physical directors in China, all very active in promoting athletics and training native personnel. The athletic programs appealed to Chinese modernizers who saw sport as an important step to achieve their goal. The YMCA introduced such sports as basketball and volleyball, promoted athletic meets in Chinese schools, created one of the first modern college physical fitness programs, and encouraged the construction of public playgrounds. Historian Clifford Putney argues that the YMCA did a better job promoting sport and fitness than in achieving conversions.

Dr. James Naismith's first classes at the International YMCA Training Institute included future missionaries. Dr. Willard Lyon, who established the first Chinese YMCA in Tianjin (Tientsin), introduced basketball to China in 1895. In 1908, the YMCA organized basketball leagues, and two years later basketball became a part of the first national athletic meet organized by the YMCA at Nanking. The YMCA organized a five-day national athletic championship held in conjunction with an industrial exposition, which symbolized Chinese efforts toward modernization. The YMCA also played an essential role in the development of the Far Eastern Championship Games in 1913, the first time that Chinese, Japanese, and Filipinos cooperated in any way.

Nonetheless, the main sport in China was baseball. There were three Chinese college baseball teams by 1895, one coached by a Chinese Hawaiian. One year later, the Tianjin Y introduced baseball, and high schools soon took up the game. Baseball was not, however, just an American game. In 1905, when physical education was introduced in the public schools, it followed a Japanese model. Thousands of Chinese had been sent to study in Japan, where they became familiar with baseball.

The strongest native proponents of sport in early-twentieth-century China were American-educated Chinese, who believed physical culture promoted modernization, manliness, and national pride. Sun Yat Sen, the first president of democratic China in 1912, attended school in Hawaii, where he became familiar with baseball. The young activist saw baseball as a convenient way to infiltrate the establishment and undermine its authority. His *Tongmenghui* (United League) formed a ball club in Changsha, capital of Hunan province, to secretly promote revolutionary activities, and their baseball skills came in handy while throwing hand grenades.

The exporting of sport to China did not alter negative American stereotypes about the Chinese people. Theodore Roosevelt at the turn of the century considered the Chinese to be decadent and unmanly. He warned Americans in 1899 that should they lose their manliness and bravery, and avoid the strenuous life, they would become as degenerate and effeminate as the Chinese.

Japan

Following the Meiji Restoration in 1868 that restored rule by the emperor and displaced the shogunate, the imperial government of Japan actively sought to modernize, end feudalism, and develop an industrialized capitalist economy. Japan decided to adopt the best elements of Western civilization to its own needs. It reformed its engineering, military, and finances based on the English model, its economics, government, and medicine based on a German model, and its education, agriculture, and animal husbandry on an American model. Their goal was to create a prestigious, proud, and powerful modern nation.

The Japanese shared with Americans a belief in the martial and manly virtues of sport. They respected traditional Japanese sports like karate and sumo wrestling more than team sports. Nevertheless, as the nation sought to modernize, the Japanese began to see Western team sports as a means to connect modern to traditional values, like the manliness of the Samurai. They also envisioned their participation in Western sport as a means to measure themselves in comparison with Westerners. In 1869, cricket was introduced to Japan by the Yokohama Cricket Club, but it was soon supplanted by baseball, just as previously occurred in the United States, because it was an easier game to play, the equipment was more accessible, the game was more exciting to play or watch, and it took up less time. Baseball embodied the social Darwinian spirit of competition and vigor, symbolized modern collectivist ideals as well as the loyalty, courage, and fighting spirit of Old Japan (*Bushido*, or "way of the warrior"), and emphasized values celebrated in civic rituals, including order, harmony, perseverance, and self-restraint. Once baseball became popular in Japan, participation enhanced the social image of elite students, its the first players, and brought status and pride to the nation whenever a Japanese squad defeated an American team.

Baseball was brought to Japan by American teachers abroad and Japanese students returning home after sojourns in the United States. The sport was first played in Japan in 1873, introduced by twenty-eight-year-old Horace E. Wilson, a Civil War veteran and baseball fan, who taught at Tokyo's *Daigaku Minamiko* (renamed *Tokyo Kaisei Gakko*), a 300-boy academy, where he had arrived two years earlier with a baseball and bat. The school trained the best and the brightest, becoming Tokyo Imperial University in 1897. Wilson taught the future elite how to play baseball, and, although they were uninterested in physical exertion for its own sake, the game became a preoccupation for them.

Japanese students educated in the United States who came home to take important positions in education and engineering also played a prominent role in promoting baseball. In 1873, three young men who had studied at the Massachusetts Agricultural College helped eighteen-year-old Albert Bates, an English teacher, give instruction in baseball to students at the newly opened Kaitakushi technical school in Tokyo. The government that year helped baseball gain widespread support by approving a primary textbook that included the rules of baseball.

The most important Japanese advocate for baseball was Hiraoka Hiroshi, a railroad engineer, who had studied in Boston, and was a fan of the Red Stockings. He organized the nation's first private baseball team in 1878, the Shimbashi Athletic Club (SAC), comprised of Shimbashi Railroad supervisors. The club charged dues, built a playing field, and wore uniforms, apparel rarely worn in Japan outside of the military, firemen, and policemen. Hiraoka's connections to railroading fused baseball and modernity in the minds of urban fans. Baseball became "modernity incarnate," appealing to a society seeking social experimentation and cultural innovation.

At first the SAC improvised their equipment, using cricket balls instead of baseballs, and kendo masks as a substitute for the catcher's mask. Fortunately, Hiroshi had valuable business connections, particularly an acquaintance from Boston, former star Red Stockings pitcher Albert Spalding. In 1884, the enterprising Spalding, an emerging sporting-goods tycoon, sent the SAC a gift comprised of balls, gloves, masks, and copies of the *1884 Spalding's Official Baseball Guide*.

The growing interest in team sports and fitness in Japan encouraged Dr. George A. Leland, a student of renowned physical educator Edward Hitchcock of Amherst College, to become the chief instructor in 1878 of the government sponsored Gymnastics Institute of Tokyo to train physical education teachers. Leland felt the Japanese were physically and psychologically not up to rigorous team sports, but more apt to play softer sports like tennis or croquet. His was hired to promote physical education for everyone, but worried his program would emphasize training a small athletic elite fostering a resurgence of the samurai legacy. The classes included military calisthenics, obstacle races, and tug of war to instill stamina and self-discipline. In the early 1890s, administrators organized extracurricular athletics to promote the school's reputation under rigorous training and strict rules. The school started out with crew, but baseball was the main sport by the late 1890s.

The first important site for Japanese baseball was at the Yokohama Athletic Club (YAC), a former cricket club, which dominated the social and recreational life of foreign residents, but barred interested Japanese. Young American businessmen and sailors enjoyed playing baseball in Japan, where it symbolized to them extraterritorial privilege and their unique cultural identity. Americans played the game to be as "American" as possible while thousands of miles from home.

The Japanese were offended by the racist YAC, which in 1891 dismissed a challenge by the elite prep school *Ichiko*, to play an American team, as unworthy. Americans disdained playing the high schoolers because that would symbolize accepting them as social equals. The students' point of view was that such a game would certify traditional values, as well as establish a new basis for national pride. The goal of playing a ball game against Americans took on the dimensions of a struggle for national honor.

In 1893 Ichiko played and lost to *Meiji Gakuin*, an Americanized Christian missionary school that symbolized the foreigners' unwelcome intrusion. This shamed the Ichiko school and led to a Spartan day-long training program. The loss of face was an important element in Japan's baseball's subculture, wherein players were taught a manly version of the sport that disdained such tactics as bunting and relief pitching as cowardly.

Finally, in 1896, Ichiko English teacher William B. Mason got the YAC to agree to a match, which the Americans expected to win easily. They demonstrated no sportsmanship before the game, taunting the opponents as they warmed up. The last laugh went, however, to the high schoolers, who embarrassed the Americans 29–4 on a diamond that had represented racism and unequal treaties imposed on Japan. Defeating the Americans at their own game, combined with the victory in the Sino-Japanese War of 1895, affirmed the nation's sense of self-worth, demonstrating their young men's manliness, and helping the nation overcome feelings of inferiority with the West. The Ichiko players became instant heroes, warriors who had defended the national honor.

Between war and baseball, the Japanese felt comfortable with the Social Darwinian concept that civilization was defined by its aggressive character. Baseball was no longer an instrument of cultural oppression by the socially and militarily superior USA, but served as the great equalizer, opening new doors to self-esteem and international respect. For several years more baseball remained primarily a sport played by elite high schools and colleges. Keio University in 1885 was the first institution of higher learning to have a standing baseball team, although there was no college league until 1914. After the end of the Russo-Japanese War of 1905–06, Waseda and Keio universities sent teams to tour the United States while the University of Wisconsin and the University of Chicago sent teams to Japan. President Theodore Roosevelt applauded the Japanese for playing America's game and learning American values, while American businessmen increasingly recognized a potential market in Japan. In 1908–09, the A. J. Reach Sporting Goods Company sent a squad comprised of major leaguers and Pacific Coast leaguers on an Asian tour to promote the sport and the company's products.

The Japanese quickly made baseball their own, with their own training techniques and spectator rituals. In 1905, they even exported baseball to their protectorate of Korea (which Japan annexed five years later). Ironically, the Imperial Government used sports, particularly baseball, along with education, to indoctrinate Koreans in Japanese ways and undermine traditional Korean values.

The Philippines and American Imperialism

As a result of the Spanish-American-Cuban-Philippine War, and the concluding Treaty of Paris, Spain ceded the Philippines, Puerto Rico, and Guam to the United States in 1899. Before the war had begun, Emilio Aguinaldo organized a revolution against Spanish rule in the Philippines, declaring Filipino independence. The United States did not, however, recognize Aguinaldo's government, which led to the Philippine-American War. The conflict, a protracted struggle in which U.S. troops faced insurgent guerilla forces, lasted until 1902, resulting in the deaths of 34,000 Filipino rebels, 200,000 civilians, many from a cholera epidemic, and 3,216 Americans. Despite the courage of the Filipino rebels, colonial officials constantly spoke disparagingly of the natives as "boys," and American soldiers commonly referred to them as "niggers." William Howard Taft, the first civilian governor of the territory (1901–03) called them our "little brown brothers." The manliness of the native Filipinos was further impugned by the jobs Americans made available to them, especially as house servants.

The United States tried to Americanize the native population, teaching English and American culture to promote their style of law and order. Government officials, military leaders, and Protestant missionaries believed it was their manly duty and obligation as representatives of a superior civilization to colonize and rule the inferior islanders. This "White Man's Burden" encompassed bringing Protestantism to the largely Catholic islanders, along with medical assistance, education, and American values like hard work and cooperation. Sport became an integral part of the effort to remake the Filipino culture and social life. U.S. soldiers used as school teachers relied on sports like baseball and boxing to regenerate civilization and supplant such vile pleasures as cockfighting, lotteries, and gambling, while sustaining racial barriers with the native people.

Spectator sports other than cockfighting were new to the islanders The first ball game in the Philippines was played in May 1898, shortly after the Battle of Manila Bay, between sailors and marines in Admiral George Dewey's fleet. The military supported baseball for enlisted men as entertainment, a source of morale, and a means to enhance martial qualities. Among the top military teams on the islands was the all-black Twenty-fifth Infantry Regiment.

American sports did not readily fit into the culture of the upper classes. Islanders opposed physical exertion for diversion and the educated classes tried to keep out of the sun to keep their skin light and hands soft. Consequently, the first Filipino ballplayers were mainly lower-class men who worked on army bases and were not worried about tans or rough hands. There were town teams by the early 1900s, and a high school league in 1905. Baseball gained so much popularity that a 1910 tournament attracted 483 teams. Manila's military commander asserted that "baseball had done more to 'civilize' Filipinos than anything else." According to Gerald Gems, baseball was employed to both promote social control and as a political tool. Americans organized ball games between Filipino and Japanese nines with the intent of redirecting Filipino hostilities against the Japanese rather than their American occupiers.

The Americans also introduced pugilism, a sport that fit the manly culture of the islands (shaken by the oppression of the American invaders) and their small physical stature, since fighters competed in weight classes. In 1910, Frank Churchill, an American fight manager, began holding weekly bouts in a Manila gym where Filipino fighters proved their manliness. In the future, professional Filipino boxers would become prominent in lower-weight divisions, notably Pancho Villa, world flyweight champion in 1923.

In 1901, U.S. military control over the islands was replaced by the Insular Government, a form of territorial government with an appointed governor general and legislature that reported to the Bureau of Insular Affairs. The civilian government encouraged education on an American model. By the mid-1900s, physical education and sport were important elements of Manila's public high school program for boys and girls. As usual, the goal was to promote health, build character, and teach such American cultural values as respect for authority, discipline, a work ethic, and community pride. In 1905, high schools had their first provincial championships.

The Insular Government altered urban spatial arrangements to promote health and other reforms, just like the Progressives back home. In 1904 Chicago architect Daniel Burnham, the director of the Columbian Exposition, was brought in to redesign the layout of Manila, the national capital, and Baguio, the summer capital, which included parks and playfields. Baguio had a substantial American population that used these facilities to swim, ride horses, and play golf and tennis.

The most important American official to promote sport in the Philippines was Governor General W. Cameron Forbes (1909–13), a Boston Brahmin and sportsman who coached Harvard's football team in 1897–98. He built a polo field and golf course at Baguio. Forbes believed sports could uplift the indigenous population and personally promoted competition, awarding uniforms to top baseball and basketball teams, and trophies in track-and-field.

The YMCA also played a big role in promoting sport, arriving after the invasion, and it became increasingly tied to the colonial government. In 1909, twenty-seven-year-old Elwood Brown was appointed national YMCA physical director in the Philippines, and he soon opened a YMCA in Manila, where basketball was played one year later. The YMCA recreation program appealed to lower-middle-class Filipinos, including Gov. Forbes' clerks, lifting their spirits and providing a constructive outlet for their energies. They were at first hesitant about doing physical activity and mussing up their clothes, so Brown got them to play volleyball and indoor baseball on government teams, and let them wear their own clothes. Then, in 1911, Brown organized the Philippines Amateur Athletic Foundation (PAAF) with Gov. Forbes as president. It was soon the biggest national sport organization in the world. Two years later the PAAF established the Far Eastern Games that included track, swimming, and tennis.

American Sport in the Caribbean

The United States made the Caribbean an American lake in the early twentieth century, less through colonization of Puerto Rico, which it acquired from Spain, and more through neo-colonialism in which weaker states retained their independence and sovereignty but the United States imposed its will by use of economic, political, and military policies. In the early twentieth century, the United States frequently intervened in the local affairs of such nations as Cuba, the Dominican Republic, and Haiti by sending in the marines. In the Caribbean, baseball was considered a benign means of imposing social control over the masses. James Mark Sullivan, minister to the Dominican Republic (1913–15), confided to Secretary of State William J. Bryan that baseball was so popular there that it curtailed revolutionary ardor: "The remarkable effect of this outlet for the animal spirit of the young men, is that they are leaving the plazas where they were in the habit of congregating and talking revolution and are resorting to the ball fields where they become wildly partisan each for his favorite team." Ironically, baseball was not brought there by Americans, but by Cubans.

Cuba
Cuba in the second half of the nineteenth century was heavily reliant economically on the United States, which bought 94 percent of the island's sugar production and was its source of technological innovations and standards of progress. Furthermore, the United States became a haven for political exiles following the failed Cuban Revolution of 1868.

Baseball arrived in colonial Cuba in the mid-1860s at a critical moment in the formation of a Cuban identity, and it served as a symbol of anti-colonialism. Young Cubans living in New York City and Key West, Florida, learned to play the game as they became familiar with admired American social norms and customs. They played ball on college teams, neighborhoods clubs, and at their workplaces. Upon returning home to Cuba, they brought the game with them, and used it to project a sense of national identity and opposition to the Spanish empire.

Nemesio Guiolo of Spring Hill College in Mobile, Alabama, is credited with bringing baseball to Cuba in 1864, returning home with a bat and ball. Four years later, he co-founded the Habana Base Ball Club. Also in 1868, eighteen-year-old Esteban Bellan, a fifth-year student at Fordham Prep, joined the Morrisania (New York) Unions, and went on the following year to play third base for the professional Troy Haymakers, which joined the National Association of Professional Base Ball Players two years later. Bellan played in the league three years, and then returned home. On December 27, 1874, Bellan played for Habana (Havana) against Matanzas in the first organized game in Cuba. He was player/manager for Habana from 1878, when the first professional Cuban league (*Liga General de Baseball de la Isla de Cuba*) was founded, through 1886, winning three league titles. Their main rival was Almendares, founded in 1878 by Cuban Fordham college students. The players then were middle-class white men.

Cubans made baseball their own game. They promoted it as a symbol of progress and democracy that promoted social mobility, social harmony, order, and national integration. This was understood as an adaptation to democratic values. Baseball was considered a meritocratic game, one in which class and race were irrelevant, and women participated as spectators. Baseball taught important qualities, such as discipline, patience, civic virtue, social responsibility, and team work, putting the group's interest ahead of the individual, qualities that would produce a successful nation. Baseball also taught such lessons as accepting defeat and then returning to practice to prepare for the next game.

Baseball for Cubans represented a democratic society compared to reactionary Spain, and Cubans unhappy with Spanish rule employed baseball to express their political view. Baseball symbolized progress and modernity in strong contrast with the barbarism, cruelty, inhumanity, and backwardness represented by the Spanish sport of bullfighting.

The colonial government recognized the game as subversive, banning it briefly first in 1869, and again in 1873. Then, when baseball was again permitted, teams were barred from adopting names that symbolized anti-Spanish sentiments. In 1881, the Rochester Hop Bitters, who played in the minor-league National Association the year before, became the first American team to tour the island. The team was owned by the manufacturer of a cure-all elixir, who encouraged his squad to tour and promote his products. Havana teams began traveling to Key West in the 1880s, and beginning in 1886, major-league teams toured the island, beginning with the Philadelphia Athletics, followed by the New York Giants four years later.

In 1890, the Habana Baseball Club constructed a home park with a seating capacity of nearly ten thousand. Baseball fever was so widespread in Cuba in the 1890s that there were more than two hundred amateur teams sponsored by urban social clubs, factories, mines, merchant seamen, and rural sugar mills. The game was so popular that there were several weekly baseball magazines. Rosters began to become more diverse, with Afro Cubans on some ball clubs.

When the Cuban War for Independence broke out in 1895, the Spanish government again banned baseball, concerned about the rhetoric associated with democracy and freedom, that a significant number of rebels were ballplayers, and that émigrés were using baseball to raise money for the revolution. As historian Louis Pérez points out, baseball "had become identified with the cause of *Cuba libre*, fully integrated into the mystique and the metaphysics of national liberation."

After the Spanish-American War, the United States ruled Cuba through 1902. The American occupiers employed baseball as an instrument to promote political order and social control, even though the sport had different meanings for the Cubans than the Americans. The U.S. Army set up leagues to occupy its soldiers, which often played Cuban nines and the results of the games were published in the daily press. Some historians, like Rob Ruck, argue that the American teams playing in Cuba were agents of soft power (a method by which a powerful nation seeks influence through co-option, often by using its culture), acting as unofficial missionaries of cultural imperialism. This contrasts with "hard power," or the employment of coercion and/or money to obtain goals. The game in Cuba became more democratic than previously. The dissolved Liga General was replaced by the Liga Cubana in 1900. An increasing number of players hailed from lower-class backgrounds, and three of the four teams, all run on a business basis, were racially mixed. The league was widely seen as a symbol of a postcolonial nation and a source of social mobility. Baseball became the national sport of postcolonial Cuba, and its players became missionaries for the sport in the Dominican Republic, the Yucatan Peninsula, and Venezuela.

In the early 1900s, Cuba was a popular site for traveling baseball teams, and Spalding's best foreign market for baseball equipment. In 1906 he even published a Spanish edition of the *Spalding Baseball Guide*. Major-league teams visited Cuba nearly every year, as did several African American teams. The major league teams did not fare well against Cuban competition. The Detroit Tigers, American League champions in 1909, went 4–8 in Cuba, while the 1910 A.L. champion Philadelphia Athletics went 4–6. Thereafter, league president Ban Johnson barred American League teams from barnstorming Cuba because their performances, often against American and Cuban men of color, were embarrassing to the major leagues. Baseball experts did recognize that some of the Cuban players were very skilled, and in 1911 the Cincinnati Reds signed Rafael Almeida and Armando Marsans, described as white "Castilians." They were the first Cubans to play in the National League. Nonetheless, the color line in baseball remained in the United States, and players identified as Afro-Cubans who wanted to play there had to limit themselves to black teams.

The American influence on Cuban sport went beyond baseball. Under the American occupation, Military Governor Leonard Wood banned cockfighting and bullfighting, but in 1902, after the U.S. occupiers left, the old sport of cockfighting resumed. Over the next few years, the upper class enjoyed American sport such as automobile racing, yachting, and horse racing, and the University of Havana played American football. The middle class participated in such American sports as roller skating, bowling, and tennis. The YMCA came to Cuba in 1904, and opened a gymnasium to promote basketball and volleyball, but the Catholic hierarchy did not welcome it because the YMCA was a Protestant organization. Reformers had less success in promoting moral uplift because there was a lot of betting on baseball, *jai alai* (a version of Basque *pelota*, which came from Spain in 1898) and horse racing at Havana's Oriental Race Track, which opened in 1915.

American sport also had a big following among the working class. Large corporations like Hershey and United Fruit transformed rural areas into company towns with athletic facilities, amusement parks, and dance halls. American corporations that owned thirteen sugar mills sponsored nearly one hundred baseball teams that provided entertainment for workers as well as a measure of social control. In 1909, a boxing academy began, and soon boxing became a popular sport. Interracial bouts disrupted the racial hierarchy, which led to the government banning the sport in 1912. The ban lasted until 1921, but was conveniently forgotten in 1915 when Jack Johnson defended his heavyweight championship in Havana against Jess Willard. Cuba in the future would become an important center of prize fighting. The growing interest in boxing was highlighted by Kid Chocolate winning the junior lightweight title in 1931.

The United States and the Olympic Games

The United States participated in a few international sporting competitions from the late nineteenth century through 1920 that promoted mutual respect and international comity. They included the Davis Cup championships in tennis (which the Americans won in 1900, 1902, 1913, and 1920), yacht races for the America's Cup, and most important, the Olympic Games, inaugurated in 1896 by thirty-three-year-old Pierre de Coubertin, a French aristocrat, who had been scarred by his nation's humiliating defeat in the Franco-Prussian War (1870–71). Americans thought that success in international sport would demonstrate American athletic excellence, giving the nation, as one magazine pointed out in 1894, a change to show off "what stuff its youth is made of." Athletic prowess was considered evidence for the superior social, cultural, and economic aspects of American civilization. Journalists, intellectuals, and academics considered sport a democratic institution that trained citizenship and unified American society, so it followed that they figured international competition would lead to the promotion of democracy and American values around the world.

For his part, Coubertin wanted to promote France's military preparation for future wars so he traveled to Great Britain, Canada, and the United States in 1889 to study each nation's athletic educational systems. He attended the Physical Training Conference in Boston that focused on sports and games in school physical education programs, and then traveled cross-country, visiting twenty-five universities, including Harvard, Yale, Princeton, and the University of Michigan, as well as other amateur sports organizations, including the New York Athletic Club. He met various ardent advocates of sport, including thirty-one-year-old Theodore Roosevelt of the U.S. Civil Service Commission, and Princeton historian William Milligan Sloane, a long-time member of the school's Faculty Athletic Advisory Committee and an officer of the Boston Amateur Athletic Association. Coubertin came away impressed by American college sports programs that fostered a sporting ethic similar to the elite British Public Schools (actually private institutions), the role model for upper-class American prep schools. Convinced of the educational value of sports and its potential for mass popularity, Coubertin determined that his homeland needed its own sporting ethic and programs of physical education to reinvigorate itself. When French educators were deaf to his propositions, Coubertin took a more international perspective, and recommended a modern athletic festival modeled on the Ancient Olympics.

In 1893, Coubertin made a four-month return visit to the United States and met with intercollegiate athletic officials from prominent eastern universities, as well as those of the fledgling University of Chicago when he attended the Columbian Exposition held a few blocks from campus. During this sojourn, Sloane became a trusted advisor, and was asked to attend the 1894 Sorbonne Conference that called for the convening of a renewed Olympic Games in 1896. Sloane, who moved to Columbia University in 1896, served on the International Olympic Committee (IOC) from 1894 until 1925, when Coubertin stepped down as IOC president. Sloane also founded the American Olympic Committee (AOC) along with other advocates of a republican sporting ideology, such as Caspar Whitney, publisher of *Outing*, a popular middle-class sporting magazine, sporting-goods magnates A. G. Spalding and Walter Spalding, and Amateur Athletic Union (AAU) leaders Gustavus Kirby, Julian W. Curtiss, and James E. Sullivan, who published *Spalding's Official Athletic Almanac*. These sportsmen were committed to using the Olympics to define American ideas about physical culture, help make sport a principal part of the way Americans defined themselves, and, for several of them, to make money.

Sloane was primarily responsible for putting together a fourteen-man team, primarily Bostonians and Princeton undergrads, to go to Athens for the Olympics. The squad also included rifleman Charles Waldstein, a Jewish New Yorker and eminent Cambridge University archeologist. The venture was financed in part by a Boston stock-broker and an anonymous donor. The first Olympic victory (then a silver medal) went to James B. Connolly of Harvard in the hop, step, and jump. Americans competed in sixteen events, primarily athletics (track-and-field), and won nine. Americans also won two pistol contests. Greece, however, won the most medals (forty-six compared to twenty for the United States).

The press tried to turn the games into an American spectacle, applauding athletic achievements as a demonstration of national superiority and interpreting U.S. success in track-and-field as making it the winner of the Olympic Games. Sloane agreed, and asserted that the modern Olympics created the same moral force as had the ancient games, uplifting "untold millions." He claimed American Olympic victories stemmed from the same traits that shaped the republic, including hard work, free competition, egalitarianism, innovation, and respect for law. Similarly, renowned author Price Collier stressed that Americans and Englishmen had learned through sports the qualities that made them world leaders in business and industry, including trustworthiness, steadiness, resourcefulness, and endurance.

The 1900 and 1904 Olympics and the Intercalated Games of 1906

The second Olympiad, staged as part of the Paris World Exposition in 1900, was an extremely chaotic and drawn-out affair that lasted five months. All athletes competed as individuals, not as members of a national team. Winners got trophies or cups (medals were awarded retroactively), and masters' level fencers competed for 3,000 franc prizes (so much for amateurism!). American participants, mainly drawn from eight colleges and the NYAC, won 19 events and came in among the top three in 47 contests, second to France with 26 championships and 101 medals. The disorganized nature of the Games was exemplified by the experience of golfer Margaret Abbott, who was touring Europe with her mother. They both entered a nine-hole tournament in Paris, which Margaret won, shooting a 47. Only later did Ms. Abbott discover she was America's first female Olympic champion.

The Americans were most successful in athletics, winning 16 of 22 events, amassing 39 medals overall, followed by Great Britain with three victories. The star was Alvin Kraenzlein, University of Pennsylvania, who became the only person to win four individual track events at one Olympic game (60- meter dash, 110- and 220-meter hurdles, and the broad jump). Ray Ewry was another star, capturing standing long jump, high jump, and triple jump. He duplicated the feat four years later in 1904 at St. Louis, and he won two events at both the 1906 and 1908 games for a total of ten Olympic victories.

Other victorious Olympians included John J. Flanagan, a migrant in 1896 from County Limerick, Ireland. He was the first of several physically imposing Irish and Irish Americans, including many New York policemen, later known as the "Irish Whales," who achieved great success in field events. Irish athletes found themselves in an awkward situation since the British did not allow Ireland to send a team to the Olympics, presumably for political reasons, although Australia, Canada, and New Zealand sent teams. Rather than compete under the hated British flag, the "Irish Whales" competed for the Stars and Stripes. Flanagan won the hammer throw at the Paris Olympics, and repeated in 1906 and 1908. The huge Irishman quit the police force in 1910 after he was switched from the Bureau of Licenses, a job that gave him a lot of time for training, to walking a beat.

Contests at Paris were staged on Sundays, which was very controversial in the United States because it violated the American custom of a strict Sabbath. The American Olympic Committee tried unsuccessfully to impose American customs on Catholic France, accustomed to a Continental Sabbath that permitted recreation on Sunday afternoons. Several American athletes agreed not to compete on Sundays, including Myer Prinstein, a Polish Jew who led the broad jump in the preliminaries. Prinstein, representing Methodist affiliated Syracuse University, was told not to compete on Sunday even though he was not Christian. A big dispute ensued among the Americans because Kraenzlein had pledged not to compete on the Sabbath, but went ahead and did so. He ended up bettering Prinstein's preliminary jump, and took first place.

Following the Paris Games, Coubertin announced that the Third Olympic Games would be held in the United States, reflecting its teams' excellent performance at the first two Olympiads, and providing an opportunity to bring the Olympics to North America. The men in charge of preparing for the games were primarily James E. Sullivan and Caspar Whitney, who welcomed the opportunity for the United States to show off. An American Olympics would demonstrate how physical culture had produced a special caliber of citizens who not only excelled in sport, but all aspects of culture.

The IOC chose Chicago as the host city for a number of reasons: because of the involvement of Albert Spalding as director of the American section on sports at the Paris Games; the positive coverage the *Chicago Tribune* gave the Olympic movement, which promoted interest among its middle-class readership; and the support of Coubertin. The baron back in 1893 had been impressed by the Columbian Exposition, as well as local interest in educational reform, and civic leaders like President William R. Harper of the University of Chicago, who believed that sport could promote peace and understanding around the world. Chicago businessmen and academics proposed a $250,000 event with funding from corporate donors, Congress, and local governments that included a 75,000-seat lakefront stadium with a retractable roof. The committee anticipated a profit of $375,000.

However, serious problems hindered the project, including difficulties in raising the proposed funding, and opposition, led by shopping catalogue magnate Montgomery Ward, to the fabrication of any buildings on the lakefront, which was barred by law. Furthermore, Chicago had an unexpected rival for the 1904 Games in St. Louis, the fourth largest city in the nation, but hardly a world-class city. The Louisiana Purchase Exposition, originally scheduled for 1903 in honor of the centennial anniversary of the Louisiana Purchase, had been pushed back to 1904. The Fair organizers planned a huge sports carnival that included the AAU championships for September that would compete with the upcoming Olympics for public attention. Coubertin unilaterally decided to switch the site to St. Louis, whose Fair planners promised to make sports its centerpiece, unlike the prior Paris Fair, whose top officials were hostile to the Olympics.

St. Louis boosters raised $5 million to host athletics at the Fair, and President Theodore Roosevelt agreed to serve as honorary president for games that depicted the virtues of the strenuous life. James E. Sullivan headed the Fair's Department of Physical Culture, having run the athletics program at Buffalo's Pan American Exposition in 1901, which had constructed the first complete athletic stadium on any American fair grounds. Sullivan's department sponsored demonstrations of athletic technology, and displayed products manufactured by A. G. Spalding.

Sullivan did an excellent job publicizing the sports program that began in May and ran through September, involving 9,000 athletes. It started with an interscholastic track meet, followed by such events as a turner mass-exercise exhibition, college baseball, traditional Irish sports, YMCA meets, and world fencing championships.

The Fair had a section of replicated villages staffed by indigenous people to represent the various stages of human progress. There was a model "Indian School" exhibit that included Native American girls from the Ft. Shaw Indian School in Montana who dominated the women's basketball exhibitions at the Olympics. Sullivan, together with Dr. William J. McGee, chief of the Fair's Department of Anthropology and Ethnology decided to examine these peoples' physicality to evaluate their level of development and test myths of aborigine athletic prowess. He arranged the "Anthropology Games" on August 12–13, which drew a lot of interest as a "test" of speed, stamina, and strength among its aboriginal competitors. The competitors, dressed in native costumes, participated in Olympic track-and-field events on the first day that included the 100-yard dash, high jump, long jump, the 56 lb. weight throw, tug of war, mile run, and shot put, as well as a baseball throw. Native Americans performed the best, which McGee attributed to their higher level of civilization. The second day's competition involved events likely more familiar to the other indigenous peoples, including pole climbing and the javelin throw, as well as a pygmy mud-ball fight. Spectators and commentators made fun of their performances in the modern sports, which were unfairly used to demonstrate the backward state of the indigenous people.

Only twelve countries outside of North America sent athletes (76), while 88 percent were from the United States (523) and Canada (52). This reflected the modest status of the Olympics, the high cost of travel, and world-shattering events elsewhere, like the Russo-Japanese War.

Americans completely dominated the sixteen-discipline competition. They won 70 of 74 track-and-field medals, 29 of 30 in rowing, and all the medals in boxing (a new event), cycling, wrestling, and women's archery. Overall, the United States captured 239 medals out of a total of 280. Participants competed as members of athletic clubs, and the team championship went to the New York Athletic Club. The American games of baseball and basketball were demonstration sports.

The top performers at the Games were Archie Hahn of the Milwaukee Athletic Club who won 60-, 100-, and 200-meter races; Ray Ewry, who won the three standing jump events; and Harry Hillman, Jr., who took the 400-meter race, 200 m. hurdles, and 400 m. hurdles. The American contingent included African Americans George Poage, who placed third in both the 200- and 400-meter hurdles, and George Stadler, who took the silver in the standing high jump.

The integrity of the competition took a hit in the marathon. American Frederick Lorz, a world-class distance runner, crossed the finish line first. He had, however, dropped out after running nine miles, and returned by car to the starting line/finishing line, ostensibly to retrieve his clothes. The actual winner was Thomas Hicks, a British brass worker running for the United States, who received strychnine sulfate mixed with brandy from his trainers to help him keep going.

Despite the lack of true international competition, the 1904 Games had a positive impact on U.S. sports by making the Olympics a major part of America's crusade for international sporting prominence. Americans continued to interpret their victories as evidence of their superior social system. Furthermore, the Games seemed to support the popular belief that sport promoted a sense of community and shared values, which helped alleviate the social divisions resulting from industrial capitalism.

In 1906, Greece staged the Intercalated Games in Athens, originally intended as a quadrennial event held two years following the Olympics, though it was never held again. Nonetheless, the 1906 Games had important innovations, such as a briefer, ten-day schedule independent of any international exposition, and extensive use of national symbols. Athletes competed for the first time under their own national Olympic committee, wore national uniforms, and marched into the stadium behind their national flag for the opening ceremonies. Winners were honored in a medal ceremony in which their national flag was raised. The American Olympic Committee raised about $15,000 to send thirty-seven athletes selected by the AAU to represent their country. Competitors wore uniforms decorated with an American shield and stars and bars.

The United States captured just 24 medals out of 236 medals in contention, tying for third in the medal count behind France and Greece, but dominated track-and-field with 11 victories and 12 other medals out of 21 events. As in St. Louis, where just slightly more than half of the team were college men, the U.S. team in 1906 had a very visible working-class ethnic contingent, strong evidence that track-and-field was less elite than long believed. The ethnic contingent included Jewish long jumpers Meyer Prinstein, who won gold, and Hugo Friend, who came in third. Fifteen years later, Friend was the presiding judge in the Black Sox trial.

The top American performer in 1906 was a 6'3", 194 lb. New York City policeman, Martin Sheridan, who had emigrated from Ireland in 1900 at the age of nineteen. He had previously competed in St. Louis, where he won the discus. In 1906, he competed in seven events, winning the discus and shot put, and placing in the standing high jump, standing long jump, and throwing the stone. Two years later, at the London Olympics, he won the discus and Greek-style discus events. Sheridan retired after setting eighteen world records.

The London Olympics of 1908

The 1908 Olympic Games at London was part of the Franco-British Exhibition. It attracted over 2,000 athletes, more than three times the number at the St. Louis Games. The U.S. national team was selected in three regional meets and a fourth exclusively for collegians, and had all expenses paid. In addition, a supplementary list of athletes were invited to also participate, but at their own cost.

A number of controversies marred the London Games, often regarded by historians as the point when the Olympics became an international relations event. The primary contentions involved the United States and the host British. On Opening Day at Shepherd Bush Stadium, the flags of all competing nations, except Sweden and the United States were flown. This inadvertent error had serious repercussions since American flag bearer Ralph Rose did not dip his pole while passing King Edward VII in the stadium reviewing stand, which had become the accepted protocol for all teams marching past the monarch. This faux pas was barely mentioned by the British press, but many American newspapers and magazines raised quite an uproar about it. There were reports that Rose or Sheridan had asserted on the spot that "This flag dips to no earthly king." Nonetheless, Rose became an American hero, creating what eventually became an American tradition, though the flag was dipped at the 1912 Stockholm Olympics, the 1924 Games in Paris, and the 1932 Winter Games in Lake Placid, and then never again.

A few days later, Lord Desborough, chairman of the Council of the British Olympic Association, apologized for the host nation's mistake for not flying the American flag. This, however, did not placate AOC leader James E. Sullivan, who was extremely critical about all aspects of British management of the Games, including allegations that sprint heats were rigged to have Americans knock each other off before the finals. The hottest debate occurred following the 400-meter run. British officials were afraid the three Americans in the final would gang up on British world-record holder Wyndham Halswelle. Late in the race, which was not run in lanes, American John Carpenter blocked Halswelle as he tried to pass, a legal tactic in the United States, but not in Great Britain. Officials immediately halted the race, and disqualified Carpenter. They called for a rerun two days later between Wyndham and the other two Americans. However, American officials kept them off the track, and so Halswelle won in the only "walk over" in Olympic history. As a result of this contretemps, officials from host nations were barred from supervising or judging future Olympic contests, the International Amateur Athletic Federation was formed to develop uniform international rules, and the 400-meters at the 1912 Olympics was run in lanes.

Another famous controversy occurred in the marathon. Judges illegally aided Italian Dorando Pietri as he staggered into White City Stadium in the lead, and then ran in the wrong direction. After he was straightened out, he fell four times, officials picked him up each time, and finally helped him cross the finish line, which was illegal. Thirty seconds later, Irish American Johnny Hayes, who worked in the sporting goods division of New York's Bloomingdale's department store, completed his race. Some two hours later, Pietri was disqualified and Hayes declared the winner.

The 1908 Games was dominated by the British who won 56 gold medals (146 overall) compared to just 23 gold (and 47 overall) for the United States. Nonetheless, Americans back home considered the performance a victory because they only cared about track-and-field, in which the United States captured 16 out of 27 medals awarded. As journalist Finley Peter Dunne's alter ego, the comical Irish American saloon keeper Mr. Dooley, noted, that while Americans won in real sports, the English won such events as "wheeloil'th' p'ramulator" and th' teadhrinkin' contest."

The 1912 Olympics at Stockholm

The 1912 Olympics in Stockholm was the most outstanding international sporting competition until the 1932 Summer Games in Los Angeles. Stockholm drew 2,407 athletes (including 48 women) from 18 countries who participated in 102 events. The American team was chosen by the AAU and the AOC based on results at eastern, central and western meets, although eastern champions received an automatic selection, reflecting the bias of AAU director James E. Sullivan.

As was par for the course, Sweden, the host nation, won the most medals (64, plus another in the art competition), one more than the United States, which won the most gold (25). The United States excelled at marksmanship, with 14 medals in eighteen contests, and track-and-field, winning 16 of 28 gold. A key component of the 174-member all-male team was the 13 members of the working-class Irish American Athletic Club (which included two Jewish runners), who captured five events and a total of ten medals. African American Howard Drew, the world-record holder in the 100-yard dash (9.6 seconds) was the favorite in the 100-meters, but pulled a tendon in the semifinals. Native Americans played a prominent role on the team, notably Lewis Tewanima, a Hopi, who won silver in the 10,000 meters, Andrew Sockalexis, a Penobscot, who came in fourth in the marathon, and Jim Thorpe, Sauk and Fox, who won both the five-event pentathlon (javelin, broad jump, 200 m., discus, and 1,500 m.), with a world record that lasted for twelve years, and the ten-event decathlon (contested over three days), with 8,413 points, a world record that stood for fifteen years. Thorpe was recognized by King Gustav VI of Sweden as "The World's Greatest Athlete."

The U.S. swimming team captured four medals, third behind Germany and Australasia (Australia and New Zealand). Hawaiian Duke Kahanamoku led the squad with a victory in the 100-meter (tying the world record of 1:02.4), and silver in the 4 x 200-meter relay. Kahanamoku competed in four Olympics from 1912 to 1932, winning three gold medals and two silver, and competed in water polo in 1932. He was also the father of modern surfing, recognized in 1999 by *Surfing Magazine* as the "surfer of the century." He became renowned for the "Kahanamoku kick," a version of the Australian crawl that employed a flutter kick. Mainlanders made the handsome swimmer a hero despite his race. In 1900, when there were only 40,000 native Hawaiians they were considered a dying race, thus no threat to white Americans, unlike African Americans.

The American team was lauded by the media and leading politicians, including all three major presidential candidates, for their accomplishments and for serving as a metaphor for American life. The achievements by minority athletes offered an opportune public relations moment for the United States to demonstrate that it was a democratic and meritocratic society. Journalists led the way, by pointing out that American success at the Olympics was due to men of different social and racial origins. Their achievements showed how sport bolstered American institutions, built national character, and promoted modernity, while preserving such traditional ideals as rugged individualism and achievement. They were "America's Athletic Missionaries" who raised U.S. prestige internationally over "inferior" races and "effeminate" Englishmen.

The Inter-Allied Games and the 1920 Olympics

The 1916 Olympics, scheduled for Berlin, was not held because of World War I. Three years later, after the end of the war (June 22–July 6), the United States organized the Inter-Allied Games in the Bois de Vincennes outside of Paris at Pershing Stadium, built by the U.S. military and the YMCA, largely under the direction of Ellsworth Brown, former YMCA national director in the Philippines, who in 1918 became athletic director for the YMCA and the American Expeditionary Force (AEF) in Europe. He developed a program as the war wound down, to keep soldiers busy and out of trouble, that included "athletics for everybody." He organized AEF athletic championships, physical pageants to demonstrate to our allies the American play spirit, and the Inter-Allied Games for men who had served in the military during the war. Eighteen nations participated in such sports as track-and-field, swimming, baseball, football, basketball, tennis, boxing, horse riding, pistol and rifle marksmanship, and wrestling. The United States as expected, dominated over the war-torn countries of Europe, taking 17 of 24 gold medals in track-and-field, and 76 medals overall. Historian Thierry Terret argues that the Military Games demonstrated American might in a postwar Europe ravaged by years of conflict.

The 1920 Olympic Games, originally scheduled for Budapest, were transferred to Antwerp, Belgium. The IOC banned the losing Central Powers, (Germany, Austria, Hungary, Bulgaria, and Turkey), while the Russian Soviet Republic, in the midst of a terrible Civil War, chose not to participate in capitalist games. The first Olympiad in eight years had important symbolic innovations, notably the athletes' recitation of the Olympic Oath, the releasing of doves to symbolize peace, and the flying of the five-ringed Olympic flag.

The American team, mainly selected from the results at the AAU championships, dominated over the other 28 nations, winning 41 gold and a total of 95 medals, far ahead of second place Sweden (19 gold and 64 medals). The United States sent 273 men (90 in track-and-field) and 14 female swimmers and divers. The United States took a disappointing 9 of 29 track-and-field events, mainly in sprints and field events. Its dominance was diminished by the success of newly independent Finland, which also won 9 gold medals, led by its long-distance stars.

The Americans did particularly well in shooting, with 13 of 18 gold medals and in swimming, with 8 of 10 gold and four world records. The men captured 5 of 7 races, led by Duke Kahanamoku, who retained his 100-meter swimming title, and set a new world record, coming in ahead of fellow Hawaiian Pua Kela Kealoha, who won the 100-meter backstroke. They both also swam a leg on the winning 4 x 200 meter, abetted by sensation Norman Ross, who took the 400-m. and 1,500-m. freestyle.

American women competed in the Olympics for the first time since Margaret Abbott in 1900, overcoming the historic AAU opposition to women athletes. The Women's Swimming Association of New York under the direction of Charlotte Epstein, who served as team chaperone, produced half of the competitors. The team was criticized for including youngsters, like fourteen-year-old diver Eileen Riggin. American women had until that time worn cumbersome uniforms that included woolen bloomers, a full-skirted overdress, and a mobcap (or bonnet) for their hair. In 1919, the outstanding fifteen-year-old aquanaut Ethelda Bleibtrey and a teammate were arrested at an event after taking off their stockings for "nude swimming." She and her teammates swam in Antwerp in one-piece woolen or silk suits. Bleibtrey swept the two individual races (100-meter and 300-meter freestyle), and led the 4 x 100-meter relay team to gold, all in world record times.

Conclusion

The United States in the era of industrialization went from a nation borrowing heavily on the athletic experience and ideology of Great Britain and western Europe to becoming an exporter of American-created sports. The diffusion of American sports, positive sporting ideology, and sporting goods overseas reflected the growing prominence of American capitalism and culture on our borders, in the Caribbean basin, and across the Pacific. On the other hand, European indifference to American sporting culture reflected the lack of influence the United States enjoyed in prewar Europe. The promotion and acceptance of American sport in several locations overseas certified back home that the United States was in fact a superior nation economically, culturally, and politically, one that carried the "white man's burden" abroad, bringing its "advanced" level of development to the "benighted" peoples of inferior lands. Americans arrived to civilize them, and make them part of their system of industrial capitalism as consumers and producers. In addition, by the end of the nineteenth century, as a United States Empire formally developed overseas through neo- and overt colonialism, the national government employed sport, as had the British before, to gain access to local elites and exercise social control over the masses through what political scientists call soft power. The introduction of sports like baseball, basketball, boxing, and volleyball was not contested, but welcomed, albeit often for reasons antithetical to the American Empire, notably the development of local nationalism.

The United States further moved on to the world stage as a leading participant in international sports competition. Prior to the coming of the Olympic Games, elite level American athletes had competed against other outstanding sportsmen primarily from Great Britain and Ireland, in such sports as boxing, crew, track, and yachting. U.S. participation in international competition expanded dramatically with the coming of the modern Olympic Games. American teams, that included men (and eventually women) from all social classes and ethnic and racial groups competed against the other nations of the world (mainly Europe), and the United States fared extremely well in sports that were important back home, particularly in track-and-field. Commentators held up that success as evidence for the superior character and manliness of Americans, and the advanced quality of our economic, political, and social system. This was not very scientific proof, but it satisfied American readers. In addition, the press and other opinion makers utilized the mixed composition of American teams as corroboration of the meritocratic nature of American society, or rather the confirmation of the myth of American social democracy.

BIBLIOGRAPHICAL ESSAY

General Surveys

A valuable introduction to the study of sport history is Allen Guttmann's *From Ritual to Record: The Nature of Modern Sports* (New
York, 1978), which examines the nature of modern sport from a
Weberian perspective by analyzing the characteristics of sport in
premodern, ancient, medieval, and modern times. He argued that
the development of sport has been a product of modernization, and
that modern sport is characterized by secularism, equality, bureau-
cratization, specialization, rationalization (logical formation and
adaptation of universal rules; application of scientific methods to
athletic training), quantification, and an obsession with records.

The principal interpretations of the rise of American sport have
emphasized the role of cities and industrialization in the process.
Scholars originally focused on the negative character of city life in
comparison to rural society and subsequently accentuated the influence of industrialization on urban life. The first scholarly analysis of
American sport history was Frederic L. Paxson's presidential address
to the Mississippi Valley Historical Society (now the Organization
of American Historians), "The Rise of Sport," *Mississippi Valley*

Historical Review 4 (1917): 143–68. A student of Frederick Jackson Turner, Paxson argued that the late-nineteenth-century rise of sport was a reaction to the deprivation of urban life in comparison to that of the countryside or frontier. Following the disappearance of the frontier, Americans needed a new release, which they found in sport, as a means to manage urban tensions and sustain harmony in congested heterogeneous cities. Paxson's deprivation thesis was slightly modified by Arthur M. Schlesinger, Sr., in *The Rise of the City: 1878–1898* (New York, 1938), who attributed the athletic boom to a reaction against the restrictions of urban life. Urbanites were deprived of traditional fresh-air recreations, and they turned to spectator sports to vicariously experience rural life. Foster Rhea Dulles reinforced the deprivation paradigm in *America Learns to Play: A History of Popular Recreation* (Englewood Cliffs, NJ, 1965), which pointed out that crowded urban conditions and the pace of industrial work "did not permit the familiar games and athletic contests of village life." Consequently, city dwellers relied on spectator entertainments, particularly sports, as an "outlet for surplus energy and suppressed emotions." Dale Somers argued in *The Rise of Sports in New Orleans, 1850–1900* (Baton Rouge, LA, 1972), a study of a wide-open southern city where all sports flourished, that the rise of sport reflected urbanization's and industrialization's transformation of the social structure. He argued along the lines of Schlesinger that the nature of urban life (weak community identities, six-day work weeks, and remoteness from the countryside) "rendered the simpler, unorganized and often spontaneous diversions of rural America unsatisfactory or inaccessible." The void was filled by organized and commercial sport, which provided a safety valve in the stifling urban environment.

A new paradigm was established by John R. Betts in his seminal "The Rise of Organized Sport in America" (Ph.D. diss., Columbia University, 1951), largely summarized in his *America's Sporting Heritage, 1850–1950* (Reading, MA, 1974). Betts argued that sport was neither a "reaction against mechanization, the division of labor, and the standardization of life in a machine civilization" nor a romantic return to a lost pristine age. Rather the rise of sport was "as much a product of industrialization as it was an antidote to it." Betts argued that industrialization and the urban movement were the principal factors in the rise of organized sport. He recognized that while American sports were originally primarily rural, simple, individualistic, and mainly for youths, sport had existed as an urban institution since the early colonial era. Among Betts' major contributions was his analysis of how a positive antebellum sport ideology helped sell sport to the middle class. He dated the boom in organized sport to the post–Civil War era, a product of industrialization that provided enormous fortunes and a higher standard of living for the middle class. Technological innovations, improved access to sports sites, lowered equipment costs and new apparatus, and the emergence of entrepreneurs who recognized potential profits in catering to urban sporting interests facilitated the rise of a national sports market.

The most sophisticated and elegant explanation of the American sporting experience is Benjamin G. Rader's indispensable *American Sports: From the Age of Folk Games to the Age of Television*, 6th ed. (Upper Saddle River, NJ, 2008). Rader seeks to explain how and why informal games evolved into modern spectator sport and identify and explain developments in the internal history of sport (rules, ethos, management, and finance). Rader examines the emergence of an antebellum sporting counterculture that sought to maintain traditional athletic pleasures; he mainly focuses on how nineteenth-century industrial capitalism, the evolution of American society and culture in an urban setting, and the particular requirements of major American sports led to the rise of organized sports. Rader emphasizes the importance of spectator sports in the period from 1890 to 1950, stressing the role of entrepreneurs, heroes, and professional athletes; voluntarism; the emergence of a consumer society; and the impact of the progressive sports creed on public behavior. His excellent analysis of postwar sport examines the continued growth of commercial amateur and professional sports, the impact of television, and the growing roles of African Americans and women in major sports.

There are a number of other overviews of American sport history. Allen Guttmann argues for the merits of a modernization paradigm in *A Whole New Ball Game: An Interpretation of American Sports* (Chapel Hill, NC, 1988), a collection of essays on such topics as

Puritans, southerners, women, and children. A more recent synthesis is Elliott Gorn and Warren Goldstein, *A Brief History of American Sports* (Urbana, IL, 2004), which examines the connections between sport and American culture and society, how developments in culture and society influenced sport, and how sport influenced class and gender identities. It is particularly strong on the nineteenth century. This was followed by Richard O. Davies, *Sports in American Life: A History*, 2nd ed. (Malden, MA, 2011), which emphasizes the twentieth century, with a text that is nearly 60 percent post World War II. He focuses on analyzing why sport has become a major institution in contemporary life. The coverage emphasizes the major college and professional sports and how they have been significant social forces for much of American history. The most recent new textbook is Gerald R. Gems, Linda J. Borish, and Gertrude Pfister, *Sports in American History from Colonization to Globalization* (Champaign, IL, 2008), which focuses on the experience of marginalized groups, as well as trying to put American sport into a more global context.

A number of outstanding scholars in the 1980s undertook extensive examination of sport as an urban phenomenon. Recent scholars, especially Melvin L. Adelman in *A Sporting Time: New York City and the Rise of Modern Athletics, 1820–70* (Urbana, IL, 1986), have gone beyond examining the city as a principal site of American sport to analyze sport as both the product of urbanization and an independent variable influencing city building. Adelman argues that the emergence of sport in the nation's leading city was a joint product of the modernization of society and of the modernization of sporting institutions. Stephen Hardy's *How Boston Played: Sport, Recreation and Community, 1865–1915* (Boston, 1982) examines such topics as interscholastic sports, elite sports clubs, boxing heroes, and park use in post–Civil War Boston. Steven A. Riess's *City Games: The Evolution of American Urban Society and the Rise of Sports* (Urbana, IL, 1989) shows how demographic growth, evolving spatial arrangements, social reform, the formation of class and ethnic subcultures, the expansion of urban government, and the rise of political machines and crime syndicates all interacted to influence the development of American sport. Sport, in turn, also influenced these social variables. For a similar analysis of British sport, see

Richard Holt's *Sport and the British: A Modern History* (New York, 1989), which examines how class structures and urban experiences molded British sport.

Over the years several review essays on sport history have provided valuable critiques of the booming literature that help make the scholarship accessible. See Melvin L. Adelman, "Academicians and American Athletics: A Decade of Progress," *Journal of Sport History* 10 (1983): 80–106; Stephen Hardy, "The City and the Rise of American Sport, 1820–1920" *Exercise and Sports Sciences Reviews* 9 (1981): 183–229; Steven A. Riess, "The New Sport History," *Reviews in American History* 18 (1990): 313–25; Jeffrey T. Sammons, "'Race' and Sport: A Critical, Historical Examination," *Journal of Sport History* 21 (1994), 203–277; and Robert M. Lewis, "American Sport History: A Bibliographical Guide," *American Studies International* 19 (1991): 35–59.

Readers seeking accessible primary sources should consult Steven A. Riess, ed., *Major Problems in American Sport History* (Boston, MA, 1997), which combines condensed secondary articles and primary documents. There is a very useful series published by Academic International entitled *Sports in North America: A Documentary History*. Volumes 3–6 includes George Kirsch, *The Rise of Modern Sports, 1840–1860* (Gulf Breeze, FL, 1992), *Sports in War, Revival and Expansion, 1860–1880* (1992); Gerald Gems, *Organized Sport, 1880–1900* (1996), and Steven A. Riess, *Sports in the Progressive Era, 1900–1920* (1998). Selections cover all the major sports in their respective era, as well as provide coverage of such matters as rules and regulations, club and association bylaws and constitutions, and contemporary articles and press accounts of major contests.

Reflecting the enormous classroom interest in sport history, a number of valuable anthologies have been published. In addition to Riess, *Major Problems in American Sport History*, they include S. W. Pope, *The New American Sport History: Recent Approaches and Perspectives* (Urbana, IL, 1997); David K. Wiggins, *Sport in America: From Wicked Amusement to National Obsession* (Champaign, IL, 1995); and Wiggins, *Sport in America: From Colonial Leisure to Celebrity Figures and Globalization* (Champaign, IL, 2010).

Industrialization, Urbanization, and the Rise of Sport

The best introduction to antebellum sport is Adelman, *A Sporting Time*, which analyzes the modernization of sport in New York between 1820 and 1870. The author's superb research into baseball, cricket, harness racing, and thoroughbred racing indicates that the rise of sport predated the Civil War era. The book also contains considerable information about boxing, pedestrianism, and water, animal, and leisure sports. John Dizikes, *Sportsmen and Gamesmen* (New York, 1981) argues that the ideas and behavior of antebellum sportsmen changed from the values of sportsmen to gamesmen. While elite sportsmen accepted the written rules and unwritten conventions of a game, bourgeois gamesmen were manipulative and tried to bend rules whenever they could in order to win. Dizikes' analysis is based on just a few biographical studies, and he unfairly stereotypes middle-class Victorians, who had more integrity than he suggests.

The dynamics of urban growth and its impact on sport has received considerable scholarly attention, particularly the development of the municipal park movement. On sport and urban space, see Riess, *City Games*. Galen Cranz, *The Politics of Park Design: A History of Urban Parks in America* (Cambridge, MA, 1982) is an overview of park history that offers a highly idiosyncratic analysis. On sport and the parks, see Riess, *City Games*, and Hardy, *How Boston Played*. On the origins and evolution of the naturalistic vision, see David Schuyler, *The New Urban Landscape: The Redefinition of City Form in Nineteenth-Century America* (Baltimore, 1986). On Central Park, see Roy Rosenzweig and Elizabeth Blackmar, *The Park and the People: A History of Central Park* (Ithaca, NY, 1992), an essential work concerned with the role of the masses in the construction and use of public space.

For a positivist interpretation of the park movement, see Gerald Marsden, "Philanthropy and the Boston Playground Movement, 1885–1907," *Social Science Review* 35 (1961): 48–58, and Betts, *America's Sporting Heritage*, and for a social control perspective, see Michael P. McCarthy, "Politics and the Parks: Chicago Businessmen and the Recreation Movement," *Journal of the Illinois State Historical Society* 65 (1972): 158–72; Joel Spring, "Mass Culture and School Sports," *History of Education Quarterly* 14 (1974): 483–95; Cary Goodman, *Choosing Sides: Playground and Street Life on the Lower East Side* (New York, 1979); and Cranz, *Politics of Park Design*. For a more moderate view that recognizes the self-lessness of the reformers, see Paul Boyer, *Urban Masses and Moral Order in America, 1820–1920* (Cambridge, MA, 1978). While these studies largely examine the park movement from the top down, recent scholarship recognizes that motivation for reformers is quite complex and that many countervailing factors are involved, including the agency of working-class urbanites. See Hardy, *How Boston Played*; Roy Rosenzweig, *Eight Hours for What We Will: Workers and Leisure in an Industrial City 1870–1920* (Cambridge, MA, 1983); and Stephen Hardy and Alan G. Ingram, "Games, Structures and Agency: Historians on the American Play Movement," *Journal of Social History* 17 (1983): 285–302. On the origins of Chicago's park system see Glen Holt, "Private Plans for Public Spaces: The Origins of Chicago's Park System, 1850–1875," *Chicago History* 8 (1979): 173–84, which demonstrates how private citizens played a crucial role in initiating municipal change. See also Elizabeth Halsey, *The Development of Public Recreation in Metropolitan Chicago* (Chicago, 1940); and Gerald R. Gems, *Windy City Wars: Labor, Leisure and Sport in the Making of Chicago* (Lanham, MD, 1997). On Frederick Law Olmsted, the leading park architect, see Witold Rybczynski, *A Clearing in the Distance: Frederick Law Olmsted and America in the Nineteenth Century* (New York, 1999); Cynthia Zaitzevsky, *Frederick Law Olmsted and the Boston Park System* (Cambridge, MA, 1982); Laura Wood Roper, *FLO: A Biography of Frederick Law Olmsted* (Baltimore, 1973); Elizabeth Stevenson, *Park Maker: A Life of Frederick Law Olmsted* (New York, 1977); and Thomas Bender, *Towards an Urban Vision: Ideas and Institutions in Nineteenth-Century America* (Lexington, KY, 1975). See also Frederick Law Olmsted, Jr., and Theodora Kimball, eds., *Frederick Law Olmsted: Landscape Architect, 1822–1903* (1922–28; reprint, New York, 1970); along with Charles E. Beveridge and David Schuyler, eds., *The Papers of Frederick Law Olmsted*, vol. 3, *Creating Central Park, 1857–1861*, and vol. 6, *The Years of Olmsted, Vaux & Company, 1865–1874* (Baltimore, 1984–92). For a critical review of some of this literature, see Daniel M. Bluestone, "Olmsted's Boston and Other Park Places," *Reviews in American History* 11 (1983): 531–36. Rosenzweig and Blackmar in *Park and the People* argue that Olmsted has been given too much credit at the expense of his colleague Calvert Vaux, and they are critical of the elitism in early park planning.

Scholars have given little attention to rural sports, emphasizing competitive urban sports. See Ted Ownby, *Subduing Satan: Religion, Recreation and Manhood in the Rural South, 1865–1920* (Chapel Hill, NC, 1990) for a discussion of field sports and cock fighting in the evangelical South. On southern hunting see Stuart A. Marks, *Southern Hunting in Black and White: Nature, History, and Ritual in a Carolina Community* (Princeton, NJ, 1991). Andrea Smalley has brought attention to women hunters in "'Our Lady Sportsmen': Gender, Class and Conservation in Sport Hunting Magazines, 1873–1920," *Journal of the Gilded Age & Progressive Era* 4:4 (2005): 355–380. On fishing, see, Colleen J. Sheehy, "The Rise of Urbanism and the Romance of the Rod and Reel," in *Hard at Play: Leisure in America, 1840–1940*, ed. Kathryn Grover (Amherst, MA, 1992), 77–92; Kevin Kokomoor, "The 'Most Strenuous of Anglers' Sports Is Tarpon Fishing': The Silver King as Progressive Era Outdoor Sport." *Journal of Sport History* 37:3 (2010): 347–364.

Over forty years ago John Higham's innovative essay, "The Reorientation of American Culture in the 1890s," in *The Origins of Modern Consciousness*, ed. John Weiss (Detroit. MI, 1965), 29–48, pointed out how the elite worried about moral and physical decline. In the 1980s, possibly a product of the fitness fad, considerable attention was given to the history of sport, fitness, and health. James C. Whorton, *Crusaders for Fitness: The History of American Health Reformers* (Princeton, NJ, 1982); Harvey Green, *Fit for America: Health, Fitness, Sport and American Society* (New York, 1986); and Martha Verbrugge, *Able-Bodied Womanhood: Personal Health and Social Change in Nineteenth-century Boston* (New York, 1988), date the rise of the health movement to the Jacksonian Era, when it was a product of urbanization, the rise of evangelical Christianity, the search for perfection, and the general thrust for social reform. These works all examine middle-class attitudes about health from that time through the Progressive Era. They further consider the health movement of the Progressive Era, produced by fears of city life, the new germ theory, social efficiency, and concerns about individual character. See also Donald Mrozek, *Sport and American Mentality: 1880–1910* (Knoxville, 1983); Kathryn Grover, ed., *Fitness in American Culture: Images of Health, Sport, and the Body 1830–1940* (Amherst, 1989); Joseph Ernst, *Weakness is a Crime: The Life of Bernarr McFadden* (Syracuse, NY, 1991), a fascinating biography of an arch-male chauvinist who was a founder of the physical fitness movement; and David L. Chapman, *Sandow The Magnificent: Edward Sandow and the Beginnings of Body Building* (Urbana, IL, 1994).

The seminal essay on the positive ideology of sport is John R. Betts, "Mind and Body in Early American Thought," *Journal of American History* 54 (1968): 787–805. See also his "Public Recreation, Public Parks, and Public Health before the Civil War," in *The History of Physical Education and Sports*, ed. Bruce L. Bennett (Chicago, 1972), 33–520. Also useful on the ideology of sport are Adelman, *A Sporting Time*; Hardy, *How Boston Played*; Roberta J. Park, "'Embodied Selves': The Rise and Development of Concern for Physical Education, Active Recreation for American Women, 1777–1865," *Journal of Sport History* 5 (1978): 5–41; and Linda J. Borish, "The Robust Woman and the Muscular Christian: Catharine Beecher, Thomas Higginson, and Their Vision of American Society, Health and Physical Activities," *International Journal of the History of Sport* 4 (1987): 139–53.

On the impact of technology on sport, see John R. Betts's article, "The Technological Revolution and the Rise of Sport, 1850–1900," *Mississippi Valley Historical Review* 40 (1953): 231–56, and his *America's Sporting Heritage*. For brief studies of the metropolitan press, see Bernard A. Weisberger, *The American Newspaperman* (Chicago, 1961); and Gunther Barth, *City People: The Rise of Modern City Culture in Nineteenth-Century America* (New York, 1980). On sports journalism, see Michael Oriard, *Reading Football: How the Popular Press Created an American Spectacle* (Chapel Hill, NC, 1993); John R. Betts, "Sporting Journalism in Nineteenth-Century America," *American Quarterly* 5 (1953): 39–56; and Norris W.

Yates, *William T. Porter and the Spirit of the Times* (Baton Rouge, LA, 1957). On cartoonists, see Amy McCrory, "Sports Cartoons in Context: Tad Dorgan and Multi-Genre Cartooning in Early Twentieth-Century Newspapers," *American Periodicals* 18:1 (2008): 45–68; and Lori A. Roessner, "Hero Crafting in *Sporting Life*, an Early Baseball Journal," *American Journalism* 26:2 (2009): 39–65.

On sport and public transportation, see e.g., Riess, *City Games*; Betts, *American Sporting Heritage*; and John B. Rae, *The American Automobile: A Brief History* (Chicago, 1975). On cycling, see David Herlihy, *The Bicycle* (New Haven, CT, 2004); Norman Dunham, "The Bicycle Era in American History" (Ph.D. diss., Harvard University, 1956); Robert A. Smith, *A Social History of the Bicycle* (New York, 1972); Hardy, *How Boston Played*; and George D. Bushnell, "When Chicago was Wheel Crazy," *Chicago History* 4 (1975): 167–75. For an excellent analysis of the social and symbolic functions of cycling in the late nineteenth century, see Richard Harmond, "Progress and Flight: An Interpretation of the American Cycling Craze of the 1890s," *Journal of Social History* 5 (1971): 235–57; and on touring, see Gary Allan Tobin, "The Bicycle Boom of the 1890s: The Development of Private Transportation and the Birth of the Modern Tourist," *Journal of Popular Culture* 7 (Spring 1974): 838–49. On religion and cycling, see Michael Taylor, "Rapid Transit to Salvation: American Protestants and the Bicycle in the Era of the Cycling Craze," *Journal of the Gilded Age and Progressive Era* 9:3 (2010): 337–63.

Sport and Class

On the American elite, see Frederick C. Jaher, *The Urban Establishment: Upper Strata in Boston, New York, Charleston, Chicago, and Los Angeles* (Urbana, IL, 1982); and Steve Fraser and Gary Gerstle, eds., *Ruling America: A History of Wealth and Power in a Democracy* (Cambridge, MA, 2005). On elite sport, see Thorstein Veblen's classic, *The Theory of the Leisure Class* (New York, 1899).

Historians have devoted considerable attention to elite sports. Essential works include E. Digby Baltzell, *Philadelphia Gentlemen: The Making of a National Upper Class* (New York, 1958);

Somers, *The Rise of Sports in New Orleans*; Hardy, *How Boston Played*; Frances G. Couvares, *The Remaking of Pittsburgh: Class and Culture in an Industrial City 1877–1919* (Albany, NY, 1984); and Mrozek, *Sport and American Mentality*. Mrozek focuses on the eastern elite and their broad influence on Ivy League colleges, and on the military; he also examines ideas of manliness, regeneration, nationalism, and social efficiency. Mrozek points out that eastern elite sons were particularly prominent sportsmen who sought physical, psychological, and sexual regeneration through football and other strenuous activities to prove their manliness and secure the future of the race. On James G. Bennett, the leading elite sportsman, see Donald Seitz, *The James Gordon Bennetts* (Indianapolis, IN, 1928), and Richard O'Connor, *The Scandalous Mr. Bennett* (Garden City, NY, 1962).

For a scholarly study of horse racing, see Steven A. Riess, *The Sport of Kings and the Kings of Crime: Horse Racing, Politics, and Crime in New York, 1865–1913* (Syracuse, NY, 2011). Adelman's *A Sporting Time* is essential for the mid-nineteenth century turf. Very informative is William H. P. Robertson, *The History of Thoroughbred Racing in America* (Englewood Cliffs, NJ, 1964); and Dwight Akers, *Drivers Up! The Story of American Harness Racing* (New York, 1938). On elite track-and-field clubs, see Rader, *American Sports*; Frederick W. Janssen, *History of Amateur Athletics* (New York, 1885); Bob Considine and Fred B. Jarvis, *The First Hundred Years: A Portrait of NYAC* (London, 1969), and Joe D. Willis and Richard G. Wettan, "Social Stratification in New York City Athletic Clubs, 1865–1915," *Journal of Sport History* 3 (1975): 45–63. On the governance of amateur sport see Richard G. Wettan and Joe D. Willis, "Effect of New York Athletic Clubs on American Amateur Athletic Governance, 1870–1915," *Research Quarterly* 47 (1976): 499–505, and "Social Stratification in the New York Athletic Club: A Preliminary Analysis of the Impact of the Club on Amateur Sport in Late Nineteenth-Century America," *Canadian Journal of History of Sport and Physical Education* 7 (1976): 41–53. On golf, see George B. Kirsch, *Golf in America* (Urbana, IL, 2009); James. M. Mayo, *The American Country Club: Its Origins and Development* (New Brunswick, NJ, 1998); and Richard J. Moss, *Golf and the American*

Country Club, (Urbana, IL, 2001). On cricket, see Tom Melville, *Tented Field: A History of Cricket in America* (Bowling Green, OH, 1998); and P. David Sentence, *Cricket in America, 1710–2000* (Jefferson, NC, 2006), as well as George B. Kirsch, *The Creation of American Team Sports: Baseball and Cricket, 1838–72* (Urbana, IL, 1989). On elite hunting, see John F. Reiger, *American Sportsmen and the Origins of Conservation* (New York, 1975). An excellent treatment of the country club appears in Hardy, *How Boston Played*. On metropolitan men's clubs, see Baltzell, *Philadelphia Gentlemen*; Hardy, *How Boston Played*; and David Hammack, *Power and Society: Greater New York at the Turn of the Century* (New York, 1982).

Middle-class sport has received relatively less attention. On the formation of the urban middle class, see Stuart Blumin, *The Emergence of the Middle Class: Social Experience in the American City 1760–1900* (New York, 1989); Cindy Sondik Aron, *Ladies and Gentlemen of the Civil Service: Middle-Class Workers in Victorian America* (New York, 1987); John S. Gilkeson, Jr., *Middle-Class Providence, 1820–1940* (Princeton, NJ, 1986); Mary Ryan, *Cradle of the Middle Class: The Family in Oneida County, New York, 1790–1865* (Cambridge, MA, 1981); and Burton J. Bledstein, *The Culture of Professionalism: The Middle Class and the Development of Higher Education in America* (New York, 1976).

Middle-class manliness has received a lot of attention. Gail Bederman argues in her gendered analysis *Manliness and Civilization: A Cultural History of Gender and Race in the United States, 1880–1917* (Chicago, 1995) that the concept of "manliness," which meant sexual self-restraint and character was altered in the late nineteenth century, replaced by the term *masculinity*, which meant physicality, aggressiveness, and sexuality, celebrating the primitive "natural" man. In both cases, white men were considered civilized and the highest form of human being. See also Steven A. Riess, "Sport and the Redefinition of American Middle-Class Masculinity," *International Journal of the History of Sport* 8 (1991): 5–27; E. Anthony Rotundo, *American Manhood: Transformations in Masculinity From the Revolution to the Modern Era* (New York, 1993); Peter Stearns, *Be A Man! Males in Modern Society* (New York, 1979); Joe L. Dubbert, *A Man's Place: Masculinity in Transition*

(Englewood Cliffs, NJ, 1979); and Gerald E. Roberts, "The Strenuous Life: The Cult of Manliness in the Era of Theodore Roosevelt" (Ph.D. diss., Michigan State University, 1970). For a comparative Anglo-American analysis, see J. A. Mangan and James Walvin, eds., *Manliness and Morality* (London, 1987). On middle-class leisure, see also Grover, ed., *Hard at Play.*

For an introduction to working-class culture and recreation, see Herbert Gutman, *Work, Culture and Society in Industrializing America: Essays in Working-Class Culture* (New York, 1976); and on the work ethic, see Daniel Rodgers, *The Work Ethic in Industrial America, 1850–1920* (Chicago, 1978); and Daniel Nelson, *Managers and Workers: Origins of the New Factory System in the United States* (Madison, WI, 1975). See also the classic study on whiteness and class, David R. Roediger, *The Wages of Whiteness: Race and the Making of the American Working Class* (London, 1991). Particularly valuable on all aspects of working-class leisure is Rosenzweig, *Eight Hours for What We Will.* For a comparative study of the quality of British and American working-class life, see Peter R. Shergold, *Working-Class Life: The "American Standard" in Comparative Perspective, 1899–1913* (Pittsburgh, 1982), who argues that British workers originally had more discretionary time.

The best place to begin on working-class sport is Elliott Gorn, *The Manly Art: Bare Knuckles Prize Fighting in Nineteenth Century America* (Ithaca, NY, 1986), an analysis of boxing from an American studies perspective that focuses on the subterranean working-class bachelor subculture. A masterful study of gender, folk history, and working-class culture, Gorn's work provides an excellent examination of some of the seedier sides of American history. He traces boxing's development from its Anglo-Irish origins, to its popularity with the antebellum subterranean working class, and finally to its resurgence in the 1880s, which was encouraged by professional promotion, the charismatic heavyweight-champion John L. Sullivan, and the rise of gentlemen-amateur boxers. Gorn elegantly describes the nature of ring combat, its development into a more modern and civilized enterprise, and the cultural meaning of pugilism. Other works that focus on working-class sport include Riess, *City Games*; and Ted Vincent, *Mudville's Revenge: The Rise and*

Fall of American Sport (New York, 1981), a largely overlooked book that examines blue-collar participation in major sports from the late nineteenth century to the 1940s. A lot of valuable information on industrial sport can be found in Betts, *America's Sporting Heritage*. For an excellent overview of British working-class sport, see Holt, *Sport and the British*, which argues that historians underestimated working-class agency in the development of their favorite pastimes.

Information on workers' sports is scattered. See, e.g., Katherine A. Harvey, *The Best Dressed Miners: Life and Labor in the Maryland Coal Region, 1835–1910* (Ithaca, NY, 1969); Duane A. Smith, *Rocky Mountain Mining Camps: The Urban Frontier* (Bloomington, IN, 1967); John T. Cumbler, *Working-Class Community in Industrial America: Work, Leisure and Struggle in Two Industrial Cities, 1880–1930* (Westport, CT, 1979); David Walkowitz, *Worker City, Company Town: Iron and Cotton Worker Protest in Troy and Cohoes, New York, 1855–1884* (Urbana, IL, 1978); Couvares, *The Remaking of Pittsburgh*; and Steven J. Ross, *Workers on the Edge: Work, Leisure and Politics in Industrializing Cincinnati, 1788–1890* (New York, 1985). For sport in southern mill towns, see Nelson, *Managers and Workers*; Donald Gropman, *Say It Ain't So Joe: The True Story of Shoeless Joe Jackson and the 1919 World Series* (New York, 1988); and Thomas K. Perry, *Textile League Baseball: South Carolinas Mill Teams, 1880–1955* (Jefferson, NC, 1993).

On welfare capitalism see Stuart Brandes, *American Welfare Capitalism* (Chicago, 1976). Sport and welfare capitalism is discussed in Gems, *Windy City Wars*. On sport at Pullman, see Wilma Pesavento, "Sport and Recreation in the Pullman Experiment, 1880–1900," *Journal of Sport History* 9 (Summer 1982): 38–62; Pesavento and Lisa C. Raymond, "'Men Must Play: Men Will Play': Occupations of Pullman Athletes, 1880 to 1900," *Journal of Sport History* 11 (1985): 233–51; Stanley Buder, *Pullman: An Experiment in Industrial Order and Community Planning, 1880–1930* (Chicago, 1977); and Almont Lindsey, *The Pullman Strike: The Story of a Unique Experiment and of a Great Labor Upheaval* (New York, 1964). For other programs, see Gerald Zahavi, *Workers, Managers, and Welfare Capitalism: The Shoemakers and Tanners of Endicott Johnson, 1890–1950* (Urbana, IL, 1988); and

John Schleppi, "It Pays: John H. Paterson and Industrial Recreation at the National Cash Register Company," *Journal of Sport History* 6 (1979): 20–28. See also such company histories as Alfred Lief, *The Firestone Story: A History of the Firestone Tire and Rubber Company* (New York, 1951).

Historians have given due consideration to saloons, the primary site of male working-class recreation, as sports centers. See Perry Duis, *The Saloon: Public Drinking in Chicago and Boston, 1880–1920* (Urbana, IL, 1983); Elliott West, *The Saloon on the Rocky Mountain Mining Frontier* (Lincoln, NE, 1979); Madelon Powers, *Faces Along the Bar: Law and Order in the Workingman's Saloon, 1870–1920* (Chicago, 1998); Jon Kingsdale, "The Poor Man's Club': Social Functions of the Working-Class Saloon," *American Quarterly* 25 (1977): 472–89; and Mark Haller's seminal essay, "Organized Crime in Urban Society: Chicago in the Twentieth Century" *Journal of Social History* 5 (1971–72): 210–34. Still useful is Herbert Asbury, *Suckers Progress: An Informal History of Gambling in America from the Colonies to Canfield* (New York, 1938), though it must be used with care. Otherwise, the secondary literature on popular indoor sports is sparse. On billiards see Ned Polsky's classic sociological study *Hustlers, Beats and Others* (Chicago, 1967); and John Grissim, *Billiards: Hustlers & Heroes, Legends & Lies, and the Search for a Higher Truth on the Green Felt* (New York, 1979), an informative, popular account. On early billiards, see Edwin A. Miles, "President Adams' Billiard Table," *New England Quarterly* 45:1 (1972): 31–43; and Adelman, *A Sporting Time*. On billiards at the turn of the century, see Riess, *City Games*. Rick Kogan, *Brunswick: The Story of an American Company from 1845 to 1985* (Skokie, IL, 1985) is a lavishly illustrated volume recounting the history of the foremost American manufacturer of table games. On bowling, see Herman Weiskopf, *The Perfect Game: The World of Bowling* (Englewood Cliffs, NJ, 1978); and Riess, *City Games*.

Sport and Women

The literature on sporting women, a rapidly growing topic, focuses on elite and upper-middle-class women. A good place to start is Allen Guttmann's *Women's Sports: A History* (New York, 1991), a prizewinning interpretive analysis of women's sport history from ancient times to the present.

A growing number of monographs have recently been published that examine women's sport and fitness. Verbrugge's *Able Bodied Womanhood* focuses on the rise of well-being among middle-class nineteenth-century female Bostonians, examining various athletic training programs, particularly athletics at Wellesley and the establishment of the city's Normal School of Gymnastics, to demonstrate their growing awareness and understanding of health issues. She does not, however, point out how such knowledge was used to improve society. Patricia Vertinsky, *The Eternally Wounded Woman: Women, Exercise and Doctors in the Late Nineteenth Century* (Manchester, UK, 1990) examines the impact of mainstream physicians on limiting the athletic behavior of Anglo-American women. On physical fitness and health, see Frances B. Cogan, *All-American Girl: The Idea of Real Womanhood in Mid-Nineteenth-Century America* (Athens, GA, 1989). Middle-class gymnastics is examined in Ann Chisholm, "Nineteenth-Century Gymnastics for U.S. Women and Incorporations of Buoyancy: Contouring Femininity, Shaping Sex, and Regulating Middle-Class Consumption," *Journal of Women's History* 20:3 (2008): 84–112. On baseball, see Gai Berlage, *Women in Baseball: The Forgotten Story* (Westport, CT, 1994); and on cycling see Patricia Marks, *Bicycles, Bangs and Bloomers: The New Woman and the Popular Press* (Lexington, KY, 1990). On basketball, see Joan S. Hult and Marianna Trekell, eds., *A Century of Women's Basketball: From Frailty to Final Four* (Reston, VA, 1991); Ralph Melnick, *Senda Berenson: The Unlikely Founder of Women's Basketball* (Amherst, MA, 2007); Pamela Grundy, *Learning to Win: Education and Social Change in Twentieth-Century North Carolina* (Chapel Hill, NC, 2001); and Pamela Grundy and Susan Shackelford, *Shattering the Glass: The Remarkable History of Women's Basketball* (New York, 2005). On sports clothing, see Patricia C. Warner, *When the Girls Came Out to Play: The Birth of American Sportswear* (Amherst, MA, 2006). Women's swimming is discussed in Linda J. Borish, "'The Cradle of American Champions, Women Champions . . . Swim Champions': Charlotte Epstein, Gender and Jewish Identity, and the Physical Emancipation of Women in Aquatic Sports," *International Journal of the History of Sport* 21:2 (2004):

197–235. On women at college, see Charles H. Wilson, III, "'No Imitations of Masculine Sports': 'Physical Culture' at a Southern Woman's College," *Southern Studies: An Interdisciplinary Journal of the South* 17:2 (2010): 69–85.

For excellent comparative studies on Anglo-American sport and gender, see Roberta J. Park and J. A. Mangan, eds., *From "Fair Sex" to Feminism: Sport and the Socialization of Women in the Industrial and Post-Industrial Eras* (London, 1987). Other valuable studies include Stephanie L. Twin, "Jock and Jill: Aspects of Women's Sports History in America, 1870–1940" (Ph.D. diss., Rutgers University, 1978); Cindy L. Himes, "The Female Athlete in American Society, 1860–1940" (Ph.D. diss., University of Pennsylvania, 1986); and Susan Cahn, *Coming on Strong: Gender and Sexuality in 20th Century Women* (New York, 1994), which emphasizes the years following the 1920s. On working-class women's sport, see Monys Ann Hagen, "Industrial Harmony through Sports: The industrial Recreation Movement and Women's Sports" (Ph.D. diss., University of Wisconsin, 1990).

Ethnic Sports

An informative source on the subject of ethnic sports is George B. Kirsch, Othello Harris, and Claire E. Nolte, *Encyclopedia of Ethnicity and Sports in the United States* (Westport, CT, 2000). There are several relevant essays in George Eisen and Wiggins, *Ethnicity and Sport in North American History and Culture* (Westport, CT, 1994). For general studies, the place to begin on ethnic sports is Riess, *City Games*; and Rader, *American Sports*. On English Americans, see Rowland Berthoff, *British Immigrants in Industrial America, 1790–1950* (Cambridge, MA, 1958); and Adelman, *A Sporting Time*. For Scottish newcomers see Gerald Redmond, *The Caledonian Games in Nineteenth-Century America* (Rutherford, NJ, 1971); and Rowland Berthoff, "'Under the Kilt': Variations on the Scottish-American Ground," *Journal of American Ethnic History* 1:2 (1982): 5–34; and Benjamin G. Rader, "The Quest for Subcommunities and the Rise of American Sport," *American Quarterly* 29 (1977): 355–69. On French Canadians, see Richard Sorrel, "Sports and the Franco-Americans in Woonsocket, 1870–1930," *Rhode Island History* 31 (1972): 117–26.

There is a considerable literature on German Americans, such as Roberta Park, "German Associational and Sporting Life in the Greater San Francisco Bay Area, 1850–1900," *Journal of the West* 26:1 (1987): 47–64. The scholarship focuses heavily on the turners. See Henry Metzner, *A Brief History of the American Turnerbund* (Pittsburgh, 1924), an informative insider's account, and the more scholarly Carl Wittke, *Refugees of Revolution: The German Forty-Eighters in America* (Philadelphia, 1952). For a more recent analysis, see Annette Hofmann *The American Turner Movement: A History from Its Beginnings to 2000* (Indianapolis, IN, 2010). On the turners and socialism, see Ralf Wagner, "Turner Societies and the Socialist Tradition," in *German Workers' Culture in the United States, 1850 to 1920*, ed. Hartmut Keil (Washington, D.C., 1988), 221–39. See also Annette R. Hofmann, "Between Ethnic Separation and Assimilation: German Immigrants and Their Athletic Endeavors in Their New American Home Country," *International Journal of the History of Sport* 25:8 (2008): 993–1009.

On the Irish, see Hardy, *How Boston Played*; Carl Wittke, *The Irish in America* (Baton Rouge, LA, 1956); William M Shannon, *The American Irish* (New York, 1963); and Michael T. Isenberg, *John L. Sullivan and His America* (Urbana, IL, 1988). On traditional Irish sport, see Paul Darby "Gaelic Sport and the Irish Diaspora in Boston, 1879–90," *Irish Historical Studies* 33:132 (2003): 387–403; Darby, "Emigrants at Play: Gaelic Games and the Irish Diaspora in Chicago, 1884–c.1900," *Sport in History* 26:1 (2006): 47–63; and Darby, "'Without the Aid of a Sporting Safety Net?': The Gaelic Athletic Association and the Irish Émigré in San Francisco, 1888–c.1938," *International Journal of the History of Sport* 26:1 (2009): 63–83. An unusual article that examines occupational discrimination against Irish athletes is E. Woodrow Eckard, "Anti-Irish Job Discrimination circa 1880," *Social Science History* 34:4 (2010): 407–443. On Irish social and athletic clubs, see Frederick M. Thrasher's classic, *The Gang: A Study of 1,313 Gangs in Chicago* (Chicago, 1928); William M. Tuttle, Jr., *Race Riot: Chicago in the Red Summer of 1919* (New York, 1974); and Chicago Commission on Race Relations, *The*

Negro in Chicago (Chicago, 1922), a report written by sociologist Charles Johnson, who compiled considerable oral testimony about the behavior and image of the Ragen Colts.

There is a growing scholarship on the sporting pastimes of the new immigrants. For all ethnic groups and baseball, see Lawrence Baldassaro and Richard A Johnson, *The American Game: Baseball and Ethnicity* (Carbondale, IL, 2002). On Slavic-Americans, see, e.g., Gems, *Windy City Wars*; Vaclad Vesta, ed., *Panorama: A Historical Review of Czechs and Slovaks in the U.S.A.* (Cicero, IL, 1970); Casimir J. B. Wronski, "Early Days of Sport Among Polish Americans of Chicagoland," in *Poles of Chicago, 1837–1937* (Chicago, 1937); Donald E. Pienkos, *One Hundred Years Young: A History of the Polish Falcons of America* (Boulder, CO, 1987); Myron B. Kuropas, "Ukrainian Chicago: The Making of a Nationality Group in America," in Peter D. Jones and Melvin Holli, *Ethnic Chicago* (Grand Rapids, MI, 1981), 165–73; and Steven A. Riess, *Touching Base: Professional Baseball and American Culture in the Progressive Era* (Westport, CT, 1980). On Italians, see John H. Mariano, *The Italian Contribution to American Democracy* (Boston, 1921); and Matthew P. Llewellyn, " 'Viva l'Italia! Viva l'Italia!' Dorando Pietri and the North American Professional Marathon Craze, 1908–10," *International Journal of the History of Sport* 25 (2008): 710–36.

On Jewish American sport, see Bernard Postal, Jesse Silver, and Roy Silver, *Encyclopedia of Jews in Sports* (New York, 1965), which has many interesting anecdotes, however a few of the subjects are incorrectly identified as Jewish. Peter Levine, From *Ellis Island to Ebbets Field: Sport and the American Jewish Experience* (New York, 1992) is excellent on Brooklyn, but the work mainly focuses on the post–1920s. There are several useful essays in Steven A. Riess, ed., *Sport and the American Jew* (Syracuse, NY, 1998), particularly on boxing, women, marathoning, and settlements. See also Benjamin Rabinowitz, *The Young Men's Hebrew Association, 1854–1913* (New York, 1948), and Cary Goodman, *Choosing Sides: Playground and Street Life on the Lower East Side* (New York, 1979), for Jewish German-American attitudes. This book, however, is marred by ideological fallacies. The negative attitudes to sport of Russian immigrants are described in Irving Louis Howe, *World of Our Fathers* (New York, 1976). On boxing, see Steven A. Riess,

"The Jewish American Boxing Experience, 1890–1940," *American-Jewish History* 56 (1985): 223–54; Levine, *From Ellis Island to Ebbets Field*; and William B. Kramer and Norton B. Stern, "San Francisco's Fighting Jew," *California History* 53 (1974): 333–45, on Joe Choynski, the first great Jewish American heavyweight. For a biography of a star working-class Jewish runner, see Alan S. Katchen, *Abel Kiviat, National Champion Twentieth-Century Track and Field and the Melting Pot* (Syracuse, NY, 2009).

The literature on African American sport is extensive and of high quality. One can find a lot of information on this topic in Arthur Ashe's encyclopedic *A Hard Road to Glory: A History of the Afro-American Athlete, 1619–1986*, 3 vols. (New York, 1988). For a survey of the literature, see David K. Wiggins, "From Plantation to Playing Field: Historical Writings on the Black Athlete in American Sport," *Research Quarterly* 57 (1986): 101–16. An invaluable source is David K. Wiggins, and Patrick B. Miller, eds., *The Unlevel Playing Field: A Documentary History of the African American Experience in Sport* (Urbana, IL, 2003). On the slave experience, see the essay by David K. Wiggins in his *Glory Bound: Black Athletes in a White America* (Syracuse, NY, 1997); and Kevin Dawson, "Enslaved Swimmers and Divers in the Atlantic World." *Journal of American History* 92:4 (2006): 1327–1355.

The fascinating history of black baseball was first explored in Robert Peterson, *Only the Ball Was White* (Englewood Cliffs, NJ, 1970). For an early history by a contemporary, see Sol White, *Sol White's Official Baseball Guide* (1907; reprint, Philadelphia, 1984). On the public image of early black players, see James E. Brunson III, *The Early Image of Black Baseball: Race and Representation in the Popular Press, 1871–1890* (Jefferson, NC, 2009). Among the best secondary works is Michael E. Lomax, *Black Baseball Entrepreneurs, 1860–1901: Operating by Any Means Necessary* (Syracuse, NY, 2003). See also James B. Bennett, *Religion and the Rise of Jim Crow in New Orleans* (Princeton, NJ, 2005); and Lawrence D. Hogan, *Shades of Glory: The Negro Leagues and the Story of African-American Baseball* (Washington, DC, 2006). An essential biography is David W. Zang, *Fleet Walker's Divided Heart: The Life of Baseball's First Black Major Leaguer* (Lincoln, NE, 1995), on baseball's first black major leaguer. See also Robert

C. Cottrell, *The Best Pitcher in Baseball: The Life of Rube Foster, Negro League Giant* (New York, 2001).

On racism and professional African American athletics, see, e.g., the essays on jockey Isaac Murphy and pugilist Peter Jackson in Wiggins, *Glory Bound*. On Joe Gans, see Colleen Aycock and Mark Scott, *Joe Gans: A Biography of the First African American World Boxing Champion* (Jefferson, NC, 2008). There are several important studies on Jack Johnson, including Al-Tony Gilmore, *Bad Nigger! The National Impact of Jack Johnson* (Port Washington, NY, 1975), who explores American fears of the black heavyweight champion. For a more sophisticated treatment, see Randy Roberts, *Papa Jack: Jack Johnson and the Era of White Hopes* (New York, 1983), which makes extensive use of classified FBI files to give a complete and well-rounded picture of Johnson; and Thomas R. Hietala, *The Fight of the Century: Jack Johnson, Joe Louis, and the Struggle for Racial Equality* (Armonk, NY, 2002). On cyclist champion Marshall W. "Major" Taylor, see his autobiography, *The Fastest Bicycle Rider in the World* (1927; reprint, Battleboro, VT, 1972), and the fine biography by Andrew Ritchie, *Major Taylor: The Extraordinary Career of a Champion* (San Francisco, 1988). On the black prominence in the nineteenth-century turf, from slavery to freedom, see Edward Hotaling, *The Great Black Jockeys: The Lives and Times of the Men Who Dominated America's First National Sport* (Rocklin, CA, 1999). On black jockeys in the early twentieth century, see Edward Hotaling, *Wink: The Incredible Life and Epic Journey of Jimmy Winkfield* (Camden, ME, 2005); and Joe Drape, *Black Maestro: The Epic Life of an American Legend* (New York, 2006). On racism and football, see John Carroll, *Fritz Pollard: Pioneer in Racial Advancement* (Urbana, IL, 1992), a biography of one of the first black All-Americans, and the first African American National Football League head coach. Black college football is examined in Michael Hurd, *Black College Football, 1892–1992: One Hundred Years of History, Education, and Pride* (Virginia Beach, VA, 1993).

Sport in black communities is briefly discussed in such works as Somers, *The Rise of Sports in New Orleans*; Allan Spear, *Black Chicago* (Chicago, 1967); Kenneth L. Kusmer, *A Ghetto Takes Shape: Black Cleveland, 1870–1930* (Urbana, 1L, 1976); and Howard Rabinowitz, *Race Relations in the Urban South, 1865–1890* (Urbana, IL, 1980). Rob Ruck, *Sandlot Seasons: Sport in Black Pittsburgh* (Urbana, IL, 1987) is a model local study that shows how sports helped Pittsburgh's black neighborhoods after the turn of the century to carve out their own arenas of creativity, expression, and organization. There is some information on the black YMCA movement in C. Howard Hopkins, *The History of the Y.M.C.A. in North America* (New York, 1951). On recreational facilities in southern cities, see James F. Murphy, "Egalitarianism and Separatism: A History of Approaches in the Provision of Public Recreation and Leisure Services for Blacks, 1906–1972" (Ph.D. diss., Ohio State University, 1972). On segregated southern parks see Rabinowitz, *Race Relations*; Somers, *Rise of Sports in New Orleans*; and Carl M. Harris, *Political Power in Birmingham, 1871–1921* (Knoxville, TN, 1977). For Chicago parks, see Chicago Commission on Race Relations, *Negro in Chicago*; Spear, *Black Chicago*; and Tuttle, *Race Riot*.

The impact of welfare capitalism on black sports is briefly examined in James Grossman, *Land of Hope: Chicago, Black Southerners and the Great Migration* (Chicago, 1989). On African American women, see Gwendolyn Captain, "Enter Ladies and Gentlemen of Color: Gender, Sport and the Ideal of African American Manhood and Womanhood during the Late Nineteenth and Early Twentieth Centuries," *Journal of Sport History* 18 (1991): 81–102.

There is a substantial literature on Native Americans. See, e.g., see C. Richard King, *Native Athletes in Sport & Society: A Reader* (Lincoln, NE, 2005); and Joseph B. Oxendine, *American Indian Sports Heritage* (Lincoln, NE, 1995). A lot of the scholarship focuses on baseball, like Jeffrey P. Powers-Beck, *American Indian Integration of Baseball* (Lincoln, NE, 2004); Tom Swift, *Chief Bender's Burden: The Silent Struggle of a Baseball Star* (Lincoln, NE, 2008), and Harold and Dorothy Seymour, *Baseball: The People's Game (New York, 1990)*. On other sports see John Bloom, *To Show What an Indian Can Do: Sports at Native American Boarding Schools* (Minneapolis, MN, 2000); Lars Anderson, *Carlisle vs. Army: Jim Thorpe, Dwight Eisenhower, Pop Warner, and the Forgotten Story of Football's Greatest Battle* (New York, 2007); Kate Buford, *Native American Son: The Life and Sporting Legend of Jim Thorpe* (New

York, 2010); Mathew S. Gilbert, "Hopi Footraces and American Marathons, 1912–1930," *American Quarterly* 62 (2010): 77–101.

For an overview on Latinos and sports, see Jorge Iber, et al, *Latinos in U.S. Sport: A History of Isolation, Cultural Identity, and Acceptance* (Champaign, IL, 2011). On baseball, see Adrian Burgos, Jr., *Playing America's Game: Baseball, Latinos, and the Color Line* (Berkeley, CA, 2007); and Samuel O. Regalado, *Viva Baseball!: Latin Major Leaguers and Their Special Hunger 3rd ed.* (Urbana, IL, 2008). On the Mexican influence on rodeo, see Mary Lou LeCompte, "The Hispanic Influence on the History of Rodeo, 1823–1922," *Journal of Sport History* 12 (1985): 21–38.

On Asian Americans and Pacific Islanders, see Joel Frank, *Asian Pacific Americans and Baseball: A History* (Jefferson, NC, 2008); and "Chinese Americans and American Sports, 1880–1940," *Chinese America: History & Perspectives* 9 (1995): 133–147; Susan G. Zieff, "From Badminton to the Bolero: Sport and Recreation in San Francisco's Chinatown, 1895–1920," *Journal of Sport History* 27 (2000): 1–29; Joseph R. Svinth, "A Celebration of Tradition and Community: Sumo in the Pacific Northwest, 1905–1943," *Columbia: The Magazine of Northwest History* 13 (1999): 7–14; Jim Nendel, "New Hawaiian Monarchy: The Media Representations of Duke Kahanamoku, 1911–1912," *Journal of Sport History* 31 (2004): 32–52; and "Surfing in Early Twentieth-Century Hawai'i: The Appropriation of a Transcendent Experience to Competitive American Sport," *International Journal of the History of Sport* 26 (2009): 2432–2466.

Sport and the Educational Process

The relationship between sport and education has received considerable attention. A good place to begin on college sports is Ronald A. Smith, *Sports & Freedom: The Rise of Big-Time College Athletics* (New York, 1988). Smith focuses on Harvard and Yale from the beginnings of intercollegiate sport through 1906, when the National Collegiate Athletic Association was established. He argues that Oxford and Cambridge provided role models for elite American colleges, that the fundamental nature of modern college sport was achieved before the turn of the century, and, somewhat elliptically, that the development of intercollegiate sports was always connected to the idea of freedom. Students were originally free to develop their own extracurricular activities, but over time freedom in intercollegiate sports meant institutional autonomy to deal with athletics as administrators felt best. See also Robin D. Lester, *Stagg's University: The Rise, Decline and Fall of Big-Time Football* (Urbana, IL, 1995), which provides a fascinating narrative of Amos Alonzo Stagg's career. He focuses on the role of the professional coach in recruiting, retaining, training, and strategizing. Lester also analyzes the purpose of establishing a high-profile sports program at a new research-oriented university, describes the life of the college star-athlete, and evaluates the impact of football on the college community.

John S. Watterson's *College Football: History, Spectators, Controversy* (Baltimore, MD, 2000) examines the turn-of-the-century football crises concerning the issues of brutality, subsidization of athletes, and growing commercialism. He points out that the number of deaths due to college football injuries were exaggerated and sensationalized by reformers who felt football was becoming too commercialized, corrupt, and professional. Oriard in *Reading Football* points out that the rise of football occurred in the late nineteenth century, simultaneously with the great boom in American newspapers and magazines. His thesis is that the daily press largely created football as a popular spectacle. He analyzes how football narratives developed often contradictory versions of what the sport meant. On the early days of Notre Dame football, see Murray Sperber, *Shake Down the Thunder: The Creation of Notre Dame Football* (New York, 1993). Popular magazines idolized the football hero as the ideal masculine model, aggressive, yet a man of gentlemanly character. According to Daniel A. Clark, in *Creating the College Man: American Man Magazines and Middle-Class Manhood, 1890–1915* (Madison, WI, 2010), football magazine fiction also emphasized a corporate mentality (teamwork) and a passionate test of manhood. See also Guy M. Lewis, "The American Intercollegiate Football Spectacle, 1869–1917" (Ph.D. diss., University of Maryland, 1963); and Patrick B. Miller, "Athletes in Academe: College Sports and

American Culture, 1850–1920" (Ph.D. diss., University of California, Berkeley, 1987), a wide-ranging study of manly values and intercollegiate sports. More specialized studies include John H. Moore, "Football's Ugly Decades, 1893–1913," *Smithsonian Journal of History* 2 (1967): 49–68 (reprinted in Riess, ed., *American Sporting Experience*), and Roberta J. Park, "From Football to Rugby—and Back, 1906–1919: The University of California-Stanford Response to the Football Crisis of 1905," *Journal of Sport History* 11 (1984): 15–40. See also Mark F. Bernstein, *Football: The Ivy League Origins of an American Obsession* (Philadelphia, 2001).

On the origins of crew, the first intercollegiate sport, see Guy M. Lewis, "The Beginning of Intercollegiate Sport," *American Quarterly* 21 (1970): 222–29; and "America's First Intercollegiate Sport: The Regattas from 1852 to 1875," *Research Quarterly* 38 (1967): 637–48.

On youth sport there is a lot of useful information in Gems, *Windy City Wars*. The best study of elementary school sport is J. Thomas Jable, "The Public Schools Athletic League of New York City: Organized Athletics for City School Children, 1903–1914," in Riess, ed., *American Sporting Experience* (West Point, 1984). For a fascinating study of the rehabilitative and character-building effects of educational fitness programs, and their impact on gender, see David S. Churchill, "Making Broad Shoulders: Body-Building and Physical Culture in Chicago 1890–1920," *History of Education Quarterly* 48 (2008): 342–70. On secondary school sport, an essential study is Robert Pruter, *The Rise of American High School Sports and the Search for Control: 1880–1930* (Syracuse, NY, 2013). Important monographs include Jeffrey Miral, "From State Control to Institutional Control of High School Athletics: Three Michigan Cities, 1883–1905," *Journal of Social History* 16 (1982): 82–99; Timothy O'Hanlon, "School Sports as Social Training: The Case of Athletics and the Crisis of World War I," *Journal of Sport History* 9 (1982): 1–14; Joel Spring, "Mass Culture and School Sports," *History of Education Quarterly* 14 (1974): 483–95; and Hardy, *How Boston Played*. On the development of physical education, see Paula Welch, *History of American Physical Education and Sport* (Springfield, IL, 2004).

Historians have analyzed the acculturating function of adult-directed play and sports at playgrounds and such institutions as the YMCA, settlement houses, and youth sport leagues. The history of the play movement is summarized by Lee Rainwater, *The Play Movement in the United States* (Chicago, 1922). On the municipal park movement in New York, see Richard Knapp, "Parks and Politics: The Rise of Municipal Responsibility for Playgrounds in New York City, 1887–1905" (M.A. Thesis, Duke University, 1968). For a study that emphasizes the role of elites, see Jerry A. Dickason, "The Development of the Playground Movement in the United States: A Historical Survey" (Ph.D. diss., New York University, 1979). The philosophical underpinnings of the play movement and structured play are examined in Donald J. Mrozek, "The Natural Limits of Unstructured Play, 1880–1914," in Grover, ed., *Hard at Play*, 18–46; Dominick Cavallo, *Muscles and Morals: Organized Playgrounds and Urban Reform, 1880–1920* (Philadelphia, 1981); Bernard Mergen, "The Discovery of Children's Play," *American Quarterly* 27 (1975): 399–420; and Mark Kadzielski, "'As a Flower Needs Sunshine': The Origins of Organized Children's Recreation in Philadelphia, 1886–1911," *Journal of Sport History* 4 (1977): 169–88.

There is an extensive literature on juvenile sports. A good place to begin is Rader, *American Sports*. An essay that examines the Progressive analysis of sport as an answer to juvenile delinquency is Robert Park, "'Boys' Clubs are Better than Policemen's Clubs': Endeavours by Philanthropists, Social Reformers, and Others to Prevent Juvenile Crime, the Late 1800s to 1917," *International Journal of the History of Sports* 24 (2007): 749–75. See also Hardy, *How Boston Played*; Paul Boyer, *Urban Masses and Moral Order in America, 1820–1920* (Cambridge, MA, 1978); David I. Macleod, *Building Character in the American Boy: The Boy Scouts, YMCA and Their Forerunners, 1870–1920* (Madison, WI, 1983); Cavallo, *Muscles and Morals*; Goodman, *Choosing Sides*; and David Nasaw, *Children of the City: At Work and At Play* (New York, 1986). For a summary of contemporary studies of street youth activities, see Alan Havig, "The Commercial Amusement Audience in 20th Century American Cities," *Journal of American Culture* 5 (1982): 1–19. The need for municipal swimming pools for urban youth is examined in Jeff Wiltse, *Contested Waters: A Social History of Swimming Pools in America* (Chapel Hill, NC, 2007).

On sports and religion, see William J. Baker, *Playing with God: Religion and Modern Sport* (Cambridge, MA, 2007), and Clifford Putney, *Muscular Christianity: Manhood and Sports in Protestant America, 1880–1920* (Cambridge, MA, 2001). On the Y movement, see Boyer, *Urban Masses*; Hardy, *How Boston Played*; Elmer L. Johnson, *The History of YMCA Physical Education* (Chicago, 1979); Hopkins, *History of the Y.M.C.A.*; Macleod, *Building Character*; Betts, *America's Sporting Heritage*; and Aaron Abell, *The Urban Impact of American Protestantism, 1865–1900* (Cambridge, MA, 1943). Evangelical Protestants were very concerned about the problem of sexual awakening. See Adelman, *A Sporting Time*; and Charles E. Rosenberg, "Sexuality, Class, and Role in Nineteenth Century America," *American Quarterly* 25 (1973): 131–53. On the impact of muscular Christianity on the adult-directed boys' sport movement, see Rader, *American Sports*. On the attitudes of Luther Gulick, see his *A Philosophy of Play* (New York, 1920); Rader, *American Sports*; Jable, "Public Schools Athletic League"; and Clifford Putney, "Luther Gulick: His Contributions to Springfield College, the YMCA, and 'Muscular Christianity,'" *Historical Journal of Massachusetts* 39 (2011): 144–69.

On the role of settlement houses in the youth sports movement, see Allen F. Davis, *Spearheads for Reform: The Social Settlement and the Progressive Movement, 1890–1914* (New York, 1967); Riess, *City Games*; Cavallo, *Muscles and Morals*; and Boyer, *Urban Masses*. See also Jane Addams, *The Spirit of Youth and the City Streets* (New York, 1909); and *Twenty Years at Hull-House* (1910; reprint, New York, 1990).

Professional Sports

A lot of excellent work has been done on professional sports. On prizefighting, one should begin with Adelman, *A Sporting Time,* for information on midcentury New York pugilism, and Gorn, *The Manly Art,* an excellent analysis of the bare-knuckle era. Jeffrey T.

Sammons, *Beyond the Ring: The Role of Boxing in American Society* (Urbana, IL, 1988) gives some coverage to boxing at the turn of the century, but the book mainly focuses on later developments. For a detailed study of boxing in two of its major loci, see Somers, *The Rise of Sports in New Orleans*; William H. Adams, "New Orleans as the National Center of Boxing," *Louisiana Historical Quarterly* 39 (1956): 92–112; and Steven Riess, "In the Ring and Out: Professional Boxing in New York, 1896–1920," in *Sport in America: New Historical Perspectives*, Donald Spivey, ed. (Westport, CT, 1985), which is especially valuable for its analysis of boxing's connections to urban political machines and organized crime. On the efforts behind the Jim Corbett–Bob Fitzsimmons championship of 1897, see Leo N. Miletich, *Dan Stuart's Fistic Carnival* (College Station, TX, 2004). See also Thomas M. Croak, "The Professionalization of Prize-Fighting: Pittsburgh at the Turn of the Century," *Western Pennsylvania Historical Magazine* 62 (1979): 333–43; and James Chinello, "The Great Goldfield Foul," *Westways* 68 (September 1976): 27–30. On the impact of World War I on the legalization of boxing, see Guy M. Lewis, "World War I and the Emergence of Sport for the Masses," *The Maryland Historian* 4 (1973): 109–22. On Madison Square Garden, see Joseph Durso, *Madison Square Garden: 100 Years of History* (New York, 1979); and Riess, *City Games*.

Biographies are an important segment of the boxing literature. See Randy Roberts, *Jack Dempsey: The Manassa Mauler* (Baton Rouge, LA, 1979); and *Papa Jack* (New York, 1983). See also Isenberg, *John L. Sullivan and His America*, a biography of the greatest nineteenth-century sports hero that also describes the male bachelor subculture that was abhorred by the respectable classes; and Robert Catwell, *The Real McCoy: The Life and Times of Norman Selby* (Princeton, NJ, 1971), an informative biography of a leading turn-of-the-century fighter. The autobiographies, John L. Sullivan, *I Can Lick Any Sonofabitch in the House!* (New York, 1980); and Jack Johnson, *In the Ring and Out* (Chicago, 1927) must be used with caution. On the early career of promoter Tex Rickard, see Mrs. Tex Rickard, *Everything Happened to Him: The Story of Tex Rickard* (New York, 1936).

For popular overviews of thoroughbred racing, see Robertson, *The History of Thoroughbred Racing in America*; C. B. Parmer, *For Gold and Glory: The History of Thoroughbred Racing in America* (New York, 1939); and William S. Vosburgh, *Racing in America, 1866–1921* (New York, 1922). For the sport's ties with gambling, see Henry Chayfetz, *Play the Devil: A History of Gambling in the United States from 1492 to 1955* (New York, 1960); and Asbury, *Sucker's Progress*. For a more scholarly perspective, see David R. Johnson, "A Sinful Business: The Origins of Gambling Syndicates in the United States, 1840–1887," in *Police and Society*, ed. David H. Bayley (Beverly Hills, CA, 1977). Adelman's *A Sporting Time* is essential for an understanding of the modernization of harness racing and the mid-nineteenth-century development of thoroughbred racing in New York. See also his "Quantification and Sport: The American Jockey Club, 1866–1867, A Collective Biography" in Spivey, ed., *Sport in America*, 51–65. Considerable attention is given to the turf in Somers, *Rise of Sports in New Orleans*. For a detailed analysis of the nexus between horse racing, politics, and gambling, see Steven A. Riess, *The Sport of Kings and the Kings of Crime: Horse Racing, Politics, and Crime in New York, 1866–1913* (Syracuse, 2011), Riess, *City Games*; and Riess, "Horse Racing in Chicago, 1883–1894: The Interplay of Class, Politics and Organized Crime," in Riess and Gerald R. Gems, *The Chicago Sports Reader: 100 Years of Sports in the Windy City* (Urbana, IL, 2009), 59–80. An outstanding examination of horse racing at one key venue is Edward Hotaling, *They're Off! Horse Racing at Saratoga* (Syracuse, NY, 1995).

The literature on professional sports is richest on baseball, which was the first sport to get serious scholarly attention. The place to begin is Harold Seymour's *Baseball*, 3 vols. (New York, 1960–90), a beautifully written, painstakingly researched (albeit unfootnoted) trilogy, co-authored with wife Dorothy. *Baseball: The Early Years* (vol. 1) and *Baseball: The Golden Age* (vol. 2) examine the emergence of baseball from a simple antebellum boys' game into a popular commercial spectator sport operated as a monopsony. Seymour regards baseball's development as a reflection of contemporary industrial capitalism. *The Golden Age* is a definitive study of major-league baseball in the period from 1900 to 1930. The third volume, *Baseball: The People's Game*, is a far-ranging study that examines all aspects of amateur baseball, including sandlots, colleges, and prisons, as well as women's participation, Native Americans, and professional black baseball. Much of Seymour's work on the major leagues is paralleled by David Voigt's *American Baseball*, a three-volume work that brings the history of major-league baseball up to the 1980s (Norman, OK, 1966–71; University Park, PA, 1983). The three volumes are summarized by Voigt in *Baseball: An Illustrated History* (University Park, PA, 1987). For single-volume histories, see Charles A. Alexander, *Our Game: An American Baseball History* (New York, 1991), and especially Benjamin G. Rader, *Baseball: A History of America's National Game*, 3rd ed. (Urbana, IL, 2008). Geoffrey G. Ward's *Baseball: An Illustrated History* (New York, 1994) was based on the script of Ken Burns' 18.5 hour documentary *Baseball* (1994). A great source for baseball documents, is Dean A. Sullivan, ed., *Early Innings: A Documentary History of Baseball, 1825–1908* (Lincoln, NE, 1995); and *Middle Innings: A Documentary History of Baseball, 1900–1948* (Lincoln, NE, 1998).

Seymour's and Voigt's analyses of the early days of baseball have been supplanted by Adelman, *A Sporting Time*; Kirsch, *The Creation of American Team Sports*; and Warren Goldstein, *Playing for Keeps: A History of Early Baseball* (Ithaca, NY, 1989). They demonstrate how a boys' game became a popular, modern, middle-class pastime, supplanting cricket as the leading team sport. Goldstein's slender work is less well researched than that of either Adelman or Kirsch, but Goldstein presents some interesting ideas. He points out that the game has both a linear and cyclical history. He also argues that in the 1860s baseball began to be played for keeps, stressing the spirit of work over the element of fun through the rise of championship seasons, scientific play, and greater demands for victory. Peter Morris, *"But Didn't We Have Fun?" An Informal History of Baseball's Pioneer Era, 1843–1870* (Chicago, 2008) focuses on the rules, tactics, and rise of the umpire. For the most exhaustively researched and detailed analysis of the origins of the national pastime see John Thorn, *Baseball in the Garden of Eden: The Secret History of the Early Game* (New York, 2011). On the Civil War era, see George

B. Kirsch, *Baseball in Blue and Gray: The National Pastime during the Civil War* (Princeton, NJ, 2003), who argues that the Civil War helped spread the national pastime.

On early professional baseball, besides Seymour, *Baseball*; and Voigt, *American Baseball*, see William J. Ryczek, *When Johnny Came Sliding Home: The Post–Civil War Baseball Boom, 1865–1870* (Jefferson, NC, 1999); Ryczek, *Blackguards and Red Stockings: A History of Baseball's National Association* (Jefferson, NC: 2006); Tom Melville, *Early Baseball and the Rise of the National League* (Jefferson, NC, 2001); and Robert F. Burk, *Never Just a Game: Players, Owners and American Baseball to 1920* (Chapel Hill, NC, 2000).

There are several specialized studies of baseball. For an examination of how baseball's ideology influenced public behavior at the turn of the century, when it was unchallenged as the national pastime, see Riess, *Touching Base*. On baseball and urban politics, see Riess, *Touching Base*; and Vincent, *Mudville's Revenge*. For additional studies of baseball and cultural values, see Richard Crepeau, *Baseball: America's Diamond Mind, 1919–1941* (Orlando, FL, 1980); and Leverett T. Smith, Jr., *The American Dream and the National Game* (Bowling Green, OH, 1975). On the composition of crowds, see Kirsch, *The Creation of American Team Sports*; and Riess, *City Games*, who argues that commercialized baseball sought and attracted a largely middle-class crowd, contradicting the conclusions Allen Guttmann draws in *Sports Spectators* (New York, 1986), asserting that spectators were mainly working class. On the first modern World Series, see Louis P. Mazur, *Autumn Glory: Baseball's First World Series* (New York, 2006). The Black Sox scandal is well examined in Seymour, *Baseball: The Golden Age*; and Daniel Nathan, *Saying It's So: A Cultural History of the Black Sox Scandal* (Urbana, IL, 2003). For histories of major league teams, a good start is Steven A. Riess, ed., *The Encyclopedia of Major League Baseball Teams*, 2 vols. (Westport, CT, 2006).

On the business history of baseball, see Burk, *Never Just A Game*, a study of labor-management conflict primarily based on secondary sources marred by questionable statistics, and Peter Levine, *A. G. Spalding and the Rise of Baseball: The Promise of American Sport*

(New York, 1985), which analyzes Spalding's ownership of the Chicago National League club, his leadership in the National League, and his entrepreneurial activities in the sporting goods industry. Eugene C. Murdock, *Ban Johnson: Czar of Baseball* (Westport, CT, 1982), examines the life of the founding president of the American League and such issues as the war for recognition with the National League, Johnson's recruitment of magnates, and labor-management disputes. See also G. Edward White, *Creating the National Pastime: Baseball Transforms Itself, 1903–1953* (Princeton, NJ, 1996), who credits the leaders of the sport with transforming it during the Progressive Era from its working-class, urban origins to a game that both protected traditional culture and adapted to modern industrial urban society. For a general analysis of sport and business, see three of Stephen Hardy's works: "Entrepreneurs, Organizations, and the Sport Marketplace," *Journal of Sport History* 13 (1986): 14–33; "Entrepreneurs, Structures, and the Sportgeist: Old Tensions in Modern Industry," in *Essays on Sport History and Sport Mythology*, ed. Donald G. Kyle and Gary Stark (College Station, TX, 1990), 83–117; and "Adopted by All the Leading Clubs: Sporting Goods and the Shaping of Leisure, 1860–1900," in *For Fun and Profit: The Transformation of Leisure into Consumption*, ed. Richard Butsch (Philadelphia, 1990), 71–101.

On major-league ballparks, see Riess, *City Games*; Michael Gershman, *Diamonds: The Evolution of the Ballpark* (Boston, 1993), an excellent illustrated history. For basic reference, see the deservedly celebrated Philip J. Lowry, *Green Cathedrals: The Ultimate Celebration of Major League and Negro League Ballparks* (New York, 2006); and Michael Benson, *Ballparks of North America: A Comprehensive Historical Reference to Baseball Grounds, Yards, and Stadiums, 1845 to the Present* (Jefferson, NC, 1989), which is largely derivative. On ballparks and their neighboring communities, see Bruce Kuklick, *To Every Thing a Season: Shibe Park and Urban Philadelphia, 1909–1976* (Princeton, NJ, 1991); and Riess, *City Games*. Gunther Barth's chapter, "Ballpark," in his *City People*, is a provocative discussion of baseball's role in promoting a homogeneous urban culture. He emphasizes the psychological impact of urbanization and the ways the park promoted a sense of shared identity among sports fans. His conclusions, however, based on dubious assumptions, erroneous inferences, and factual misstatements, are unreliable.

On labor relations, see Lee Lowenfish, *The Imperfect Diamond: A History of Baseball's Labor Wars*, rev. ed. (New York, 1992). Excellent interviews of early-twentieth-century ballplayers appear in Lawrence Ritter's *The Glory of Their Times* (New York, 1966). For biographies of prominent players see Charles C. Alexander's *Ty Cobb* (New York, 1984) and *John J. McGraw* (New York, 1988); Ray Robinson, *Matty: An American Here: Christy Mathewson of the New York Giants* (New York, 1994); and Marshall Smelser, *The Life That Ruth Built: A Biography* (New York, 1975). On baseball and professional sports as an avenue of social mobility, see Riess, *City Games*; and "Sport and Social Mobility: American Myth or Reality," in Kyle and Stark, eds., *Essays on Sport History*, 83–117.

On early professional basketball, see Robert W. Peterson, *Cage to Jump Shots: Pro Basketball's Early Years* (New York, 1990); and Vincent's *Mudville's Revenge*. On early professional football, see Marc S. Maltby, *The Origins and Development of Professional Football, 1890–1920* (New York, 1997); Robert Peterson, *Pigskin: The Early Years of Pro Football* (New York, 1997); J. Thomas Jable, "The Birth of Professional Football: Pittsburgh Athletic Clubs Ring in Professionals in 1902," *Western Pennsylvania Historical Magazine* 62 (1979: 136–47); and Tom Bennett et al., *The NFL's Official Encyclopedic History of Professional Football* (New York, 1979).

The literature on professional track is pretty sparse, but Vincent, *Mudville's Revenge* is particularly good on nineteenth-century working-class track-and-field. Vincent reported some extraordinary professional records, but without attribution. On long-distance running, see Pamela Cooper, *The American Marathon* (Syracuse, NY, 1998); John Cumming, *Runners & Walkers: A Nineteenth-Century Chronicle* (Chicago, 1981); and John A. Lucas, "Pedestrianism and the Struggle for the Sir John Astley Belt, 1878–1879," *Research Quarterly* 39 (1968): 587–95.

The scholarship on American sport and globalization hardly existed when the first edition of this book was published. While scholars were aware that the United States participated in the modern

Olympics, it was mainly a topic explored by European historians, and the focus was on the 1936 Games, often referred to today as "The Nazi Olympics," which goes beyond the scope of this book. There was barely any scholarship on transnational aspects of American sport, other than the occasional contests with Great Britain and Canada, and the sporting culture that colonists and immigrants brought to the United States. Today, however, the study of the diffusion of sport across borders has become a major subject of American sport history.

For an overview of the subject of sport and imperialism, see Allen Guttmann, *Games and Empire: Modern Sports and Cultural Imperialism* (New York, 1994). British historians, not surprisingly, given the preeminence of their nation in eighteenth- and nineteenth-century sports, and the growth of the Empire, became interested in the expansion overseas of British sports before American historians did. One of the first books to examine the topic was John Ford, *This Sporting Land* (London, 1977), which was produced in conjunction with a documentary on the Thames Network. Major credit for bringing awareness of this topic to historians goes to J. A. Mangan's *The Games Ethic and Imperialism: Aspects of the Diffusion of an Ideal* (Harmondsworth, UK, 1986). He argues convincingly that there was a concerted effort by British colonial officials to import the games ethic taught at the top English public schools to their colonial elites to instill character and tighten their bonds to London. Mangan has edited other books on British imperialism and sport, including *Pleasure, Profit, Proselytism* (London, 1988), a collection of fourteen essays on cultural diffusion; and *Cultural Bond: Sport, Empire, and Society* (London, 1992), covering the years 1860–1914. A very accessible analysis of the British experience can be found in Richard Holt's excellent, *Sport and the British: A Modern History* (Oxford, 1988).

American sports in the late nineteenth and early twentieth centuries were becoming adopted in foreign nations. A great place to start is Gerald R. Gems, *The Athletic Crusade: Sport and American Cultural Imperialism* (Lincoln, NE, 2006). This essential book examines the role of sport in American engagements abroad. His volume mainly covers the late nineteenth and early twentieth centuries.

Gems demonstrates how the military, missionaries, and educators brought American sports with them to civilize nations overseas. They tried to run U.S. colonies, and otherwise control weaker states in the Caribbean, through sports. These subject societies adopted American sports, but they often tried to use it to fit their own needs, not those of the Americans. In some cases, the natives learned the games so well they beat the Americans, a matter of great pride. Gems examines cultural imperialism with chapters on China, Japan, the Philippines, Hawaii, Cuba, Puerto Rico, and the Dominican Republic. He also examines cultural diffusion in China and Japan, where cultural imperialism did not apply. He goes too far in focusing on cultural imperialism, which fits some situations but not all. For an interpretive analysis, see Steven W. Pope, "Rethinking Sport, Empire and American Exceptionalism," *Sport History Review* 38 (2007): 92–120.

The main sport being promoted overseas was baseball, albeit by private interests and not the government. Robert Elias, *The Empire Strikes Out: How Baseball Sold U.S. Foreign Policy and Promoted the American Way Abroad* (New York, 2010), argues that baseball contributed significantly to the rise of the United States as a world power. The evidence does not, however, support his argument. On baseball's world tour of 1889, see Mark Lamster, *Spalding's World Tour: The Epic Adventure That Took Baseball Around the Globe — and Made It America's Game* (New York, 2006), a popular account, and the more scholarly Thomas W. Zeiler, *Ambassadors in Pinstripes: The Spalding World Baseball Tour and the Birth of the American Empire* (Lanham, MD, 2006). Zeiler explores the ways in which the Spalding World Baseball Tour drew on elements of cultural diplomacy to inject American values and power into the international arena, but probably goes too far in claiming its role in foretelling American imperialism. Zeiler sees the baseball players and their entourage as "tourists" who disseminated American culture abroad and brought global influences back home. He claims the tour helped build up an imperial U.S. identity that laid the roots of the empire soon acquired due to the Spanish-American War, but the thesis is more claimed than proven. The trip was made possible by such forces as economic growth, a search for overseas markets, and growing cultural interchange that was pushing the United States out into the world, but that did not make it part of the march toward imperialism. The trip is also covered in Peter Levine, *A.G. Spalding and the Rise of Baseball*; and Albert G. Spalding, *America's National Game* (New York, 1911). On the tour of 1913–1914, see James E. Elfers, *The Tour to End All Tours: The Story of Major League Baseball's 1913–1914 World Tour* (Lincoln, NE, 2003).

For American influence on sport on the borders, with Mexico, see William H. Beezley, *Judas at the Jockey Club* (Lincoln, NE, 1987); and Beezley, "Bicycles, Modernization and Mexico," in Joseph L. Arbena, ed., *Sport and Society in Latin America: Diffusion, Dependency, and the Rise of Mass Culture* (Westport, CT, 1988), 15–28. In Canada, see Alan Metcalfe, *Canada Learns to Play* (Toronto, 1987); William Humber, *Diamonds of the North: A Concise History of Baseball in Canada* (Don Mills, ONT, 1995); Nancy Bouchier and Robert Barney, "A Critical Examination of a Source on Early Ontario Baseball: The Reminiscence of Adam E. Ford," *Journal of Sport History* 15 (1988): 75–90; Colin Howell, "Baseball and Borders: The Diffusion of Baseball into Mexican and Canadian-American Borderland Regions, 1885–1911," *Nine: A Journal of Baseball History & Culture* 11 (2003): 16–26; Colin Howell, "Baseball, Class and Community in the Maritime Provinces, 1870–1910," *Histoire Sociale: Social History* 22 (1989): 265–286.

On baseball in Latin America, see Michael M. Oleksak and Mary Adams Oleksak, *Beisbol: Latin Americans and the Grand Old Game* (Grand Rapids, MI, 1991). On Cuba and United States baseball, see the outstanding essay by Louis A. Perez, "Between Baseball and Bullfighting: The Quest for Nationality in Cuba, 1868–1898," *Journal of American History* 81 (1994): 493–517, an essential study on sport and cultural diffusion. The most detailed study of Cuban baseball is Roberto Gonzalez Echevarria, *The Pride of Havana: A History of Cuban Baseball* (New York, 1999). On other areas in the Caribbean, see Alan M. Klein, "Sport and Colonialism in Latin America and the Caribbean," *Studies in Latin American Popular Culture* 10 (1991): 257–71; Alan M. Klein, *Sugarball: The American Game, the Dominican Dream* (New Haven, CT, 1991); Rob Ruck,

The Tropic of Baseball: Baseball in the Dominican Republic (Westport, CT, 1991); and Burgos, *Playing America's Game.*

On the coming of baseball to Hawaii in its era of independence, see Monica Nucciarone, *Alexander Cartwright: The Life Behind the Baseball Legend* (Lincoln, NE, 2009); Frank Ardolino, "Missionaries, Cartwright, and Spalding: The Development of Baseball in Nineteenth-Century Hawaii," *Nine: A Journal of Baseball History and Culture* 10 (2002): 27–45. Joel S. Franks has studied sport in Hawaii and the Pacific Islands for years. See *Hawaiian Sports in the Twentieth Century* (Lewiston, NY, 2002); *Crossing Sidelines, Crossing Cultures: Sport and Asian Pacific American Cultural Citizenship* (Lanham, MD, 2000); and *Asian Pacific Americans and Baseball: A History* (Jefferson, NC, 2008).

For the American influence on sport in Asia, see Gems, *Athletic Crusade*; Allen Guttmann and Lee Thompson, *Japanese Sports: A History* (Honolulu, HI, 2001); the seminal essay Donald Roden, "Baseball and the Quest for National Dignity in Meiji Japan," *American Historical Review* 85 (1980): 511–34; Sayuri Guthrie-Shimizu, *Transpacific Field of Dreams: How Baseball Linked the United States and Japan in Peace and War* (Chapel Hill, NC, 2012); Joseph Reaves, *Taking in a Game: A History of Baseball in Asia* (Lincoln, NE, 2002); Gael Graham, "Exercising Control: Sports and Physical Education in American Protestant Mission Schools in China," *Signs: Journal of Women in Culture & Society* 20 (1994): 26–48; and Janice A. Beran, "American Sports in the Philippines: Imperialism or Progress Through Sports?" *International Journal of the History of Sport* 6 (1989): 62–87.

The United States and the Olympics

On the history of the Olympic Games, see Allen Guttmann, *The Olympics: A History of the Modern Games* (Urbana, IL, 1992); and 1st Century Project, *The Olympic Century: The Official 1st Century History of the Modern Olympic Movement*, vols. 1, 3–7 (New York, 1996–2000) that cover the Olympics through 1920. (Volume 2 on the 1896 Olympics has not been produced to date due to copyright litigation with the National Olympic Committee of France.) The series consists of twenty-three gorgeously produced, well-written volumes, with superb appendixes, produced at a cost of $11.5 million. On the origins of the games, and the American role, see John MacAloon, *This Great Symbol: Pierre de Coubertin and the Origins of the Modern Olympic Games* (Chicago, 1981); on the first games in Athens, see Richard Mandell, *The First Modern Olympics* (Berkeley, CA, 1976).

On the early years of U.S. participation in the Olympics, see Mark Dyreson, *Making the American Team: Sport, Culture and the Olympic Experience* (Urbana, IL 1998). Dyreson argues that intellectuals, social reformers and political leaders believed that sport could revitalize the "republican experiment," forming a new sense of national identity to bind the country together and foster community and a healthy political order. This was exemplified by American views of the early Olympic Games (1896–1912). Prominent American thinkers defined the United States as a sporting republic. They saw sport as an athletic technology that could help make a national culture strong enough to shape political culture and help the people cope with modernization. Sport was the common language most Americans shared, plus it was an institution that would revitalize a nation in flux, promoting equity, democracy, and public virtue. For a further discussion, see also Steven W. Pope, "American Muscles and Minds: Public Discourse and the Shaping of National Identity during Early Olympiads, 1896–1920," *Journal of American Culture* 15 (1992): 83–94.

There is a substantial literature on the 1904 Games in St. Louis. See George R. Mathews, *America's First Olympics: The St. Louis Games of 1904* (Columbia, MO, 2005); S.W. Pope, *Patriotic Games: Sporting Traditions in the American Imagination, 1876–1926* (New York, 1997); Robert K. Barney, "Born from Dilemma: America Awakens to the Modern Olympic Games, 1901–1903," *Olympika: The International Journal of Olympic Studies* 1 (1992): 92–135; Mark Dyreson, "The Playing Fields of Progress: American Athletic Nationalism and the 1904 St. Louis Olympics," *Gateway Heritage* (1993): 4–23.

On the Anthropological Games, see Lew Carlson, "Giant Patagonians and Hairy Ainu: Anthropology Days at the 1904 St. Louis

Olympics" *Journal of American Culture* 12 (1989): 19–26; and Mati Goksyr, "'One Certainly Expected a Great Deal More from the Savages': The Anthropology Days in St. Louis, 1904 and their Aftermath," *International Journal of the History of Sport* 7 (1990): 297–306. For a sophisticated and thorough analysis of all aspects of the event, see the award-winning Susan Brownell, ed., *The 1904 Anthropology Days and Olympic Games: Sport, Race, and American Imperialism* (Lincoln, NE, 2008), with eleven essays by various experts and an introduction by Brownell.

On the United States and subsequent Olympics, see John Lucas, "The Hegemonic Rule of the American Amateur Athletic Union 1888–1914: James Edward Sullivan as Prime Mover," *International Journal of the History of Sport* 11 (1994): 355–71; Lucas, "American Involvement in the Athens Olympic Games of 1906—A Bridge Between Failure and Success," *Stadion* 6 (1980): 217–228; George R. Mathews, "The Controversial Olympic Games of 1908 as Viewed by the *New York Times* and the *Times* (London)," *Journal of Sport History* 7 (1980): 40–53; Matthew McIntire, "National Status, the 1908 Olympic Games and the English Press," *Media History* 15:3 (2009): 271–286. On the issue of dipping the flag in 1908 at London, see Mark Dyreson, "'This American Flag Dips for no Earthly King': The Mysterious Origins of an American Myth," in Dyreson, *Crafting Patriotism for Global Dominance: America at the Olympics* (London, 2009). For a history of the London Olympics, see Rebecca Jenkins, *The First London Olympics, 1908* (London, 2008).

Two of the stars of the 1912 Olympics were Duke Kahanamoku and Jim Thorpe. See Jim Nendel, "New Hawaiian Monarchy: The Media Representations of Duke Kahanamoku, 1911–1912," *Journal of Sport History* 31 (2004): 32–52; and Kate Buford, *Native American Son: The Life and Sporting Legend of Jim Thorpe* (New York, 2010).

On the United States and post–World War I international events, see Thierry Terret, "The Military 'Olympics' of 1919: Sport, Diplomacy and Sport Politics in the Aftermath of World War One," *Journal of Olympic History* 14:2 (2006): 22–31; and John A. Lucas, "American Preparations for the First Post World War Olympic Games, 1919–1920," *Journal of Sport History* 10 (1983): 30–44.

INDEX